T0333622

The Hidden Life of Clothing

Also by Rachel Worth and published by Bloomsbury

Fashion for the People: A History of Clothing at Marks & Spencer
Clothing and Landscape in Victorian England
Fashion and Class

The Hidden Life of Clothing

Historical Perspectives on Fashion and Sustainability

Rachel Worth

BLOOMSBURY VISUAL ARTS
LONDON • NEW YORK • OXFORD • NEW DELHI • SYDNEY

BLOOMSBURY VISUAL ARTS
Bloomsbury Publishing Plc
50 Bedford Square, London WC1B 3DP, UK
1385 Broadway, New York, NY 10018, USA
29 Earlsfort Terrace, Dublin 2, Ireland

BLOOMSBURY, BLOOMSBURY VISUAL ARTS and the Diana logo are trademarks of
Bloomsbury Publishing Plc

First published in Great Britain 2023

Copyright © Rachel Worth, 2023

Rachel Worth has asserted her right under the Copyright, Designs and Patents Act, 1988,
to be identified as Author of this work.

For legal purposes the Acknowledgements on p. ix constitute an extension of
this copyright page.

Cover design by www.paulsmithdesign.com
Cover image: Lace 'patchwork' pieces stitched onto silk backing using feather stitch
© Rachel Worth

All rights reserved. No part of this publication may be reproduced or transmitted in any
form or by any means, electronic or mechanical, including photocopying, recording,
or any information storage or retrieval system, without prior permission in writing
from the publishers.

Bloomsbury Publishing Plc does not have any control over, or responsibility for, any third-
party websites referred to or in this book. All internet addresses given in this book were
correct at the time of going to press. The author and publisher regret any inconvenience
caused if addresses have changed or sites have ceased to exist, but can accept no
responsibility for any such changes.

A catalogue record for this book is available from the British Library.

A catalog record for this book is available from the Library of Congress.

ISBN: HB: 978-1-3501-8098-7
PB: 978-1-3501-8097-0
ePDF: 978-1-3501-8094-9
eBook: 978-1-3501-8095-6

Typeset by Deanta Global Publishing Services, Chennai, India
Printed and bound in India

To find out more about our authors and books visit www.bloomsbury.com and sign up for
our newsletters.

Contents

Illustrations

Acknowledgements

The Covid-19 pandemic put paid to face-to-face interviews, engagement with colleagues and students and to physical attendance at conferences. It did, however, encourage wide reading beyond the discipline where I might otherwise have taken my research. Online libraries and purchases from book retailers therefore proved invaluable. Meanwhile, lockdown walks and bike-rides in my immediate environment – the (mostly) traffic-free area around Dorset where I am fortunate enough to live – made me reflect deeply on the issues I address in this book. I was repeatedly reminded of past textile industries that once flourished and of clothing production that frequently relied on localised networks of trade. My thoughts turned to the deep continuities and discontinuities that the contemporary fashion industry has with its history.

Like many of us working from home since 2020, without the need for a formal 'working wardrobe', I began to question the number of clothes I possess as well as my shopping habits. Given that it is all too easy to buy new clothes cheaply and easily, I noticed how the skills of making and mending I learnt in my teens I no longer practised on a regular basis. I have since begun to sew again.

Heartfelt thanks to Frances Arnold at Bloomsbury Publishing, with whom I first discussed this project in 2019 and for her encouragement and expert editorial eye throughout the writing process. Thanks also to her assistant Rebecca Hamilton for keeping me on schedule in the preparation of the text and images prior to production. To the late Christina Strutt of Cabbages & Roses, who gave generously of her time when I met with her in January 2022, my gratitude. Last, but by no means least, thank you to my 'Gen-Z' son Sam, who gives me hope that the future of 'fashion' can be better than its past.

Introduction

In what has become a classic study of clothing, Quentin Bell tells us: 'Our clothes are too much a part of us for most of us ever to be entirely indifferent to their condition: it is as though the fabric were indeed a natural extension of the body, or even of the soul.'[1] Meanwhile, Stewart Brand posits that 'in the hands of users, garments have lives of their own.'[2] Taken together, these observations highlight two central tenets of this study: that clothing is central to what it is to be human, and, being worn next to the body, pertains intimately to our sense of self. Inextricably linked to our group and individual identities, clothing becomes part of us, while also maintaining a 'life' of its own, which we extend when we mend and care for an item of clothing. Crucially, however, that life is directly impacted by its makers and 'users'/wearers. It is shaped by the fibre from which it is made; the fabric influencing its design, cut and style; how and where it is made; and the way in which it is worn and cared for, which may change as it is passed from one wearer to another over time. Finally, a garment may be repurposed or upcycled, or, the fabric from which it is made, recycled, but eventually – and increasingly and tragically this is the case – some or all of it may end up in landfill. Orsola de Castro laments: 'Judging by how many things are left unused and unloved, the less we know about the clothes we buy, the less we make an emotional connection and the easier it is to get rid of them.'[3] Caring for our clothes amounts to caring for our environment.[4]

This book sets out to explore the hidden life of clothing, particularly as it relates to current dilemmas we face, as 'producers' and 'consumers'/'customers' – or, as I prefer to describe us – *makers* and *wearers* of clothing. As the economist Kate Raworth has observed, in the twentieth century, the use of the term 'consumer' grew steadily in public life, policymaking and the media until it outstripped the word 'citizen'. (By the mid-1970s 'consumer' was used widely in English-language books and newspapers.) Why does this nomenclature matter? Because unlike that of the 'citizen', the 'consumer's' means of expression is limited. As Raworth says: 'While citizens can address every aspect of cultural, social and economic life, consumers find expression only in the market place.'[5] It is precisely the commercialisation (and marketing) of clothing as 'fashion' that is at the heart of contemporary debates around the irreconcilability of the making and wearing of sustainable clothing. The idea that 'fashion' is a commodity rather than holding to the fact that clothing can connect us – through making and wearing – has distanced us from its creative and aesthetic qualities. And it is this that makes sustainability such a complex conundrum in relation to the future of fashion because clothing can be discarded so easily especially when it is the product of impersonal and opaque production processes.

So where does one begin writing about *The Hidden Life of Clothing*? And what does this phrase and the ideas it connotes even mean? One way to start is to focus on the separate words of the title with their different potential meanings – the 'keywords' in twenty-first-century terminology:

- *Hidden*: what cannot be seen or easily understood, either because it is not obvious or is deliberately obscured, or both of these;
- *Life*: the idea that something has an existence, which, by definition, is dependent on other 'lives';
- *Clothing* (note, *Fashion* came later!): fabrics/materials made into various wrappings for the body, whether for warmth, protection, modesty, display or all of these.

Woven into the fabric of the title, these broad definitions inform the ideas that are the focus of this study. The 'life of clothing' assumes an interest in how a garment is made and what it is made from; its journey from the place of making to the location from which it is purchased or acquired; its complex life in relation to its wearer or wearers (in particular how it is cared for – washed, mended and so on) and what happens to it when it is no longer wanted, whether it is given to charity, recycled or repurposed, or whether it ends up in landfill or is burnt. This book is not only about the life but the *life cycle* of clothing. And, crucially, it is about how clothing per se is given value and meaning in our own lives. It reveals that there is much to be gained by delving into that life – both in the contemporary context and in the historical context of the development and evolution of the clothing systems with which, in the West and increasingly globally, we are most familiar – and, above all, in relation to complex questions surrounding our understanding of sustainability. Our clothes – where they come from, how they are made and cared for and what happens to them when they are no longer useful to us – are closely linked to our economic and cultural values.

Of the supposed 53 million tonnes of textiles produced globally every year, shockingly over 75 per cent are discarded, both in the production phase and at post-consumer level.[6] According to Greenpeace, the average Western customer towards the end of the second decade of the twenty-first century bought 60 per cent more clothes a year and kept them for about half as long as fifteen years prior.[7] In the UK alone, the fashion industry is estimated to be worth about £32 billion, providing more than 850,000 jobs.[8] Fashion has frequently been cited as the 'second most polluting industry': in 2018, more than 8 per cent of global greenhouse-gas emissions were produced by the apparel and footwear industries and around 25 per cent of globally produced chemical compounds were utilised in the textile-finishing industry.[9]

In a climate of increasing anxiety about the environmental and social impact of the global fashion industry, this book explores the hidden life of clothing by deepening our understanding of history so that we might think in new ways about what sustainability actually means when we apply it to the fashion industry, and how this knowledge can help us influence the future of fashion. I am not seeking to find 'solutions' from the past, or to apply past practices out of context to our present dilemmas, but, paradoxically, I want to comprehend better some key issues in the evolution of fashion in order to throw new light on current debates. I look to history to assist in contextualising the challenges we face in making decisions about the clothing that fills our wardrobes. In so doing, I draw on dress and art history, philosophy, fictional literature and, not least, current thinking in economics. (How can one even talk about fashion without mentioning the latter?) In 1924, the economist J. M. Keynes argued that 'the master-economist must possess a rare *combination* of gifts. He must be mathematician, historian, statesman, philosopher'. (Far from claiming expertise in all of the disciplines mentioned earlier but, given that our relationship with our clothes impacts on so many areas of our lives, I have tried to touch on them as I see them influencing the choices we can make in obtaining, wearing and caring for our clothes.) Crucially, Keynes went on, 'he must study the present in the light of the past for the purposes of the future'.[10]

By laying bare the hidden life of clothing, I want to encourage awareness of the issues at stake when we make the decision to buy a new item of clothing or when we decide how to dispose of one that we no longer want to keep. How might it be possible to bridge divides between knowledge of the past, current individual choice and future directions? While considering the economic aspects of clothing production and retailing, this study suggests that we as wearers, by 'negotiating' what are often considerable pressures to choose *fashion* over sustainable clothing, can, by our individual behaviours, shape the future fashion industry. We need to tell the industry what we want from our clothes, *not* the other way around. Why should we accept without question manufacturers' and retailers' adoption of 'green-washing' practices or the public-relations spin which makes companies seem more caring of the environment than they truly are? Education and knowledge – knowing what are our choices and what influences them – are key to making 'sustainable' decisions. And we, as customers, hold the power to influence the fashion industry and fashion brands, if only we could reverse the hold that they seem to have over us. In short, history introduces alternative frameworks to those presented to us when we find it hard to see the horizon that lies beyond a contemporary perspective.

Readers, you might respond here that rather than *thinking* about a complex problem, surely it is *action* that makes the difference. I began writing this book in April 2020 with the UK three weeks into a lockdown as a result of the Covid-19 pandemic. Because of the enforced social isolation we have been experiencing, reflection becomes a powerful tool, perhaps even more powerful sometimes than all the 'action', which, until recently, was theoretically possible. My telephone and 'virtual' conversations with many people both during and since those lockdowns seem to bear this out.

Why do clothes matter so much, and at what point in our lives do they start to do so? The global and cultural historian Giorgio Riello points out that while for us textiles have 'quintessentially a consumer value', many of those imported to Southeast Asia in the Middle Ages (and beyond) were used for a variety of purposes including curing diseases, death and religious rights, the sanctification of icons and ceremonial and diplomatic exchange, suggesting that the use of cloth was not simply practical (covering one's body) or decorative (as fashionable apparel) but served to 'connect people across space and time'.[11] Anthropologists, meanwhile, hold that there are significant 'conditions' that separate humans from animals, such as storytelling and bipedalism, along with the fact that we clothe ourselves.[12] At birth when we are separated from the warmth of the womb, one of the first things that is done for us is wrapping us in cloth; and with this simple action, our nakedness becomes our 'otherness', while our clothed body is the one that most of us, for the majority of our time on this planet, will inhabit. Clothing has symbolic meaning in creation stories. In the Judaeo-Christian tradition, putting on clothing for the first time signified a loss of innocence: Adam and Eve became aware of their nakedness only after disobeying God and eating of the Tree of Knowledge of Good and Evil. Clothes also convey to others our perceptions of beauty and aesthetic choice. Dynamic and subject to change, the meanings we attach to particular items of clothing or specific looks or styling are culturally specific. Whether we are talking about the habit worn by a Christian nun, the hijab worn by a Muslim woman or the joggers and hoodies of

Generation Z, clothes act as an outer, second 'skin' – the skin with which we face both the social world and our own reflection in the mirror. Much of the time, we take their significance for granted. Yet, depending on the country, culture and climate into which we are born, clothes provide warmth (or, conversely, keep us cool), comfort, security, modesty and a sense of belonging and/or identity with, or difference from, social groups. As the sociologist Theodore Veblen observed, 'the need of dress is eminently a "higher" or spiritual need'.[13] Not only are material goods (including clothes) essential for our basic material needs but they also enable us to 'participate in the life of society'.[14]

In the West, and, increasingly in societies where there are developing fashion industries, we are required constantly to shape our identities through the medium of 'fashion'. The irony perhaps is that many of us seek to do so through what we are told is the current trend. Why is it a compliment to be described as being 'on trend' rather than an indication of a lack of individual style? Why do we 'need' followers on social media, or, indeed, to be the followers? Why do we want even to be influenced by the banality of the idea of 'influencers'? Thirty years ago, Malcolm McLaren observed in the early 1990s in inimitable radical fashion:

> It started with Levi's in the fifties. America has been marketing the workwear look – denim, dungarees, T-Shirts, and work shirts – ever since. But it doesn't impart any sophistication or individualism, any mystery or romantic notion, and ultimately it puts you on the production line with everybody else. It's irrelevant and boring . . . If we can wear something handmade and individual, it's a touch closer to reality, to roots. And this will be the beginning of a turnaround not only in fashion, but in all of culture.[15]

Whatever our personal clothing choices and style, our lived experiences of clothing become so much part of us that we are often unconscious of the subtle ways in which over time they both reflect and influence who we are. These experiences have often been kept opaque perhaps partly because sewing, making and caring for clothing have in the past frequently been associated with femininity and women's lives: as Virginia Woolf wrote in *A Room of One's Own* (1929), 'it is the masculine values that prevail', whereas the worship of fashion and the buying of clothes is so often considered 'trivial'.[16] Clothing tells us so much about the economics of past histories: in eighteenth-century Warwickshire, for example, as many as 6 per cent of the total number of apprentices taken on were girls, some of those as apprentices to women, chiefly in trades connected with sewing.[17]

Each of us will have our own particular autobiography in which a clothing narrative speaks to us and shapes both memory and current choices. Mine is as a child of the 1960s, growing up at a time when many people in the UK still made their own clothes. However, it was fast becoming cheaper and more 'convenient' to buy them ready-made, as a result of changes in retailing practices and fabric technologies that brought into the mainstream those man-made and synthetic fibres that we are now so familiar with, most notably nylon, acrylic, polyester, Lycra, and which we now see have become a significant part of the fast-fashion conundrum (see Chapters 2 and 3). This was the time when teenagers might be said to have been 'invented' and, with them, styles distinct from what are often described as the staid and dowdy clothing of parents (which, actually, in my experience, was anything but). What factors awakened my interest – and perhaps that of many others of my generation – in clothes, how they were acquired/made and cared for? Memories stand out seemingly randomly albeit significantly. I recall my father coming home from work as a personnel manager in the early 1970s; he changed immediately from his Marks & Spencer suit, shirt and tie to more casual clothing for the evening, and I recall the care with which he removed the change from his trouser pockets and then hung his jacket up. (I was shown by my mother how to iron – using a damp cloth placed over the fabric – and hang formal trousers, making sure the centre creases were in precisely the correct place.) Born in 1921 and having left formal education aged fifteen, my father, like so many of his generation, had a military training and lived through the chaos of the Second World War, parachuting into Normandy on the eve of D-Day; his organization and appearance were impeccable. He valued his (very few) clothes, choosing a new tie (a relatively frugal way of adding 'newness' to an old, well-worn suit) with care. These purchases were an occasion and a luxury, given that after he left the army and as a married man, he was on a low income. By the time I was born, there were already three older siblings. My mother meanwhile – aged fourteen when the war ended and therefore used to wartime shortages which continued into the 1950s – loved clothes and like many of her generation, taught herself to sew and make do as a young woman.

I loved the picture my mother painted for me of the young woman taking the train from Salisbury to London for the day in the early 1950s wearing the 'charcoal grey wool suit' she had made, along with a pair of shop-bought 'dusky' pink gloves, hat and shoes, at a time when coordinating accessories was the 'fashion', rather than the deliberate mix-and-*don't*-match approach favoured seventy years later. Like army personnel taking care of their kit and appearance in the mud of the trenches, or women wearing high-heeled shoes as they surveyed the debris of their shattered lives among the destruction of the London Blitz, it was as if a sense of personal neatness and coordination in the years following the Second World War was a way of creating order out of the devastating and random chaos that had been unleashed over the preceding years.

Like many women of her time, my mother made her own wedding dress when she married in 1955. Not only did she continue to make her own clothes when she became a mother, eventually, of five children, but she also made dresses for my three sisters and me when we were young, often out of the same fabric. Dressing siblings – especially daughters – alike was not unusual and meant that one could minimise waste in the cutting out of precious fabric. However, the long-term effect on me – the youngest and least vocal of four sisters – was urgently to establish a sense of self through my own (different) clothes. And I desperately wanted *more* clothes than the very minimal wardrobe I possessed. (Only when I became a buyer for Marks & Spencer in the early 1990s with more disposable income and 'overdrafts' from university study finally paid off was this dream fulfilled.)

One of my earliest clothing memories was of identical yellow-and-white cotton gingham, high-waisted 'best' dresses my mother made for my three sisters and me and which we wore for the first time on a visit to our grandmother. Having devoted so much time and endless patience to making four of the same dresses differing only in size and length (my eldest sister is seven years my senior), my mother must have been distraught when tiny flecks of black tar covered our dresses as we walked past road works on Salisbury High Street where road resurfacing was taking place. I don't remember wearing the dress again after that: no amount of washing (my mother had a twin tub which meant coming into contact with the clothes while they were being washed as one slopped the washed clothes into the spin-dryer) and rubbing the fabric in the affected areas would remove the stains. But I do remember being upset as a result of the despoiling of one of our very few items of summer clothing. Nobody thought of asking for 'compensation' then and in any case, how would one put a monetary value on dresses into which the efforts of a time-starved young housewife had been lavished? Apart from this dress, I remember owning a couple of pink cotton sleeveless dresses that I cherished because none of my sisters had worn them: handed down by a family friend, they fitted only me.

The first time I had a brand new, ready-made outfit was in the mid-1970s when my mother bought me for my twelfth birthday a turquoise Crimplene flared trouser suit from the store Owen Owen[18] in Weston-Super-Mare. I have not forgotten the intense excitement of that shopping trip! She also made me a coordinating floral blouse in cotton to wear underneath it with a large 'fashionable' collar. To complete the outfit, I bought a pair of plastic platform shoes (from either Dolcis[19] or Freeman, Hardy and Willis[20]) and a number of knee-length white nylon socks with different patterns from Littlewoods,[21] which I adored. I dread to think what I *actually* looked like, but wearing this outfit as I entered my teenage years transformed how I felt – different from my former self and perhaps part of the 'fashionable' crowd. A similar, transformative effect of clothing in an earlier generation is captured brilliantly by George Orwell in *The Road to Wigan Pier* (1937): 'You may have three-half-pence in your pocket and not a prospect in the world . . . but in your new clothes you can stand on the street corner, indulging in a private daydream of yourself as Clark Gable or Greta Garbo.'[22] Our clothes both shape and reflect dreams of who we want to be.

The memories of my own world of clothing as I grew up thus reflect the period of transition that the 1970s represent. Although ready-made clothing was becoming more widely available, it was still often cheaper to make one's own clothes. While I disliked domestic science classes at school where we made aprons and shoe-bags, my imagination was unleashed by the sight of rolls of wonderful, tactile fabrics in 1970s department stores as well as the abundance of paper patterns. These fabrics – all kinds of silks; cottons, including ginghams and lawn; wools of different weights and patterns along with rows of matching artificial silk lining fabrics – were objects of beauty in their own right and utility was not necessarily the primary consideration when making a purchase. Learning to sew on my mother's 1950s solid and reliable electric Singer sewing-machine (it seemed that the tension never had to be adjusted whatever the fabric being sewn), I adapted pattern pieces from 'Style', 'Simplicity', 'McCalls' and 'Very Easy Vogue' and added trimmings to plain styles to make something individual. Rather than be prescribed what to make (as at school), I wanted to invent new outfits and looks. It was probably the mention of 'notions' on the back of paper pattern envelopes that drew me towards haberdashery, spending pocket money in our local store, Walker and Ling.[23] Like so many department stores of its time, this shop was a mecca for dress fabrics and haberdashery, the latter including ribbons of all widths and materials – 'modern', synthetic nylon but also more expensive silk and cotton velvets, the latter nowadays available in such variety only in specialist haberdashery store V. V. Rouleaux.[24] These were laid out in orderly rows on reels displayed according to colour/shade and width in a beautiful glass-fronted wooden cabinet unit. To me, the sales assistant – whose job was to measure and cut the ribbons that were interleaved with fine white paper streams, on the haberdashery unit's inlaid brass yard measure – had the best job in the world. Lynn Knight observes that a 'prosaic list cannot begin to convey haberdashery's pleasures':

> Ardern's Crochet Cotton; Clark's Embroidery Thread; tuppenny packets of Flora Macdonald needles; Stratnoid Knitting Pins; floral paper baskets opening to reveal rows of needles and pins; knitting wools; feathers, ribbons, beads and braids ... comprise some of the many items needed for decorative and functional sewing.[25]

The choice of knitting wools, fabric, paper patterns and accompanying 'notions' (thread, zips, buttons, interlining) helps to visualise the item of clothing, a very different process from buying it ready-made where the wearer is disassociated and distanced from its manufacture.

Personal selection of design, fabric and trimmings creates a strong thread connecting maker and finished garment. In his novel *The Woodlanders* (1887), Thomas Hardy observed that 'there can be hardly anything less connected with a woman's personality than drapery which she has neither designed, manufactured, cut, sewed, nor even seen'.[26] At the time when Hardy was writing, ready-made clothing was beginning to come into its own in the UK. Not only did the technology, retailing and marketing practices that made this possible change the way clothing was produced and purchased, but, ultimately, it affected how we *feel* about our clothes, along with the attachments we have – or often don't have – to them. From the early nineteenth century the democratisation of the clothing industry in the United States of America and Western Europe began to make more affordable clothing available to growing populations. In theory, working- and middle-class wearers had *greater* choice in terms of where and what they bought, but correspondingly and increasingly over time, *less* control over how their clothing was made. One of the consequences of this complex process has been our disconnection from the creative and human aspects of the making of clothing so that clothing becomes a commodity rather than an extension of our bodies, personalities and souls. According to community textile artist and curator, Clare Hunter, we should mourn both the lack of visibility of textiles and that of the process of sewing in our lives: 'The act has become separate from the object, the maker from what they have made, and with it we have lost its emotional and social potency.'[27]

In the twenty-first century, economic models of growth have fed our expectations, which in turn translates into increasing acquisition of clothing at relatively low prices. Quality meanwhile seems far less important or relevant than it did because clothing is not expected to last. (Ironic perhaps, given that, as we shall see in Chapter 2, a significant factor holding back the burgeoning ready-made clothing industry in its early days was its association with poor quality.) As a result, in high-income and industrialised nations the market has become saturated with clothing about which wearers know little in terms of its fabric and provenance. Arguably clothing is valued less for its inherent aesthetic qualities or because of the hours spent in its making, but more for the extent to which it serves current trends. And since the end of the twentieth century, *fashion* has more often than not become synonymous with *fast fashion*. Unsurprisingly we have become increasingly disassociated from the clothes that we wear, not only because we have not designed or made them ourselves but also because of the way we *buy* and will *dispose* of them. The advent of ready-made, machine-made and mass-produced clothing that has gained momentum since the late nineteenth century, along with our current obsession with 'fast' fashion, has become a metaphor for our increasingly fast-moving and restless twenty-first-century state of mind. One more piece for our wardrobe is like one more dopamine-inducing fix from our email inbox or social media feed.

For me there was a discernible shift in my habits of clothing acquisition in the 1980s: in my twenties working as a knitwear buyer at Marks & Spencer head office gave me insights into the processes that produce mass-produced clothing. Fascinating though this was, the pressure to wear a different outfit each day in the office – in short, to 'look the part' – combined with being in an environment where the success of the department was measured by the level of percentage increase on the previous week's sales figures nurtured extreme discontent with my own material possessions and put me on a wheel of acquisition that became self-fulfilling; the more variety in my wardrobe, the more I got tired of clothes that I had worn only half a dozen times and the more I wanted to replenish. Perhaps the relative 'deprivation' of clothing during my childhood fuelled my desire to consume and this might be the case for many of us born after, but still experiencing, a culture of frugality in the post–Second World War period. On Saturdays (no doubt like many other young people in the 1990s encouraged to have credit on store cards) I often spent the day shopping for clothes; 'researching' trends, yes, but really what I was after was the acquisition of 'stuff'.

The advent of online clothes shopping has succeeded in distancing us even further from the connection we might otherwise have with our clothes. We invest very little in that item of clothing before acquiring it; not much more perhaps than one 'click' on our mobile devices, having perhaps selected it from the seemingly endless 'choices' available that have, in fact, been styled for us by manipulative advertising and marketing undertaken by brands and increasingly promoted by influencers. We do not get to feel the fabric of the garment in advance or try it on for fit. This clothing also seems relatively 'cheap' (to us) in purely monetary terms and so if we wear it only a dozen times, it does not find its place into our hearts or become associated with important routines or particular periods in our lives and, because we have so much already, it can become just one more disposable commodity with which we fill our already overflowing wardrobe. Necessity does not require us to remake it into something else or cut it into patchwork pieces for, say, a quilt or a cushion cover as would so often have been done in the past. Arguably it is the prospect of acquiring an item of clothing that gives us that addictive dopamine rush. And it seems so much easier to buy something new rather than care for or cherish what we already have! And so we can dispose of the 'old' without a thought and very little, if any, guilt. How many people say 'thank you', Marie Kondo-style, for the 'joy' that an item of clothing has brought them before, at worst, throwing it into the rubbish destined for landfill or, at best, giving it to charity or selling it on, say, Ebay or Depop?[28] The value we might attach to our clothes and the gratitude we have for the purpose that they have served seem to have vanished (Figures I.1 and I.2).

Figure I.1 Abandoned clothing near railway at Charing Cross, London, UK, January 2019. Photo by Rachel Worth.

Figure I.2 Textile recycling bank, Dorchester, UK, January 2022. Photo by Rachel Worth.

This book explores the historical contexts and processes that have influenced our clothing choices since at least the eighteenth century, beginning (in Chapter 1) by highlighting hidden aspects of the life of clothing: the subtle but complex ways in which the language of clothing was woven into the rhymes, proverbs and idioms encountered by children but that went on to shape the adult view of the world. Chapter 2 traces the origins of Western fashion systems that exploited new industrial, technological and retailing practices that made it possible from the early nineteenth century for the poor and less well-off to buy new, ready-made clothing. The latter was seen as a 'good thing' and not just because it made huge profits for businesses and entrepreneurs alike: the relative cheapness of mass-produced clothing enabled working-class people to buy, for example, shoes for their children rather than have them go barefooted, or to acquire two sets of clothes rather than have only one. Not only did clothing serve basic human needs for warmth and protection, but it added colour to people's lives and facilitated means of display, self-expression and identity – both as individuals and as social groups. However, while initially providing a positive solution to combating (clothing) poverty and inequality in the face of expanding populations and changing patterns of demand, 'democratisation' also held within it the seeds of inequality, not only because of the slave, sweated and 'outsourced' labour upon which it came to depend and which fundamentally broke the threads that link makers of clothing to wearers, but also because of the waste and promotion of overconsumption upon which such industrial growth models rely. What 'sustainability' actually means and how it has evolved as a concept in relation to fashion and later fast fashion (and the backlash against fast fashion) are discussed in Chapter 3. In the nineteenth century, recycling and reuse of both clothing and fabric were commonplace but the advent of fast fashion encourages us to reconsider 'sustainable' practices from the past. There is a full discussion of some of the environmental and ethical considerations around the production of both natural and man-made/synthetic fabrics and the use of fur, as well as issues of 'transparency' as these relate to the provenance of contemporary, mass-produced garments. Chapter 4 brings the discussion of sustainability in fashion more fully into the contemporary arena, in particular by problematising the ways in which fashion became embroiled in dominant business models and economic paradigms privileging growth and profit that have paved the way for ever-increasing and ultimately unsustainable levels of production while perpetuating the terrible working conditions of textile and garment workers that should have been eradicated once and for all in the past.

This segues into an exploration in Chapter 5 of some fascinating narratives that draw threads linking clothing with the natural world and, in Chapter 6, with new 'philosophies' of dress in which 'dress' and 'clothes' became the focus of a backlash against the drive towards consumerism and the commodification of fashion and retailing/shopping. Some of these most trenchant objections to both fashion – and to the processes of mass production that produced it – were voiced in the cause of 'nature' and are exemplified by the work of designer William Morris and adherents of the Arts and Crafts Movement as well as by the views expressed by exponents of the Aesthetic Dress Movement both in the nineteenth century and into the twentieth.

Finally, I conclude by looking to some alternatives to the limitations posed by unsustainable practices and to the human and aesthetic potential unleashed by individuals and organisations that creatively challenge fast fashion. I suggest that the more we know, and the more we know how to care about, our clothes, the less likely we will wear an item of clothing only a few times before 'replenishing' it with newer purchases. By taking ownership of our own clothing choices rather than feeling pressurised by sophisticated marketing or remaining blind to the inherently limiting tastes of 'influencers', how might we rethink our wardrobes in philosophical and practical ways that create a sense of order and beauty in our lives, wresting control back from the chaos of seemingly endless choice that perpetuates unsustainable, impersonal fast fashion? Looking to history helps us to trace the threads that link past to present, and, ultimately, to the future of fashion. In this respect we urgently need this future to be better than the past. As the late economist Manfreed Max-Neef tells us, by looking to the past we can imagine the routes that we did not take and in this we may find alternatives: 'And then it may be wise to unearth the alternative map of the route we did not navigate, and see whether we can find in it orientations that can rescue us from our existential confusion.'[29]

1

The hidden language of clothing

I am a poor old man, come listen to my song.
Provisions now are twice as dear as when that I was young;
When this old hat was new and stood above my brow,
Oh! what a happy youth was I when this old hat was new.

(Traditional verse)

The (natural) fibres used to weave the fabrics that have made human clothing are older than the language that has evolved to define and describe it. Evidence of the use of flax fibres by 'modern' humans, including for clothing – some of which were twisted and dyed – has been found at the Dzudzuana cave in the Caucasus Mountains in the Republic of Georgia. The fibres are dated to around 34,500 years ago. Linen, meanwhile, has been found in the Valley of the Kings in Egyptian tombs which were constructed from around 3100 BCE.[1] Early silk production in China has been dated to before 2750 BCE, while wool used by the Vikings (for sails and probably for clothing too) has been dated to 850 CE.[2] Scholars have suggested that cotton originated in India and was first cultivated in the Indus Valley in 3200 BCE with cotton cultivation reaching sub-Saharan Africa and southern Europe by the tenth century.[3] As we have seen, the history of man-made and synthetic fibres is much more recent, dating from the late nineteenth century (see also Chapter 3).

The language that has evolved as a result of sourcing fibres, developing fabric and making and mending clothing reveals how richly woven our language is with metaphors, proverbs and idioms that refer to our material experience of making and wearing clothes, both reflecting and influencing how we see and experience the world. Kassia St Clair writes:

> When we talk of lives hanging by a thread, being interwoven or being part of the social fabric; or, if we want to help someone in danger of unravelling . . . we are part of a tradition that stretches back many thousands of years. Fabric and

its component parts have long been a figurative stand-in for the very stuff of human life.[4]

Metaphors describing 'being on tenterhooks' or 'spinning a yarn' reveal, observes St Clair, how the language of textiles is 'like the ticking of a clock in a room: inescapable once noticed'.[5] This 'rich tapestry of oral wisdom' is repeated all over the world: in France and Italy, respectively, 'retourner sa veste' refers metaphorically to the age-old habit of wearing your jacket inside out to make it last longer, and 'volta gabbana' describes someone who has changed their mind; in Spain something simple to do is as easy as 'cortar y coser' (cutting and sewing) and in Kazakhstan you congratulate someone by bidding them to 'wear it a long time'.[6] Significantly, many of these metaphors 'are themselves becoming over-stretched and threadbare, because most of us have very little experience or understanding of their original meanings'.[7] Metaphors, far from being mere figures of speech, structure our most basic understanding of our experience, and, as George Lakoff and Mark Johnson argue in their classic book, become 'metaphors we live by', reflecting and shaping our perceptions of the world.[8] This chapter is about how nursery rhymes/songs and the idioms and proverbs of everyday speech reveal some of the ways in which this 'language' of clothing became a vital and colourful part of our consciousness and of the complex ways in which clothing thus shapes our adult view of the world. If those clothing metaphors have lost their meaning for us, because the world they reflect and describe no longer exists as a result of our increasing disconnection from our clothing, this surely has wider implications for how we tackle the impasse that is fast fashion. The world referred to and illuminated by such language in rhymes is one before the widespread democratisation of clothing that is described in subsequent chapters and is therefore a fitting prequel to a narrative that describes a world on the brink of industrialisation of the textile and clothing industries.

Nursery rhymes, fabric and clothing

Scholars have delved into the meanings of nursery rhymes, the first stories set to what often become familiar tunes to young children. Most parents probably introduce these seemingly innocuous stories to their children without knowing what Clemency Burton-Hill has described as the 'shockingly sinister backstories'.[9] The earliest nursery rhymes probably date from the fourteenth century, although the 'golden age' probably came later in the eighteenth century. The earliest known English nursery rhyme book, *Tommy Thumb's (Pretty) Song Book*, was published for the 'Diversion of all Little Masters and Misses' in 1744, and was issued in two volumes, priced at sixpence a volume, bound and gilt-edged. Like many of its successors in the next eighty years it was of midget proportions, with pages 3 in. by 1¾ in., each page containing a single rhyme usually headed by a miniature engraving. This layout was adopted at the beginning of the nineteenth century for the little nursery rhyme chapbooks which were sold up and down the country, in marketplaces and at cottage doors, for a penny or a halfpenny.[10] A little over a century later Edward Rimbault published a collection of nursery rhymes, which was the first one to include notated music.[11]

Some form of rhyming ditties for children seems to be a universal practice among many human cultures, the distinctive sing-song metre, tonality and rhythms thought to have a proven evolutionary value, serving to aid a child's mental development and spatial reasoning, foster emotional connections and cultivate language and 'complete' the world. Parents singing nursery rhymes to their children are said to create a special bond. Furthermore, in a time when to caricature royalty or politicians was punishable by death, nursery rhymes proved a potent way to smuggle in coded or thinly veiled messages in the guise of children's entertainment. In largely illiterate societies, the catchy sing-song melodies helped people remember the stories and, crucially, pass them on to the next generation.[12] In this way, they have become an enduring legacy of oral history.

Some of the best-known rhymes reference such topical themes as plagues (the subject of 'Ring a Ring O' Roses' is thought to refer to the horrors of the Great Plague of 1665[13]), political intrigue and taxes. A case in point is 'Baa Baa Black Sheep', which can be read as a statement of class injustice:

> Baa baa black sheep,
> Have you any wool?
> Yes, sir, yes, sir,
> Three bags full;
> One for the master,
> One for the dame,
> And one for the little boy
> Who lives down the lane.[14]

This rhyme reflects the importance of wool to the English economy in the medieval period. Albert Jack points out that until at least 1765 (when it was included in *Mother Goose Melody*, published by John Newbery), the last line of the rhyme read, 'And none for the little boy who cries in the lane'. So 'rather than being a gentle song about sharing things out fairly, it's a bitter reflection on how unfair things have always been for working folk throughout history'.[15] It was probably changed to the current version in order to make it less gloomy and a song more suitable for children. The prosperity of medieval England owed much to the flourishing wool trade: in 1086 the Domesday Book recorded that many flocks across the country numbered more than 2,000 sheep with English landowners including the church counting their wealth in terms of sheep, which were tended by dozens of shepherds. By the late twelfth century Guildford, Northampton, Lincoln and York had become thriving centres of production, with wool finding a healthy domestic market as well as being exported to Europe where it was dyed and woven into high-quality cloth. In order to pay for his military campaigns, Edward I, on returning from the Crusades in 1272, imposed new taxes on the wool trade: in 1275 the Great Custom was introduced in the shape of a royal tax of six shillings and eight pence per wool sack (approximately one-third of the price of each sack). It was this wool tax that is said to be the basis of the rhyme: the tax was divvied up between the master (king) and the dame (the monasteries) but none went to the shepherd ('the little boy who cries in the lane') who had tirelessly tended and protected the flock.[16]

The origins of the lyrics of other nursery rhymes are disputed, but many contain either direct or oblique references to different aspects of the textile and clothing trades: 'Half a Pound of Tuppenny Rice' became a popular music hall song, performed throughout Victorian London's many theatres:

> Half a pound of tuppenny rice,
> Half a pound of treacle,
> That's the way the money goes,
> Pop goes the weasel.

In the textile industry, a spinner's 'weasel' is a device used for measuring out a length of yarn; the mechanism made a popping sound when the correct length was reached. No doubt during this highly repetitive and boring work, the spinner's mind would wander, only to be brought back to harsh reality when the weasel went 'pop'. However, the third verse of the same rhyme suggests an alternative origin, which is based upon the use of London cockney rhyming slang;

> Up and down the city road,
> In and out the Eagle,

That's the way the money goes,
Pop goes the weasel.[17]

To 'pop' is a London slang word for pawn, while 'weasel' can be traced to the cockney rhyming slang of 'weasel and stoat', or coat. Even a very poor Londoner in Victorian times would have had a Sunday best coat or suit that could be pawned (perhaps on a cold and damp Monday morning when times were hard), only to be retrieved on pay day. (Melanie Tebbutt has shown how the regular pawning of clothing to raise much-needed ready cash/credit – which might include money for beer at the pub – was still common practice in the Victorian period.[18]) 'The Eagle' may refer to the Eagle Tavern (2, Shepherdess Walk, N1), a pub located on the corner of City Road and Shepherdess Walk, in the north London district of Hackney.[19]

A number of nursery rhymes thought to reference particular historical events use clothing both symbolically and also to construct the narrative of the rhyme. It is thought that 'Hark, Hark' is about the dissolution of the monasteries, the aftermath of which saw a surge in poverty as the traditional role of the monasteries in providing hospitality and charity to the many poor people in Tudor England disappeared: that is why 'the beggars are coming to town' with some of them in rags although it isn't clear why one of them should be in a 'velvet gown':

Hark, hark,
The dogs do bark,
The beggars are coming to town;
Some in rags,
And some in jags,
And one in a velvet gown.[20]

An alternative theory is that the rhyme evolved from a countrywide hue and cry and that the 'one in a velvet gown' refers to William of Orange, who landed in Plymouth in 1688 and marched his 'Beghards' through the towns and villages of England to victory over James II.[21]

Another well-known rhyme, 'Yankee Doodle', is now the official anthem of Connecticut although it was made up by British army officers in the late eighteenth century to mock their badly disciplined Yankee counterparts during the French and Indian War (1754–63) between Britain and France over their respective territories in the North American colonies (part of the Seven Years' War). The word 'macaroni' seems first to have appeared in the 1760s and became associated with a group of men purportedly obsessed with fashion, and who wore exaggerated versions of contemporary styles and were consequently lampooned by contemporary caricaturists.[22] In the rhyme, fun is being poked at someone who thinks that he is the very height of fashion (a macaroni) on account of the fact that he has stuck a feather in his cap.[23]

> Yankee Doodle came to town,
> Riding on a Pony;
> He stuck a feather in his cap
> And called it macaroni.[24]

Like many nursery rhymes that evolve as a result of being sung in a slightly different form over generations, 'Here We Go Round the Mulberry Bush' has an uncertain origin. Mulberry trees – the leaves of which are the preferred food of silkworms – have been associated with prisons since the early nineteenth century, when many prison governors entered the profitable British silk industry.[25] The particular mulberry tree of the rhyme has been associated with Wakefield (now a high-security) prison in the West Riding of Yorkshire, whose origins date back to the 1590s when it was established as a House of Correction. The tree – which has now died and was removed in 2019 – was thought to date to the nineteenth century, so it may be that the rhyme was recited originally by female inmates of the House of Correction given that subsequent verses reference repetitive and mundane domestic tasks, many of which specifically refer to the care of clothing: 'This is the way we wash our clothes', 'iron our clothes', 'mend our clothes' and so on. While such tasks were traditionally a female domain in many societies, crafts such as shoemaking and tailoring were usually associated with men:

> Cobbler, cobbler, mend my shoe;
> Get it done by half past two;
> Stitch it up and stitch it down,
> Then I'll give you half a crown.[26]

Tailors were also traditionally male, as in the rhyme about the one-eyed tailor of Bicester:

> The tailor of Bicester
> He has but one eye;
> He cannot cut a pair of galligaskins,
> If he were to die.[27]

Galligaskins were loose breeches, so the point being made is probably that the tailor cannot see well enough even to make an item of clothing that doesn't need to fit snugly.

Rhymes about clothing and class

Nursery rhymes are often stereotypically gendered: while the idea of a man obsessed with style and clothing is ridiculed in the reference to the macaronis previously mentioned, the vast majority of rhymes themed around either an interest in clothing or the care of clothing are reminders of the intimate connections built mostly between women and clothing as in the rhyme 'Washing Day':

> The old woman must stand
> At the tub, tub, tub,
> The dirty clothes
> To rub, rub, rub;
> But when they are clean,
> And fit to be seen,
> She'll dress like a lady,
> And dance on the green.[28]

Clean clothing confers, at the very least, respectability but also – as in the last four lines of this rhyme – the ability to move into a different class, the rhyme thereby providing an incitement to cleanliness. Before the advent of washing machines or modern detergents, washing clothes was a time-consuming and laborious task.

There are many allusions in nursery rhymes to the ways in which clothing and fabric signify class and social status and the power of appearances in raising people out of the class into which they were born, as well as the performative properties of particular fabrics to bring about class levelling, for example:

> Hush-a-bye, baby, they're gone to milk,
> Lady and milkmaid all in silk[29]

In the main, however, rhymes in which clothing and fabrics feature bear witness to the inequalities in society, such as in the game of counting cherry stones – the number of cherry stones denoting the girl 'predicting' when she will get married (this year, next year, sometime, never), to whom she will get married (tinker, tailor, soldier, sailor, rich man, poor man, beggar-man, thief) and in what fabric she will get married (silk, satin, cotton, rags). The latter reveals the hierarchy of fabric in terms of expense and class association prior, that is, to the democratisation and levelling brought about gradually from the late eighteenth century with the industrialisation of the cotton industry. One of the measures of higher social status was the acquisition of superior skills in needlework: in George Eliot's novel *Adam Bede*, Hetty Sorrel longs to reach out of her own humble class; next best to becoming a lady is to become a lady's maid and to that end she receives instruction from Mrs Pomfret to learn to do 'lace-mending' and 'stocking-mending' in a way that 'you can't tell it's been mended'.[30] The accomplishment of being able to 'sew a fine seam' is suggestive of being lifted out of one's current social status whether by a change in fortunes or, as in the well-known rhyme 'Curly Locks', through marriage:

> Curly locks, curly locks,
> Wilt you be mine?
> Thou shalt not wash dishes,
> Nor yet feed the swine;
> But sit on a cushion
> And sew a fine seam,
> And feed upon strawberries,
> Sugar and cream.[31]

On the other hand, some rhymes in which the narrator is wooing his sweetheart (and it is invariably this way around rather than women doing the wooing), the narrator makes seemingly impossible demands, such as that for a cambric (cotton) shirt without any seams so presumably woven in one piece:

> Can you make me a cambric shirt,
> Parsley, sage, rosemary, and thyme,
> Without any seam or needlework?
> And you shall be a true lover of mine.[32]

In the Early Modern period, people were expected ordinarily to remain in the social position into which they were born – the social order of things and the status quo thought to be ordained by God. Dressing above one's station, therefore, was often expressed in ways that border on the absurd. But human nature and ambition being what they are, the age-old desire to 'better oneself' is also reflected frequently in nursery rhymes. Perhaps those rhymes that seem either, on the one hand, to support the status quo, or, on the other, to upset it, are not saying anything unusual, but that they should do so with reference to clothing and fabric is testament to a world we have lost:

> What shall I wear to the wedding,
> Billy, my own sweet lad?
> You have your apron and gown,

If you think it is good.
Shall I wear nothing that's finer,
Billy, my own sweet lad?
Would you wear satin and silk?
I think that the girl is gone mad.[33]

Rhymes with an advisory or cautionary (clothing) theme

A number of other nursery rhymes with a catchy and jaunty metre use clothing to show how the world or at any rate individuals are 'gone mad', such as 'Diddle, diddle, dumpling, my son John', who goes to bed 'with his trousers on':

One shoe off, and one shoe on,
Diddle, diddle dumpling, my son John.[34]

In the case of the well-known alliterative 'Wee Willie Winkie' who 'runs through the town / Upstairs and downstairs in his nightgown', the rhyme was presumably supposed to have the effect of persuading young children of exhausted parents to get to bed at a reasonable time (nothing changes!):

Rapping at the window, crying through the lock,
Are the children all in bed, for now it's eight o'clock?[35]

Eight o'clock seems quite early in our electricity-/television-/internet-'enabled' world, but when parents had much to do in the evenings in preparation for the following day and staying up late in the autumn and winter meant lighting precious candles, there was an incentive to get children to bed, especially as they were up earlier in the morning, particularly in the summer months, in order to make use of precious daylight.

So, nursery rhymes are not the flippant, light-hearted ditties that we might assume them to be: indeed, they sometimes offer a cautionary tale or give advice which makes 'sense' only when we understand the context. So, for example, in an age before central heating and when large swathes of the population, engaged in agricultural pursuits, spent much of their time outdoors, it makes perfect sense to remember to button up one's clothes to the chin as soon as the autumnal weather of October begins and not to take off, put away or dispose of a 'clout' (originally a garment or a piece of cloth/patch with which to mend a hole) until the end of May:

Button to chin
When October comes in;
Cast not a clout
Till May be out.[36]

Some rhymes are exhortations to mend one's clothes and again this makes sense when we consider that clothing was not disposable or throwaway in previous times when people often had very few material possessions, which were often handed down or made at home. Ally this with the belief that waste of any kind was anathema and the following rhyme strikes one as less implausible:

Hold up your head,
Turn out your toes,
Speak when you're spoken to,
Mend your clothes.[37]

Other rhymes offer guidance for acquiring and caring for clothes. Grown in many cottage gardens, and sold on provincial streets and markets, lavender is a traditional way of keeping marauding moths at bay and it was also stored with clothes to make them smell nice, as noted in the song 'Sweet Blooming Lavender':

You buy it once you will buy it twice;
It will make your clothes smell sweet and nice.[38]

Before clothes driers, the natural – and only – way of keeping clothes white was to hang them outside to dry after washing or even to lay them on the grass to dry (see later). This practice is probably what lies behind the rhyme:

Down by the river
Where the green grass grows,
Pretty Polly Perkins
Bleaches her clothes.[39]

Some rhyming stories such as 'Old Mother Hubbard and Her Dog' (in which Old Mother Hubbard goes to the tailors to buy her dog a coat; to the hatters to buy him a hat; to the barbers to buy him a wig; to the cobblers to buy him some shoes; to the seamstress to buy him some linen; to the hosier's to buy him some hose) seem prosaic or even bizarre but, in fact, offer valuable insights into the acquisition of clothing and the way in which retailing was highly specialised before the advent of department stores and changes in retailing in the nineteenth century.[40]

While a number of nursery rhymes offer 'advice' on the practicalities of caring for clothes, others are cautionary tales to children, suggesting punishment for damage done to, or loss of, precious clothes. Shocking as these are to a contemporary reader, they give us further insight into the value placed on clothing, because it represented the spending of hard-earned wages or else time-starved personal resources if made at home:

Little Polly Flinders
Sat among the cinders,
Warming her pretty little toes;
Her mother came and caught her,
And whipped her little daughter
For spoiling her nice new clothes.[41]

Other rhymes transfer the focus of the story to animals, often to cats, perhaps partly because they would have been the most common domestic pets – performing a practical service to a household by catching mice, rats and other 'vermin' – but also because of the playful (and sometimes destructive) nature of cat behaviour! But in 'Pussy Cat Mole' they are also given human characteristics and emotions:

Pussy cat mole jumped over a coal
And in her best petticoat burnt a great hole.
Poor Pussy's weeping, she'll have no more milk
Until her best petticoat's mended with silk.[42]

In the well-known tale of the 'Three Little Kittens', the kittens lose their mittens, with their mother punishing them by not giving them any pie; however, when they find their mittens they are allowed some pie. Similarly when they soil them but later wash them, they are restored to their mother's favour and become 'good kittens'.[43] One wonders if Beatrix Potter, in her *Tale of Peter Rabbit*, had nursery rhymes in mind when she tells us how Peter – feeling unwell having disobeyed his mother by going into Mr McGregor's garden and eating too many radishes and lettuces, at the same time losing his clothes – gets back to the safety of home and is put to bed early by his mother with chamomile tea whereas his siblings who 'were good little bunnies' have milk and bread and blackberries.[44]

The expense of items needed for making clothing such as pins and needles (as well as the clothing itself) helps to explain the anathema to waste in such well-known cautionary rhymes as 'See a Pin':

See a pin and pick it up,
All the day you'll have good luck;
See a pin and let it lay,
Bad luck you'll have all the day.[45]

The 'warning' becomes more meaningful when we appreciate that pins and needles were expensive items and that they were a necessity for the fastening of clothing and the arrangement of dress accessories in the sixteenth and seventeenth centuries; their importance for women as a personal requirement and expense is reflected in the term pin-money, which refers to the sum originally allocated to meet this essential cost. Before the mid-sixteenth century the finest pins were imported from France but their manufacture in England was encouraged under Henry VIII: in 1543 an 'Act for the True Making of Pynnes' was passed which aimed to control their quality and price. The Victoria and Albert Museum, London (V&A) has examples of pins made of silvered brass made between 1662 and 1800 possibly in Gloucestershire and London, both of which became the main centres of the English pin-making industry.[46] Even though pins are not the necessity that they were for our ancestors, to this day, I always pick up a pin if I see one on the floor . . . just in case!

A number of the best-known rhymes operate on two levels, such as 'Lucy and Kitty':

Lucy Lockit lost her pocket,
Kitty Fisher found it;
Not a penny was there in it,
Only ribbon round it.[47]

On a superficial level this could be a straightforward story about the loss of a pocket: before the advent of handbags separate 'pockets' for carrying personal effects were worn by women under their dresses in the seventeenth, eighteenth and (briefly again) in the nineteenth centuries. These pockets were flat, fabric bags, usually made of linen or cotton, with openings on the front face only. They were generally worn in pairs and tied around the waist, beneath the skirts of a dress which had slits, or pocket holes, at the sides to permit access.[48]

A more complex and less literal interpretation of this rhyme, however, is that it is about prostitution.[49] As Marcia Pointon has explained, the Kitty Fisher of the rhyme is likely to be the celebrated eighteenth-century courtesan whose portrait was painted variously by Nathaniel Hone (1765) and by Sir Joshua Reynolds in 1759 and again in the 1760s. To corroborate this, Pointon has alluded to John Gay's *Beggar's Opera* (1728) in which a Lucy Lockit appears:

The content of the rhyme appears to allude to some kind of succession in relation to the loss of virtue for purposes of monetary gain: the pocket or purse or jewel case commonly features in monetary exchanges for sexual favours . . . We may understand the nursery rhyme as a cautionary tale about the financial instability of women of easy virtue: Kitty will fill the purse she has inherited but it may soon be as empty as when she received it.[50]

Rhymes about clothing poverty

Unsurprisingly, many nursery rhymes use descriptions of clothing to signify poverty. In 'The Legacy', the narrator lists all the worldly goods of his late father, which includes a pair of leather breeches:

My father died a month ago
And left me all his riches;
A feather bed, a wooden leg,
And a pair of leather breeches;
A coffee pot without a spout,
A cup without a handle,
A tobacco pipe without a lid,
And half a farthing candle.[51]

Given widespread poverty until at least the mid-nineteenth century, the majority of people did not leave wills as such although they could leave a list of bequests, which reflects the very few (in this case mostly damaged in some way) items that a poor person might leave behind on their death; one suspects that the above 'list' was replicated by many thousands of poor people.

Like nursery rhymes, street songs – various versions of which were traditionally sung by street criers in order to advertise what they had to sell – often contain references to clothing. Before the advent of the rapid growth of the ready-made clothing industry from the end of the eighteenth century, old clothes were currency among the poor and large sectors of the population bought second-hand clothing rather than new. Garments that had reached the end of their life as clothing were habitually sold as rags, recycled for the burgeoning ready-made clothing industry or even used as manure. Nothing was wasted if it could be made into something useful. So the following street song refers to the poverty that was indicative of both someone who had to sell, and/or someone who had to wear, old clothes:

If I'd as much money
As I could tell,
I never would cry,
Old clothes to sell!
Old clothes to sell!
Old clothes to sell!
I never would cry,
Old clothes to sell![52]

We would probably find it difficult to imagine a song written nowadays about a child buying clothing, at least partly because such an experience is rarely founded in actuality. But the following song reminds us not only of how few clothes poor people would have had in the past and how they must have gone without (verse 1) but also what an important occasion it would have been to make a trip to the nearest large provincial centre to buy something (verse 2). Cloaks and petticoats were some of the first categories of clothing items to be bought ready-made partly because an exact fit was not vital. The 'gown' in verse 2 could refer to the fabric needed to make a gown rather than the made-up gown:

When I was a little girl,
About seven years old,
I hadn't got a petticoat,
To keep me from the cold.

So I went into Darlington,
That pretty little town,
And there I bought a petticoat,
A cloak, and a gown.[53]

Meanwhile accessories and haberdashery, including buttons, garters and ribbons, were habitually bought from travelling pedlars on special occasions or at certain times of the year, for example at fairs: this practice is evident in the following plaint about why Johnny is so long at the fair in the song, 'What Can the Matter Be?'

He promised to buy me a pair of sleeve buttons,
A pair of new garters that cost him but two pence,
He promised he'd buy me a bunch of blue ribbons
To tie up my bonny brown hair.[54]

Some rhymes are less literal and make associations between animate and inanimate things. This is the case with the strange rhyme about what little girls are made of ('Sugar and spice / And all things nice') contrasted to what little boys are made of ('Frogs and snails / And puppy dogs' tails'), while young women (sometimes mothers) are 'made' of 'Ribbons and laces / And sweet pretty faces'.[55] It is rather like the game in which people have to articulate what a person would be if they were a piece of furniture, a piece of music and so on, while the person designated as 'it' has to guess who the person is by these inanimate associations!

Interestingly, clothing is frequently described in ways that link it to the natural world, or vice versa, where the natural world is compared to clothing, such as in the riddle of 'Daffy-Down-Dilly [who] is new come to town / With a yellow petticoat, and a green gown'.[56] Daffy-Down-Dilly is, of course, a daffodil. Similarly, the following riddle is created by the way in which the object being presented in metaphorical terms on first reading seems to be described in human terms but by the third line we are suspicious of the 'strange' behaviour ('In Summer more clothing I wear'); by the last line we are in no doubt that this is not a human but a tree:

In Spring I look gay,
Decked in comely array,
In Summer more clothing I wear;
When colder it grows,
I fling off my clothes,
And in Winter quite naked appear.[57]

In their subject matter, some riddles extend not just to clothing but to haberdashery items as well as the actual process of stitching. The riddle of 'Old Mother Twitchett' (who is, in fact, a needle and her 'tail' is the thread) is much less likely to be solved by a twenty-first-century audience than by someone who was familiar with the daily round of sewing and mending:

Old Mother Twitchett has but one eye,
And a long tail which she can let fly,
And every time she goes over a gap,
She leaves a bit of her tail in a trap.[58]

For working-class men and women, whose work was manual and/or agricultural and done mostly outdoors and for whom walking long distances was habitual, boots were essential items of practical clothing when roads were often stony and muddy for much of the year. They were also very expensive and required a significant initial outlay, often a large proportion of wages, saved for over many weeks. They needed to be cared for and mended often. Thus, the following riddle uses metaphor to take the reader beneath what might otherwise appear its superficiality:

> Two brothers we are,
> Great burdens we bear,
> On which we are bitterly pressed;
> The truth is to say,
> We are full all the day,
> And empty when we go to rest.[59]

The 'great burdens' alluded to refer not just to the physical weight of their wearers in conditions described earlier (stony, muddy terrain) but also, on a less literal level, to even heavier burdens that working long hours for low wages entailed, along with the fact that those wages had to support parents and/or wife and children. The boots therefore become emblems of work, brotherhood and the means to survival.

Finally, tongue trippers and apparently nonsense rhymes[60] often feature clothing and accessories, such as the one about the 'three-cornered cambric country-cut handkerchief':

> My grandmother sent me a new-fashioned three-cornered cambric country-cut handkerchief,
> Not an old-fashioned three-cornered cambric country-cut handkerchief,
> But a new-fashioned three-cornered cambric country-cut handkerchief.[61]

Handkerchiefs were essential accessories – and, as the tongue tripper implies, they were *fashion* items, changing over time as trends in fabric and decoration/embroidery came and went – in days before people carried disposable paper tissues. Furthermore, a knotted handkerchief was habitually used as a reminder of an important event or of something not to be forgotten to be done, when for most people routine was the order of most days and grocery shopping as such was repetitive and fairly basic: it isn't difficult to remember what to buy if choices are limited, obviating the need for lists! But the knot in one's handkerchief could suffice as a reminder for anything beyond the everyday!

Aside from nursery rhymes, proverbs and idioms featuring clothing or skills associated with clothing, have found their way down the centuries into contemporary conversation. I find it fascinating that words about clothing and the skills that create it were reiterated so frequently and easily that they have slipped into common parlance and have remained even when the original meanings and contexts are either hidden or are no longer directly relevant. The themes of a number of these pick up on some of those already discussed in relation to nursery rhymes.

Even though the specific clothing associations mean less to us than they did to our forebears, they remain part of common parlance and many of us – having been introduced to them as children – know instantly what they mean without having to think about the individual words. Proverbs such as 'a stitch in time saves nine' may guide our actions in adult life: if we mend an item of clothing or darn a pair of socks before the hole gets too big, we save ourselves a much bigger job later on. Of course, this can be taken as literal (and good) advice about sewing, but it is also a more general admonition to be organised and ahead of the game: by doing something at the first sign of trouble and not ignoring it (a debt that when ignored just gets bigger and bigger), we avoid increased work or hardship in the future. We are advised not to 'air' our 'dirty linen in public': we now use this proverb to mean that we should not make public what should remain private. Thus 'dirty linen' can also refer to ugly emotions, dark secrets, diverse misunderstandings, all of which, we are told, we should keep private. However, the derivation of this proverb says a lot about past social mores as well as highlighting the importance of 'linen'.

Even among poor households, the whiteness of 'linen' (a generic term encompassing linen and later cotton fabrics, made into bedding, undergarments and nightdresses) was a measure of respectability and, quite apart from the question of hygiene, the widely held idea that 'cleanliness is next to godliness' made it a moral issue as well. In days before tumble driers, household linen was habitually dried outside, either on a clothes line or on the grass, or draped over hedges; in urban areas, a rudimentary clothing line might be suspended across a narrow street and affixed on either side, perhaps to a window, washing on display for all to see with the reputation of the household at stake if its linen is not white as the driven snow (Figure 1.1).

I love William Fiennes's inspirational account of a trip to the United States in search of snow geese. Fiennes meets Jean on his Greyhound coach journey northwards and she tells him:

> I don't have a drier. I hang things on a line in the garden. We visited Venice a few years ago. We walked down lots of these alley-ways with beautiful old houses on either side and washing-lines strung between the houses. There was all this fresh laundry hanging over our heads – shirts, sheets, dresses, brassieres, colours and whites with the sun in them. All those bright colours. The shirts were waving like flags. When I walked under those clothes-lines I felt like a bride walking under arches of fresh flowers.[62]

Figure 1.1 Clothes drying in the sun, Venice, Italy, May 2022. Photo by Marzia Caramiello/ KONTROLAB/LightRocket/via Getty Images.

Before domestic washing machines became more affordable from the 1950s in the United States, Britain and much of Western Europe, washing in the home was mostly done by hand. Because of the upheaval washing caused, especially in small, humble households with little space for drying, 'wash-day' was restricted to one day of the week, traditionally Mondays. In large houses, for centuries maids worked in the laundry to wash, dry, fold and iron (Figure 1.2). These days washing machines enable us to do washing more frequently while other tasks are undertaken, and washing can be fitted easily into work and domestic routines. Hanging washing outdoors (as described in the quotation from William Fiennes above), allowing sunlight and/or night air to miraculously remove stains is the most sustainable way of drying and whitening clothing, often more effective than any modern chemical detergents or bleaching agents. A speciality of the Dutch countryside in the past, washing was placed outside on the grass where the alchemy of sun and air over several days would whiten the fabrics. Such a scene can be seen in a painting by Pieter Brueghel (1568–1625) *Flemish Market and Washhouse*, *c.* 1625 (Prado Museum, Madrid). The mostly white sheets, tunics and what look like collars, neck ruffs and accessories are laid out beautifully in rectangles, each area arranged by the laundresses like a carefully composed jigsaw puzzle (see also Figure 1.3).

Figure 1.2 *Interior with Women beside a Linen Cupboard*, by Pieter de Hooch (1629–c. 1683), 1663. Oil on canvas. Rijksmuseum, Amsterdam, Holland. Photo by PHAS/Universal Images Group/via Getty Images.

Figure 1.3 *Clothes Drying*, by Helene Schjerfbeck (1862–1946), 1883. Oil on canvas. Finnish National Gallery, Helsinki, Finland. © Finnish National Gallery/Bridgeman Images.

Less a cautionary saying but more an encouragement to kindness is the advice to 'put yourself in another's shoe', which is to say that we should try to empathise with others. To put the boot on the other foot is a similar piece of advice or it can mean seeing things from an alternative perspective. Footwear – especially boots – figure frequently in idiomatic phrases and this reflects their central importance to all working wardrobes, those of both men and women. So, the idiom, to be as 'tough as old boots' is to be strict in one's dealings with people as well as being perhaps a derogatory comment, meaning that the person about whom it is said is lacking in emotion and therefore empathy. To be 'too big for your boots' is to be arrogant and cocky. In the novel by Wilkie Collins (1824–69), *No Name* (1862), Captain Wragge frequently comments to his wife that she is 'down at heel'. The earliest known use of the idiom is thought to be in William Darrell and George Hickes's *A Gentleman Instructed in the Conduct of a Virtuous and Happy Life* (1732). The phrase is derived from the literal sense that having worn-down shoe heels was the most visible indication that someone was poor and could not afford new clothes, but it came to imply that someone was generally badly off and perhaps that one's economic standing has been reduced from a previously wealthier one.

Though relatively unimportant today, headgear was essential for men and women for many centuries as an indicator of respectability, status and social position, especially important when being seen outside the home. To 'have a feather in your cap' denotes being proud of an achievement; we have seen how wearing feathers could imply – as in the case of the macaroni – an 'unhealthy' interest in fashion or luxurious dress, so wearing a feather in one's *cap* might imply at the same time that someone is dressing above their station. To go 'cap in hand' means to be respectful and even submissive because to remove one's hat in the presence of a woman or a social superior was accepted etiquette.

Some idioms describe a state of mind or personality trait: to have a 'bee in your bonnet' is to be agitated while to be 'all buttoned up' is to be aloof and unable to express feelings or emotions.

Accessories such as gloves feature frequently in idiomatic phrases. Gloves were essential items and protected the hands from cold, dirt and the sun (having tanned hands denoted manual labour and so was associated with working-class status) as well as being high fashion garments in their own right. Kid gloves were made from fine goatskin and were soft and pliant so that they fit snugly and showed off the contours of the wearer's hands: the phrase to 'handle with kid gloves' means to treat someone with care. Glove stretchers were used to gently stretch and shape the gloves to fit the hands. This is where the phrase to 'fit like a glove' comes from (which phrase can be and has been applied to any close-fitting garment that perfectly fits the body). It also appears in the rhyme 'Billy Boy', who, when asked if his 'lady gay' is fit to be his love, replies:

> She's as fit to be my love
> As my hand is for my glove[63]

The language of clothing has become ingrained over time in the rhymes, riddles, proverbs and idioms that make up our day-to-day communication. The result is a richness of visual metaphor suggested by these references, whether by acknowledging important historical events (and the part clothing has played in them) or by passing on knowledge about the practical chores and everyday tasks of caring for our clothes, many of which have been lost over time as we have become increasingly detached from making and caring for our own clothing. On another level, these references take clothing into a different landscape and function as metaphor for more elaborate and wider meaning, reflecting the importance of clothing as a vital albeit often hidden presence in our lives. While the cultural and social contexts have changed over time, there is much we can take from the past, not only on a practical level (by transporting the advice given in proverbs into other areas of our life) but also by nurturing our awareness of how our clothes are made and of how we can mend and care for them. In so doing, we can thus develop a closer relationship with them, acknowledging their usefulness and importance to us, the way that they enrich our lives and contribute to our aesthetic values. In sum, we can become more aware by listening to the words and phrases that we find in our everyday conversations.

From democratisation to fast fashion

A world before democratisation – illuminated by the language and metaphors of rhymes discussed in Chapter 1 – may be contrasted with the world shaped by industrialisation in Western economies from the mid- to late eighteenth century. Just as the economic crisis of 2008 is better understood by examining economic history and the history of economic thought,[1] the impasse in the contemporary fashion system is seen more clearly in the context of the social and economic history of dress. Significantly, publications since the 1980s have challenged orthodoxies in economic history with its emphasis on supply- or production-focused perspectives. For example, Neil McKendrick, John Brewer and J. H. Plumb's 1982 study *The Birth of a Consumer Society: The Commercialisation of Eighteenth-Century England* and John Brewer and Roy Porter's 1993 study *Consumption and the World of Goods* offer critiques of historical approaches that have been far more interested in explaining 'how and why supply increased than in explaining how and why the products of that rising tide of industrial production were absorbed by the market'.[2] Neil McKendrick argues that, as early as the eighteenth century, fashion filtered down to all classes.[3] The origins of fast fashion can be traced further back than is often assumed: its evolution has relied on the complex interplay between increasing production made possible by new technologies in tandem with changing tastes and the human desire to acquire and consume. In other words, the democratisation of the clothing system from the late eighteenth century held within it the seeds of twenty-first-century fast fashion.

Neil McKendrick arrived at his conclusions about the relevance of the 'trickle-down theory' in fashion by examining the supposed emulation by domestic servants of upper-class styles (rather than describing the specific consumption habits of the working classes), and has been criticised by some for so doing. Even so, his work highlights the significance of clothing in history at a time when it was mostly given short shrift by 'serious' historians, and his analysis calls into question any simplistic correlation between poverty and unfashionable clothing and its converse – wealth and access to fashionable clothing. The phenomenon of fast fashion shows democratisation arrived at its logical conclusion: it can be afforded by the majority, irrespective of wealth and class, and relies on multiple and frequent purchases.

Seen out of historical context, the expectation that we should continually 'refresh' and 'replenish' our wardrobes, while filling the coffers of retailers and satisfying their shareholders and, at the same time, depleting global resources and destroying seas, rivers and forests, makes absolutely no sense – *unless* short-term financial profit for manufacturers and retailers is the principal concern. This 'no sense' stance has been adopted by the movement gaining momentum that is not just anti-*fast fashion* but anti-*fashion*. In autumn 2018 I participated in a 'Discourse on Fashion, Design and Sustainability' organised by the Centre for Sustainable Fashion (established in 2008) in partnership with the Global Fashion Conference and hosted by the London College of Fashion (University of the Arts, London). Bringing together experts from education and industry (representing both global brands as well as independent companies), the discussions over two days brainstormed pioneering approaches to 'sustainable fashion'. If there was an omission, it was that there was no appraisal of how and why we had arrived at this moment in time, specifically, no articulation of the historical background to democratisation that paved the way for fast fashion. Although an understanding of history alone is not sufficient, it does, however, provide a useful roadmap for considering the directions that have been taken along the route to the fast-fashion impasse. This chapter describes the industrial, technological and retailing changes in the UK that made it possible from the late eighteenth and early nineteenth centuries for the less well-off to buy new, ready-made clothing, thus adding colour to otherwise limited and drab wardrobes. While we may condemn contemporary fast fashion, R. S. Thomas's 1966 poem 'Hafod Lom' reminds us not to dismiss the desire that poor people in the past (who, as he laments in the poem, 'wore their days raggedly') would have had for more to eat and to wear, in order to supplement empty plates and meagre wardrobes in contrast to the rich, who had access to plentiful food and clothing:

> It is hard
> To recall here the drabness
> Of past lives, who wore their days
> Raggedly, seeking meaning
> In a lean rib. Imagine a child's
> Upbringing, who took for truth

That rough acreage the rain
Fenced; who sowed his dreams
Hopelessly in the wind blowing
Off bare plates.[4]

And, further back, we read of such accounts as this one of children working in the Staffordshire Potteries in the 1840s:

During this inclement season I have seen these boys running to and fro on errands, or to their dinners, without stockings, shoes or jackets, and with perspiration standing on their foreheads, after labouring like little slaves, with the mercury 20 degrees below freezing . . . many die of consumption, asthma and acute inflammations.[5]

More recently, the consumption of fashion in industrialising countries has become appealing not just to those on high incomes but particularly to poorer families whose disposable income, after accommodation and food have been paid for, is extremely limited. While, in the twenty-first century, one can still pay thousands of pounds for, say, an item of 'designer' clothing or accessory, inexpensive clothing is ubiquitous and cheaper in relation to average incomes than it has ever been in the past. How has this happened? Because the clothing industry has been 'democratised' and because of the sustained impact this has had on access to more and cheaper clothing. But the terrible irony of all this is that those who benefited/benefit from that democratisation (in terms of being better able to acquire affordable clothing) were/are also enslaved by it by providing the sweated and factory labour that produces it. Furthermore, the twenty-first-century fast-fashion industry has 'outsourced' the accompanying abuse of labour and human rights overseas.

Democratisation here describes 'an eventual standardization of clothing in which social class differences would be less visible or non-existent',[6] and, as 'the process by which fashion and style, rather than being primarily the preserve of the rich, became increasingly accessible to a broader range of people than hitherto, in a diverse range of social and economic circumstances'.[7] In simple terms it means that more people have easier access to clothing and more of it, along with increased choice (although we shall return to the question of 'choice' later). This did not happen overnight but, rather, it is a complex process that occurred first in the United States and Western Europe – in other words, in those countries that were first to industrialise on a large scale and where capitalism took a hold. The key point is that fashion became available not just to elites – who had always had the privilege of access to it and for whom sumptuous clothing was a status symbol – but to more and more people across the whole social spectrum. With mass production came standardisation, initially of quality (a good thing in the main) but also of style (arguably *not* such a good thing).

Traditionally historians have placed the huge expansion of the fashion industry in the context of the development of the cotton spinning and weaving industries associated with the British 'Industrial Revolution' beginning in the late eighteenth century. This expansion also depended on the opening up and expansion of trade networks that facilitated exponential increases of imports of raw cotton for manufacture of the woven fabric, as well as changes in the market and in people's preferences along with a willingness for large sections of populations to adopt new fabrics, textures, colours and styles. In the nineteenth century, changes in the organisation of the industry and the application of steam power to cotton spinning and weaving machinery led to large numbers of people moving from mainly domestic work settings to regimented factory employment, often accompanied by appalling working conditions. The introduction of a viable sewing machine with the potential to facilitate the mass production of clothing from the mid-nineteenth century led to further growth. Alongside this were new retailing and advertising practices that made the products of the industry desirable to an ever-increasing market.

While these changes need not be underestimated (and will be considered in more detail in what follows), research by historians has confirmed that the seeds of democratisation were sown well before the mid- to late nineteenth century, at which point there was a concerted move to make clothing in factories using the sewing machine. In fact, the origins of the ready-made clothing industry predate the introduction of either factory-made clothing or that made using the sewing machine; the earlier history of the industry has been underplayed, with Beverly Lemire arguing that the mass market was well established by 1800 with the dissemination of popular fashions bringing about a narrowing and blurring of visual distinctions between different ranks.[8] Lemire's account of the expansion of the cotton industry details the history of the demand for, and sale of, cheaper cotton clothing – for example, ready-made cotton gowns – and accessories made from a huge range of prints and colours from about the 1760s onwards.[9] The products of the cotton industry and the manner in which they were sold and used marked new patterns of consumer activity that 'altered the appearance of a nation'.[10] By the late eighteenth century there were complex distribution and retailing networks that brought such goods to working-class populations in town and countryside, fuelling increased desire for novelty and consumption of the products of the Lancashire cotton industry. There was also an increase in the publication and distribution of pocketbooks and memorandum books with engravings of fashionable figures displayed on the front pages after the monopoly (established in 1704) for the publication of women's almanacs by the Stationer's Company was broken in 1770 as well, in that year, as the publication of the first edition of the *Lady's Magazine*. This arguably also led to an increased standardisation of dress.[11]

The technological progress that made all this possible went hand in hand with population growth, thus increasing demand and stimulating a reciprocal relationship of supply and demand.

It is important to distinguish between developments in the textile industry and those in the clothing industry and each will be considered in turn. In fact, the ready-made clothing industry, partly on account of its origins, suffered from both 'production' issues as well as an 'image problem' and second-hand clothing was actually considered superior throughout much of the nineteenth century. The technical application of machinery to the clothing industry as a whole (i.e. textiles and apparel) was uneven. On the one hand, the *textile* industry evidences at this time all the classic features of mass production: it was heavily capitalised, highly concentrated and operated in large-scale production units.[12] On the other hand, the *apparel* industry was labour-intensive, and continued to rely on the individually operated sewing machine well into the twentieth century.[13] It is significant that both these elements are replicated in the contemporary fast-fashion industry.

Technological change and the cotton industry

The origins of poverty and class inequality within the international fashion industry can be traced to the particular (technological) developments in the cotton industry in England during the 'Industrial Revolution' and, in turn, linked to contemporary ethical issues around fast fashion. Andrew Brooks, for example, argues that the 'international circulation of cotton/ cotton products became key to catalysing the Industrial Revolution in the north of England'. He continues: 'The history of capitalism is bound up in the progress of textile and apparel production in Europe and North America in the eighteenth and nineteenth centuries.'[14] Giorgio Riello argues that cotton 'contributed significantly to the phenomenal economic growth of the world in the last thousand years, but it is also partly to blame for the intensification of inequality'.[15] The paradox hidden beneath the surface of this history is that, on the one hand, cotton has made a massive contribution globally to economic growth over the past millennium and has helped define our understanding of the democratisation of fashion – the ability of all classes to afford washable, breathable, 'fashionable' cotton clothing. But, on the other hand, the love affair with cotton holds within it the intensification of massive social *inequalities* and environmental degradation: its dependence on the slave trade in the past and its direct links to the exploitation of modern factory workers; its contribution to the destruction of natural ecosystems through overproduction (e.g. the desertification of the Aral Sea); and its indiscriminate use for throwaway fast fashion, in particular the manufacture of jeans and the ubiquitous cheap T-shirt. But at the time of the exponential development of the cotton industry from the late eighteenth century, it was its potential for stimulating economic growth and for delivering vast profits to entrepreneurs as well as its benefits for humankind that were of significance. Democratisation is characterised by the making and wearing of more affordable, 'fashionable' clothing in both industrialising and industrialised populations. However, from the late eighteenth century, it relied on the slave trade for cheaper and plentiful supplies of raw cotton in the southern states of America. Even with the abolition of slavery, inequalities have continued, with 'modern slavery' perpetuated in the factories that produce fast fashion in the twenty-first century. Modern slavery is not only a scandal in Asian countries but also a contemporary feature of textile factories in the UK (e.g. in areas that have for centuries been economic heartlands such as the Midlands counties).

Social and economic historians have described the mechanisation of the cotton industry of the late eighteenth and early nineteenth centuries as a key feature of British industrialisation. According to Beverly Lemire, 'the choices made by British consumers directed the way in which the cotton industry would grow and determined the sorts of goods that would be produced'.[16] In other words, market demand stimulated the spinning and weaving inventions for the textile industry (see later), which were aimed at increasing productivity in order to meet the changing demands of a growing population. Although accounting for a tiny percentage of Europe's textile production in the mid-eighteenth century, by the early decades of the nineteenth century cotton became the most important textile in the West, characterised by new mechanised and urbanised structures of production.[17] The European drive to develop cotton textile production may have had less to do with taste and consumer desires than the need to clothe an increasing population and the necessity of switching from a high energy-intensive fibre (wool) to a low energy-intensive fibre (cotton).[18] And instead of machinery bringing about poorer quality (the accusation sometimes levelled at mechanisation), it actually improved it.

The challenge prior to the 1770s was to improve yarn quality such that a pure cotton cloth in which cotton yarn was used for both warp and weft could be produced rather than a mixture of cotton and linen, traditionally called 'fustian'. The following inventions that have become associated so closely with the 'Industrial Revolution' and eulogised in the historiography of the late eighteenth century are normally given credit for the huge increase in productivity – and, ultimately, the quality – of cotton: John Kay's 1733 flying shuttle (a weaving machine), John Wyatt and Lewis Paul's roller spinning machine (1738), James Hargreaves's spinning jenny (1765; patented 1770), Richard Arkwright's water frame (1767; patented 1769), Samuel Crompton's spinning mule (1779) and Edmund Cartwright's power loom (1785). The spinning machine, for example, enabled one late-eighteenth-century European woman to produce as much yarn as three hundred women working by hand in India.[19] In the last decade of the eighteenth century, Eli Whitney patented his cotton gin in 1793: this separated cotton fibre from cotton seeds and whereas previously a skilled cotton picker could get through one pound of cotton per day, an average of fifty pounds could now be completed in the same time using the cotton gin.[20] However, as Giorgio Riello points out, the momentous changes in the cotton industry took place only because the industry was already a 'global commodity'.[21] Although Britain (specifically England) was the focus of the transformation of the cotton industry, the network of markets that supported these developments was global while a fourteenth-century cotton textile fragment that survives in the Ashmolean Museum, Oxford, produced in Gujarat in India and excavated in Old Fustat, Egypt, reminds us that globalisation was also medieval.[22]

Burgeoning trade and the impact of the technological developments itemised earlier brought about vastly increased output: in 1770, the export of English-produced cottons (£200,000) was 4 per cent that of woollen textiles (£5 million), but by 1802, cotton exports actually surpassed those of wool, England's staple fabric that had clothed all classes for centuries.[23] Significantly, these innovations also reduced prices: in the fifty-year period between 1780 and 1830, the production cost of a yard of calico fell by 83 per cent and that of a yard of muslin by 76 per cent.[24] In spite of disruption in the supply of raw cotton during the American Civil War (1861–5), raw cotton imported from the southern states of America increased by 6.6 per cent in the period between 1800 and 1860 while its price fell by 0.5 per cent per annum during the same period.[25]

Notwithstanding the significance of technological innovation per se – the extent to which it can transform an industry, society or the way in which people dress and the amount of clothing they can acquire – Giorgio Riello has challenged the impact which it may have had on its own, without the contribution of other factors. In the case of the transformation of the cotton industry over time, Riello considers technological innovation as one factor, others being changes in customer demand and the development of international trade networks over many centuries, affecting the supply (import) of raw cotton to England and the export of finished cotton products, all of which contributed to a complex narrative. Riello integrates the economic value of cotton within a 'larger palette' which he hopes 'approximates a (real) world in which the economic, the cultural, the social are never separated or mutually exclusive'.[26] Riello builds on Beverly Lemire's research, which focuses on the rising demand for cotton products among all classes, especially the labouring/working classes, as the key to the development of the British cotton industry from the seventeenth century onwards.[27]

The evolution of global cotton production and trade therefore constitutes a critical part of this story. As we have seen, cotton is thought to have been cultivated first in the Indus Valley in 3200 BCE, reaching both sub-Saharan Africa and southern Europe around the tenth century, with small quantities of cotton imported from Venice to England around 1200. From the second decade of the sixteenth century, cotton was imported directly from the Levant to Britain and used for quilting, stuffing and as yarn for candlewicks. By the mid-seventeenth century Lancashire had become an important fustian-producing region, manufacturing the majority of the 40,000 pieces of fustians (cotton and linen mixes) produced in England every year, mostly by using raw cotton imported from Smyrna and Cyprus.[28] By the eve of the French Revolution, Daniel Roche has shown that 40 per cent of Parisian wage earners' wardrobes included cottons and fustians;[29] however, what Riello has described as the 'full triumph of cotton' had to wait until the end of the *Ancien Régime* and the mechanisation of its production (Figure 2.1).[30]

The cotton industry that evolved in Europe in the period between *c.* 1500 and 1750 was facilitated by the complex trade that developed between Britain, Africa and America. This triangular trade consisted of the exchange of slaves from Africa for cloth produced in Europe and, in turn, the exchange of slaves (who worked on the American cotton plantations) for raw cotton imported into England.[31] Riello, in fact, 'renames' this triangular trade (describing it as a 'diamond' trade) to include India because of the latter's long history of exporting cottons.[32]

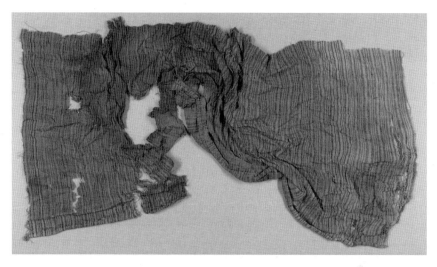

Figure 2.1 Blue and white cotton fragment, Coptic, fourth to seventh century. Made in Kharga Oasis, Byzantine, Egypt. Courtesy of the Metropolitan Museum of Art, New York, USA (Rogers Fund, 1925).

The shift from consumption of Indian to European cloth from the 1740s and 1750s was closely linked to this expansion of African and American markets and the demand for white Indian cloth that was finished (printed) in Europe.

The emergence of a cotton industry in Britain and Europe owed its development to an established trade in cottons with India (via the English East India Company for most of the seventeenth and eighteenth centuries) as well as to the application of techniques learned from India. For example, knowledge of Asian printing and dyeing techniques as well as an appreciation of both domestic and foreign tastes were crucial in nurturing a domestic industry. European printing techniques developed to such an extent that in the late seventeenth century printers learned the Indian techniques of waxing and tepid indigo fermentation but by the early eighteenth century they were actually experimenting with techniques unknown in Asia.

Meanwhile, in England, an Act of 1721 – following a partial ban in 1702 – banned totally the sale and use of all Indian cottons with the exception of muslins and blue-dyed calicoes.[33] By the 1780s Britain had relaxed its ban and France was importing muslin from its colonies in the West Indies. Although the ban had been intended as a measure to destroy the rising demand for cotton by replacing Indian cottons with printed linens and mix cottons produced in Europe, Britain, in fact, developed a thriving domestic cotton industry as a result.[34] Washable and relatively inexpensive, new coarse cotton clothing could be afforded for the first

Figure 2.2 Printed cotton, British, *c.* 1780. Courtesy of the Metropolitan Museum of Art, New York, USA (Rogers Fund, 1923).

time by the poorer classes, while the upper classes enjoyed fine cotton block- and copper-plate printed textiles.[35] These landmarks provide the context for the innovations in the mechanisation of cotton spinning and weaving described previously (Figure 2.2).

Developments in the making and retailing of ready-made clothing

Mechanising *textile* production is one thing; making *clothing* on a large scale, another. The industrial manufacture of women's clothing (considered in what follows) was way behind that of men's clothing, even at the close of the First World War. The 'tradition' of manufacturing men's clothing – which lent itself more readily to the standardisation of sizing required later for mass-production methods – goes back to the eighteenth century when ready-made male clothing could be purchased from special 'show shops'. Sailors, for example, demanded clothing of simple construction that could be worn immediately, and these ready-made clothes were often referred to as 'slops'. By the beginning of the nineteenth century, 'slop shops' had become well established.[36] The Napoleonic Wars (1793–1815) stimulated growth in government contracts for cheap army and navy clothing. Even so, the ready-made clothing industry developed relatively slowly partly because it was associated with poor quality and had a bad reputation at a time when respectability was everything. Indeed, the word 'shoddy' described the actual fabric from which the products of the early ready-made clothing industry were made: recycled wool, cotton and mixtures became the staple of the industry and 'shoddy' has, of course, come to mean 'poor quality' in everyday parlance. Although it has attached itself to other areas of our life (or is a general description of a poorly executed piece of work), we tend not to use the word these days specifically or exclusively in relation to clothing. Indeed, the fast-fashion industry has compelled us to think about clothing in a different way: 'shoddy' is not a word we associate with it (although perhaps it should be!) but the key thing is that it is affordable and makes us look like everybody else.

In the early days, men's second-hand clothing dealers were often also providers of ready-made clothing. This fact may account for the fact that 'slops' can confusingly refer to both second-hand clothes and also to early ready-made ones. The supply of ready-made men's clothing for working- and middle-class men stepped up several gears with the entrepreneurial advances of two highly successful companies (both founded by Jews) that combined manufacture and retailing: Hyam & Company and E. Moses & Son, both of which eventually opened up London West End branches. In 1828 Hyam's advertised ready-made clothing for working men, including, for example, fustian trousers, jackets, beaverteen trousers and coats.[37] The Hyam clothing 'dynasty' goes back to 1775 when Hyam Hyam was born in Ipswich, the son of Simon Hyam, an immigrant born in Hamburg who settled in Suffolk with his wife Rose in the early 1770s. By 1800, Simon was operating (with his son) as a pawnbroker and salesman in Carr Street, offering for sale a large assortment of men's, boys' and women's new and second-hand clothes. Early in 1803 the partnership between Simon and Hyam ended, with Hyam carrying on trading. By 1817 he had left Ipswich and two years later he was operating as a pawnbroker and clothier at St Botolph's Street in Colchester. It is not clear what happened after this, but according to a surviving advertising handbill (*c.*1828), his business appears to have been prospering. Hyam Hyam retired from the business in 1842, with his sons Moses and Simon managing the business, and their premises in St Botolph's Street and Queen Street were extended. The trade was healthy, and they were soon joined by a clutch of competitors. By 1845, the enterprise could boast of a string of retail 'emporiums' around the country. The Hyam family was thus at the forefront of the ready-made clothing industry, and the Colchester trade may have preceded that of Leeds (see later).

Meanwhile, insurance policies held at the London Metropolitan Archives show that in 1829, E. Moses & Son, clothiers, were at various London locations: 6 Houndsditch; in 1831 at 18 Bury Street; and in 1832 at 154 Minories.[38] Premises included 154, 155, 156 and 157 Minories, and 83, 84, 85 and 86 Aldgate, and the emporium expanded in part as a result of the growth in demand for emigrants' outfits to the colonies in the early 1840s. In 1849, branches of E. Moses & Son were opened in the northern towns of Bradford and Sheffield. In 1850 a London West End branch was opened on the corner of Hart Street and New Oxford Street, and in 1860 another in Tottenham Court Road.[39] Pioneering new advertising and marketing techniques, the success of Moses & Son is illustrated by William Makepeace Thackeray's illustrated poem, 'Mr Smith and Moses', published in *Punch* on 25 March 1848 and describing a 'veteran gent' just arrived from Paris in 'a tattered old hat and a ragged old pea-coat' and being fitted expertly with clothes ('a vest, coat and trousers') by Moses & Son of Aldgate ('the peer or the peasant, we suit everyone'). The company's 'business model' (to use twenty-first-century speak) was one of high turnover combined with low cost margins, which became the principal feature of the mass retailing of clothing from the nineteenth century (Figure 2.3).

Along with fashionable off-the-peg garments for men who aspired to dress like those in higher social classes, this new wave of retailers also supplied uniforms, servants' liveries, work-wear, outfits for emigrants, mourning clothes and some women's clothing.[40] Meanwhile, prices were often fixed so that customers did not have to haggle, and excellent customer service was in imitation of the best bespoke tailors. To increase production, subdivision and specialisation in the manufacturing of standard garments was taken to new lengths by makers of ready-made garments in the 1830s and 1840s. Jobs were generally contracted out to small workshops, where conditions of work prompted cries of outrage by the Christian socialists in the early 1840s. The subject of sweating will be explored in Chapter 4.

In the 1860s Leeds became an important centre for the ready-made clothing industry: production was divided between the manufacture of trousers (mostly in factories housing early sewing machines which stitched only straight lines) and of jackets (performed mostly in Jewish workshops by skilled Jewish tailors).[41] The suit in all its various forms was the default 'outfit' for men for most of the nineteenth, and at least half of the twentieth, century. Large-scale production of ready-made suits was augmented by the manufacture of wholesale

E. Moses & Son invite attention to The following Price List of Boys' Clothing :

Knicker-bocker Suits	Eton Suits.	Brighton Suits.	Harrow Suits.
9s. 6d.	15s.	18s.	18s.
13s. 6d	19s.	23s.	23s.
16s. 6d.	21s.	26s.	26s.
21s.	26s.	32s.	32s.
26s.	30s.	36s.	36s.
30s.	36s.	48s.	48s.
Also at other Prices.	Also at other Prices.	Also at other Prices.	Also at other Prices.

E. Moses & Son beg to remind

the public that the cheapness of an article depends entirely on its quality, and they venture to say that their prices will compare favourably with those of any other house in England.

Figure 2.3 E. Moses & Son, price list for boys' clothing, 1870. Photo by Universal History Archive/UIG/via Getty images.

bespoke suits – made-to-measure garments that could be sold at the same price as their ready-made equivalent. From the mid-1880s, both Joseph Hepworth & Sons and William Blackburn (established 1867) began to sell ready-made and made-to-measure garments through their own retail outlets. David Little was one of the first companies to recognise the potential of developing a 'special measure' or 'special order' department, whereby customers' measurements and selection of cloth were conveyed to one of the factories or workshops of the large wholesale companies for making up.[42] Like Michael Marks (co-founder of Marks & Spencer), Meshe David Osinsky (born 1885) was an immigrant and pedlar and his staple was the sale of flannel suits. Having first opened a hosiery and drapery shop in Chesterfield in 1904, Montague Burton – as he now called himself – entered the bespoke trade in 1906 and advertised in the *Derbyshire Times* in the same year: men's suits were noted for their 'hard wear and perfect fit' (prices from 11s. 9d.) while boys' suits were available 'in endless variety' and retailed from 1s. 9d.[43] The distinguishing feature of the multiple tailors, as they became known, was the integration of manufacturing and retailing. They opened networks of shops supplied by their own factory production, playing an important part in 'extending the social and geographical distribution of men's tailored outerwear', so that for the first time, ordinary working people could afford to buy the new tailored woollen clothing comparable to that worn by the middle and upper classes (Figure 2.4).[44]

Women's clothing, on the other hand, through most of the nineteenth century, was subject to rapid changes of style. A perfect fit implied respectability and gentility and this made it difficult to mass-produce and to standardise sizing in place of fitting clothing individually. (Compare, for example, the body-hugging torso shapes of the second half of the nineteenth century with the loose, unstructured styles of hoodies and T-shirts in the early twenty first century!) But the services of a dressmaker or, more exclusively, a couturier, could be afforded by only the upper classes and aspiring middle classes. However, when it came to accessories, ready-made stockings, shawls or mantles were acceptable purchases 'ready-made' from a department store. So this explains why the sectors of the women's ready-made clothing industry that developed rapidly were those where fit was relatively unimportant, where the garment was loose fitting (a cloak or a mantle) or where it could be sold partly made up (a skirt or bodice) and then altered according to the wearer's individual measurements. The earliest wholesale mantle manufactory in the City of London is thought to have been

Figure 2.4 Burton shopfront, Abergavenny, UK, January 2018. Photo by Rachel Worth.

D. Nicholson of King William Street in 1837. Even before this, however, it was possible to buy part-made dresses, which the customer's own dressmaker could finish to fit,[45] with part-made bodices for sale in the 1830s[46] (and, as mentioned previously, working-class dresses as early as the 1760s). Meanwhile, women's underwear could be bought ready-made from the 1840s, although it was, for the most part, stitched by hand well into the twentieth century. Manufacturers did not start to explore the full potential of ready-to-wear clothing for women until the 1870s,[47] with Lou Taylor showing how the provision of clothing by well-known mourning warehouses such as Jay's in Regent Street, London, encouraged its development for middle- and upper-class clients with completely ready-made dresses, which were available by 1910.[48] Only in the twentieth century did ready-made women's clothing become widely available for all classes as a result of far-reaching developments in retailing. Eventually it also became more *desirable* than second-hand clothing.

Adoption of the sewing machine

The introduction of a viable sewing machine that could be applied to large-scale factory production was key to facilitating the large-scale development of the ready-made clothing industry in the second half of the nineteenth century. The earliest known patent for a sewing machine was granted in 1790 to Thomas Saint, a London cabinet-maker. However, the patent was applied to ideas and theoretical drawings rather than to a viable sewing machine, which, as far as we know, Saint never actually constructed.[49] In the United States, meanwhile, there were many patents for sewing machines and accessories: between 1842 and 1895, 7,339 in total.[50] However, the first practical sewing machine was patented by Elias Howe in 1846, a machine which produced only a lockstitch. Five years later, Isaac Merrit Singer introduced a sewing machine from the United States into Britain, developing for the first time in 1854 a machine with a continuous stitch and forward cloth-feed.

Although the first entirely machine-made dresses are likely to have been made in the home, by the mid-late 1850s, factories were beginning to house the new sewing machines. John Barran's famous clothing factory in Leeds – where the clothing trade was one of the most advanced in the country – was probably the first to use the sewing machine, around 1856.[51] In the 1840s Barran had two Leeds workshops producing both bespoke (made-to-measure) and some ready-made garments, but in the 1850s Barran opened his first factory in Alfred Street, producing ready-made garments on a large scale. By 1867 he had moved to larger premises with stock to the value of £10,000; by this date almost all the goods were ready-made.[52] The sewing machines were linked to a central shaft that provided steam power. Gas and, later, electricity powered the factories by the 1870s. Other important processes were later mechanised with the introduction of, for example, buttonholing machines and in 1875, button sewers, both of which increased the speed at which tailoring tasks could be carried out. The introduction of the steam-powered cutting or band knife in the 1870s meant that machinists could be supplied much more efficiently with the requisite quantities of cut-out pieces of fabric.[53]

Notwithstanding the importance of these technical innovations, in particular the sewing machine and the band knife, in facilitating the growth of the ready-made clothing industry, further expansion depended on increasing labour intensification, especially the exploitation of female labour.[54] As the industry developed, productivity relied on the employment of women paid starvation wages by middlemen to produce garments in large quantities in their own home.[55] The 1881 census revealed that, after domestic service and the textile industry, the clothing trades occupied the largest single category of paid work for women, either in workshops or in their own homes on an outwork basis,[56] and the distribution of technology and factory work in the clothing industry was uneven for many years. In other words, the trade in ready-made clothing (as distinct from the textile industry, which, as we have seen, was heavily mechanised) continued to rely more on the cheap and plentiful supply of labour, than it did on technology. The fashion for mass-produced shirtwaists (blouses) in the late nineteenth century exploited female labour.[57] Women still dominated the industry even when it shifted to factory production: in Leeds in 1891, for example, women comprised between 70 and 80 per cent of the clothing workforce. While machining formed the bulk of women's work, other tasks normally assigned to women included binding, trimming, buttonholing and finishing.[58] A similar pattern of exploitation is evident in the fast-fashion clothing industry in the twenty-first century: the historical perspective is once again useful in linking the threads of past and present (see Chapter 4).

Retailing revolution (I)

The new technologies in the eighteenth and nineteenth centuries described previously combined with changes in retailing in which the products of the new consumerism were sold, marked a turning point in the democratisation of fashion. Some have located the 'birth' of modern fashion in Paris in the mid-nineteenth century with the novelty shop, *Au Bon Marché*, founded in 1838 to sell lace, ribbons and buttons (haberdashery) among other goods. The entrepreneur Aristide Boucicaut became a partner in 1852, changing how goods were marketed and instituting fixed prices and guarantees that allowed exchanges and refunds; he introduced advertising and a much wider variety of merchandise, all of which became encapsulated in the idea of the department store. In the United States one of the first and most ambitious department stores was Marshall Fields in Chicago, established in 1852, in which Gordon Selfridge rose to become a partner before eventually travelling to London where he opened Selfridges in 1909 at the west end of Oxford Street, which became a place to meet for lunch and to shop, and which served the material dreams of the aspiring middle classes. Over time Selfridges, according to Dana Thomas, has 'metamorphosed into the most ecologically responsible department store on earth'.[59] But its whole *raison d'être* is still to stand as a potent symbol of consumerism, however 'responsible' and democratic it may have become. John Lewis (established in 1864) began life as a small drapery store on London's Oxford Street and later bought control of Peter Jones on Sloane Square in 1905, followed by other acquisitions in the pursuit of the John Lewis empire. William Whiteley's business was also initially in drapery: having undertaken an apprenticeship he arrived in London, opening a drapery store in Westbourne Grove in 1863 and eventually transforming this into a department store.

Interestingly, those retail chain stores that widened their market to appeal to a wider social spectrum also originally sold haberdashery although that is as far as the comparison with department stores goes. The British chain Marks & Spencer is a case in point. Its founder Michael Marks was a Jew from Bialystok (then Russian Poland) who arrived in Leeds in the 1880s and who, like so many immigrants, brought expertise and innovation by establishing businesses that have since become widely associated with 'Britishness'.[60] Out of sheer necessity (he spoke no English and needed work) he became a licensed hawker, selling haberdashery and drapery around the Yorkshire countryside, thus bringing vital goods to poor people living in remote villages and hamlets. Then he opened a stall on the open and, later, covered Leeds Kirkgate market, where he told customers in his well-known slogan, 'Don't Ask the Price; It's a Penny', thus avoiding the practice of haggling. Instead, a fixed price policy simplified everything, both from his, and his mainly working-class customers' point of view, and it also largely determined the type of goods that would fit into the (penny) price-point, rather like the store Poundland today. The goods sold on Marks's market stall reflected the practical necessity of home dressmaking even at a time when, as we have seen, second-hand goods were prized and middle-class people were able to acquire the products of the developing ready-made clothing industry. But for poor people, access to decent and affordable new clothing remained largely in the future. It was this massive gap in the market that Marks & Spencer filled in Britain, especially from the 1920s onwards. Along with its principal competitors, F. W. Woolworth (founded 1909), Littlewoods (founded 1923) and British Home Stores (founded 1928), Marks & Spencer expanded rapidly in the first half of the twentieth century and by 1939 these stores together had around 1,200 outlets in Britain and commanded nearly 20 per cent of the total sales for multiple retail organisations.[61]

Having opened thirty-six branches of the 'Penny Bazaar' chain by the end of 1900, Marks & Spencer became a limited company in 1903. However, it was not until the late 1920s, when women's fashions – partly as a result of changing domestic roles and employment patterns after the First World War – became less fitted and formal and Simon Marks (the founder's son) had made a formative trip to the United States to see the relatively advanced state of the ready-made clothing industry there, that mass production of women's clothing really took off. The role of Marks & Spencer was pioneering during both the interwar and post-war period: the company, among other innovations, invested in research into new processes and fabrics (increasingly man-made and synthetic); forged direct relationships with suppliers and bypassed the middlemen in order to reduce costs; and established a textile laboratory (1935) where fabrics were tested for quality (wear and colour fastness) before they were utilised for mass production. In addition, the company introduced an in-house design department (1936) with the express aim of keeping abreast of the latest trends – particularly those in Paris, the focus of Western high fashion until the outbreak of the Second World War. The *quality* and *value* of merchandise were key components of the Marks & Spencer offer. Not only did ready-made clothing eventually become desirable and accessible to larger sectors of the population, with new synthetic fabrics such as polyester and acrylic popular for their easy-care qualities, but shopping habits also changed, such that the high street became a focus of British culture. While Marks & Spencer failed to capture the emerging youth market (catered for by the new boutiques such as Mary Quant and Biba), its market share nevertheless grew and by the late 1980s, and into the 1990s – before the much-publicised downturn in profits – the clothing sold by Marks & Spencer became 'fashionable' with supermodels employed and a focus on advertising to boost the company's image. From the early 1990s, however, with increasing competition on the high street and under intense pressure to reduce cost margins, Marks & Spencer, like so many other retailers, began a relentless and misguided outsourcing campaign. This decision represents a tragedy that continues to unfold: the tenets on which the company built its solid reputation – quality and value – and its well-publicised policy of supporting British manufacture have disappeared and its clothing offer, made increasingly abroad, in any case seems unable to compete with fast-fashion companies such as Zara and H&M.

The democratisation of shoe production

For working-class people in the eighteenth and nineteenth centuries and prior to the development of mass production, boots and shoes were by far the most expensive and, for those working in field and factory, the most important single 'clothing' purchase and investment. In households where occupants might walk miles to a place of work and/or worked out of doors for much of the year, we would assume that boots and shoes were an essential part of the wardrobe, so it comes as a shock to read accounts of poor people not having shoes (such as in Frank McCourt's 1996 memoir *Angela's Ashes*) or of the difficulty of affording them so that they were often paid for out of extra, one-off earnings such as after lambing or harvesting. Seen in this context the development of the ready-made shoe industry and the manufacture and retailing of shoes was a critical aspect of the democratisation of clothing.

By the end of the eighteenth century, ready-made footwear could be acquired in many parts of England. As George Barry Sutton has pointed out in his fascinating study of the company C. and J. Clark, which became one of the largest and most successful British shoe 'chains', 'the development of large-scale production of ready-made footwear, and the acceleration of this growth by new techniques, helped to revolutionise footwear retailing and distribution in Great Britain after 1830'.[62] Shoemaking became concentrated in the counties of Northamptonshire and Somerset: in the latter, in 1821, one person in sixty-seven of the population worked in the industry.[63] The village of Street (Somerset) was a small agricultural community in the early nineteenth century, but it was transformed into an important shoemaking 'hub' and, by 1914, a prosperous industrial town with a population of over 4,000. Here, shoemaking developed out of the rug-making trade developed by Cyrus Clark, whose brother, James, was apprenticed by Cyrus at the age of sixteen when James left school. To earn some pocket money, James made slippers and socks (the 'sock' was the inner lining that was stuck into the shoe, to protect the underside of the foot from the insole) from sheepskins which were too short in the wool for rugs.

At Clarks, the company endeavoured continually to improve standards with the aim of manufacturing the same or similar quality in a pair of ready-made shoes as in bespoke ones. By the late 1940s, the shoemaker's number was stamped into the shoe's 'waist' (the narrowest part of a shoe's sole) to give a 'careless' maker's identity; as early as 1858, a mark or number on the sole identified the individual workman and was thus a guarantee against poor materials and bad workmanship. In 1914, William Stephens Clark wrote that the 'wear' of shoes was guaranteed and that a new pair would replace a shoe that did not give fair wear.[64] Furthermore, a range of fittings and sizes were introduced in 1848 to try to compete with bespoke footwear: by 1855, all ladies' footwear was sold in three fittings and in every size and half size from one to seven.[65]

As with the clothing industry, ready-made shoes predated machine-made shoes: not until 1855, when there was a labour shortage, did the first machinery enter the footwear department of the Clarks factory.[66] In 1856, sewing of shoe uppers by machine began, after a representative of the Singer Company persuaded Cyrus and James Clark to try one of their machines.[67] Just as in the clothing industry machinery was developed for related tasks such as the cutting of fabric and buttonholing, in the shoe industry machinery was adopted subsequently for sole-cutting, riveting and last-making.[68] Although leather prices rose in the 1850s, by the 1860s there were large price reductions announced as a consequence of the adoption of machinery.[69] Nevertheless, the transition to machine-made was not total or immediate: in 1876, twenty years after the first 'Singer' had been introduced, 20 per cent of C. and J. Clark's footwear still had hand-sewn uppers.[70] However, increasing mechanisation over time has sped up shoe production and reduced prices exponentially.

Retailing revolution (II)

The meaning of democratisation is relative to what has gone before and to what will be. When I was a teenager in the late 1970s and early 1980s, and then working in the fashion retailing industry in the early 1990s, there was a marked 'hierarchy' in the world of fashion. At the 'top', there was exclusive couture – even though for the late 1990s, Susannah Frankel estimated that there were fewer than 2,000 customers worldwide who bought the most expensive made-to-measure clothing[71] – and beneath that was ready-to-wear, with designers, however, providing the inspiration for trends, style and colours. The fashion year was dictated to a large extent by the bi-annual collections shown, traditionally, at Paris, New York, London and Milan Fashion Weeks. Retailers took their cues from these shows – to which only a relatively few influential figures in the fashion world were invited – and from the trade fairs such as Première Vision. They then 'interpreted' what might otherwise be unwearable designs into accessible and affordable attire for the masses. With this came the inevitable 'dumbing down' of design. However, from the 1950s, trickle-up influences from sub-cultural groups gained momentum – Mods, and Punks in the 1970s and 1980s and anti-fashion trends exemplified by Grunge and Deconstruction in the 1990s – and these challenged traditional hierarchies, although at no point did these trends become mainstream. All this has changed. The creative work of designers seems to have become less 'relevant' than ever, and the trends seen in the first decades of the twenty-first century are derived more directly from brands at all price levels, and their influencers. That this has even been possible is due largely to the internet and to social media. In the early twenty-first century, it is not necessary to gain access to exclusive fashion shows (which, in any case, have become less exclusive and more accessible, with designers choosing more unusual settings to stage shows, such as in underground stations); travel to urban centres as buyers; or subscribe to *Vogue* or *Harper's Bazaar* to know what is 'on trend' and how to wear it.

E-fashion has democratised fashion to an unprecedented extent and some see this as a 'good thing'. Global fashion e-commerce hit $481.2 billion in 2018,[72] with Amazon Fashion becoming the largest online retailer of apparel in the United States in 2019. In 2006 the e-marketing giant acquired Shopbop, followed by Zappos in 2009, and later grew its fashion category by launching its own clothing brands in 2016 and introducing Prime Wardrobe in 2018, a service designed to compete against online personal styling service Stitch Fix. Although it built its success in fashion retailing terms on the sale of basic and mid-market apparel, in 2020 it launched a new platform for selling luxury fashion brands. The reach of e-fashion has been extended by the powerful and ubiquitous social media platforms that have made the sharing and circulation of fashionable styles and trends so much a part of contemporary culture: without Facebook (launched 2004), Twitter (launched 2006), Instagram (launched 2010) and not least the introduction of the iPhone (2007) and the 'app' revolution that came with it, fashion and the speed at which ideas and 'looks' can be circulated would be insignificant by comparison. However, e-fashion has also led to increasing homogeneity in design and style and although some would say that to be able to view and order clothing online (and return it just as easily if it is not fit for purpose), particularly in a time of Covid-19 lockdowns and the decimation of the high street, is the 'only' way to go, the transportation networks that support this system carry a huge carbon footprint: think of the clocking up of 'clothing miles' with clothing transported from and back to warehouses and distribution centres at the customer-click of a button. And while some brands such as higher-priced Aspiga package their products in compostable material and try to discourage indiscriminate bulk orders by *not* offering free returns,[73] the majority of retailers still use plastic and non-recyclable packaging when sending out online orders on their journeys. Furthermore, the majority of online returns do not get resold, contributing to the huge waste of resources within the fashion system. Whereas in the past, clothing was returned to the store and mostly went out on to the sales floor once again, Orsola de Castro believes that it is misguided to think that it is all right to return things bought online because, 'shockingly, most online purchases that are returned, end up as rubbish.'[74]

As a counter to the consumption of *new* clothing, there has been a renewed interest in vintage and second-hand, and a proliferation of websites that sell either pre-loved designer clothing or accessories: for example, Vestiaire Collective (a French company launched in 2009 which has since grown into a global one) and HEWI London (hardlyeverwornit.com) launched in 2012 in London. The latter is similar to Ebay but sells exclusively items that are in excellent condition and, as its name implies, have hardly ever been worn. In the United States, The RealReal (founded in 2011) is an omni-channel platform based in San Francisco selling Chanel suits and Louis Vuitton shoes, for example, at affordable prices.

When it comes to alternative ways of accessing high fashion, the United States has led the way: namely, renting rather than buying. In 2009, Rent the Runway was founded in New York. The cost to rent an item is 10 to 20 per cent of full retail. Customers sign up to a monthly 'package' for which, depending on the level of their subscription, they can rent a set number of items of clothing per month and they do not have to think about washing or dry-cleaning as this is done for them as part of the service. According to its founder Jennifer Hyman, the company's ambition is to 'put Zara and H&M out of business'[75] while its mantra is 'rent; reduce; reuse'. Not dissimilar to Rent the Runway, COCOON (launched in 2019) is a London-based subscription service for handbag lovers, allowing customers to sell their pre-loved luxury bags and receive payment in the form of cash or credit towards site membership which allows them to rent different handbags each month. Such services constitute an interesting concept:

although they reduce customer acquisition of clothing, it could be argued that they continue to feed the customer a 'dopamine rush' for continually changing looks. Because they do not own the item of clothing there is no connection built with the wearer, which can be said to discourage, rather than encourage, sustainable approaches to clothing. Furthermore, excessive dry-cleaning or washing makes renting a less sustainable alternative.

Democratising colour

Contemporary fashion is in part defined by changing colour trends and relies on the widespread availability of colour choices irrespective of class and status. But it was not always thus. Before the mid-nineteenth century, colours were limited for the most part to those that were produced using 'natural' products – either animal or vegetable dyes. New colours had been discovered by chance since ancient times: Royal or Tyrian purple brought prosperity to the city of Tyre (now in the Lebanon) from around 1500 BCE. Prohibitively expensive, the dye came from molluscs (*Murex brandaris* from the Italian coast and *Murex trunculus*, located first on the Phoenician coast) and it remained the most exclusive animal dye that money could buy. It came to symbolise sovereignty and the highest offices of the legal system.[76] Meanwhile, of the other animal dyes the most popular was cochineal, the crimson dye from cactus insects. Introduced into Europe by the Spanish from Mexico (then New Spain) in the sixteenth century, it was widely used as cloth dye, artists' pigment and, later, as a food colourant, but required a huge seasonal harvest – about 17,000 dried insects for a single ounce of dye. What may have been the first English dye house was established for cochineal in Bow, East London, in 1643, and the scarlet became known as Bow-Dye.[77]

Vegetable dyes tended to be cheaper and in greater supply than animal dyes: before the introduction of synthetic, aniline dyes, the most common were madder and indigo, the ancient red and blue dyes used for cloth and cosmetics. Found in the cloth of mummies and mentioned by Herodotus, madder comes from the roots of some thirty-five species of plants found in Europe and Asia.[78] Before the colonisation of America, indigo came predominantly from India in the form of dye-cakes: it is derived from the leaf of *Indigofera tinctoria*, a shrub-like plant that can be soaked in water and then beaten with bamboo to hasten oxidation, during which process the liquid turns from dark green to blue, after which it is then heated, filtered and formed into a paste, and although there were several other important dyes – carthamus, woad, saffron, brazilwood and turmeric – together these represented a relatively narrow range of colours: red, blue, yellow, brown and black.[79] The supply of plant dyes was often limited to a specific region and hampered by a nation's attempts to monopolise production, with fabric dyers and clothes manufacturers forced to use the colours available in the dyers' vats: 'trends in colour were fashioned less by taste than by the vagaries of war and efficiencies of foreign ports.'[80] Meanwhile, dyeing processes had not changed much in centuries and were complex and time-consuming. William Partridge's 1832 publication, *A Practical Treatise on Dyeing of Woollen, Cotton and Skein Silk, with the Manufacture of Broadcloths and Cassimeres Including the Most Improved Methods in the West of England*, was for thirty years the standard text.[81]

The first artificial or aniline dye to be derived from coal tar was discovered by William Perkin (1838–1907), who had worked at the laboratory in the Royal College of Chemistry, Oxford Street, London, 1853–6. Patented in 1856, Perkin first called his mauve 'Tyrian purple' in order to elevate its worth,[82] referring to it as 'mauveine' in his contributions to the science journals.[83] Prior to Perkin's breakthrough, some chemists had deliberately produced artificial dyes, observing how well they had coloured silk or wool, but had not attempted to manufacture them in commercial quantities. The first had been the picric acid made by the Irish chemist Peter Woulfe in 1771 from indigo and nitric acid (it dyed silk bright yellow) and in 1834 the German chemist Friedlieb Runge had used carbolic acid to make aurin (a red colour), while pittacal (a deep blue) was obtained from beechwood tar.[84]

Perkin's mauve derived from waste coal tar from the gas industry. Gas had been used for street lighting since the beginning of the nineteenth century and was derived from the distillation of coal: oily tar was one of the by-products along with foul-smelling gas water, both considered waste for many years and abandoned in streams where they poisoned the water and killed the fish.[85] In the 1820s in Glasgow, Charles Macintosh found a use for the coal tar, developing a method of waterproofing cloth, using it to prepare a special solution of rubber, which was applied to two pieces of coat fabric, which were made into a raincoat or, after the name of the inventor, a 'macintosh'.

Perkin described how he came upon his mauve dye:

> I was endeavouring to convert an artificial base into the natural alkaloid quinine, but my experiment, instead of yielding the colourless quinine, gave a reddish powder. With a desire to understand this particular result, a different base of more simple construction was selected, viz. aniline, and in this case obtained

a perfectly black product. This was purified and dried, and when digested with spirits of wine gave the mauve dye.[86]

Perkin stained a silk cloth with his discovery, realising a brilliant and lustrous colour, which he found did not fade with washing or prolonged exposure to light. Mauve successfully dyed silk but initially it was much harder to dye cotton. Perkin and Robert Pullar (of the family dye firm Pullars of Perth, with whom Perkin collaborated) both independently found a tannin mordant with which to apply mauve to cotton and fasten it against water and light.[87] Perkin claimed that one pound of his mauve could dye 200 pounds of cotton.[88]

As a consequence of the development and expansion of the cotton industry from the late eighteenth century, Perkin's discovery came at a time when 'the state of technical advance in Britain's dye and printing works was ideally poised to exploit it'.[89] Two important factors are thought to have changed the course of Perkin's fortunes by encouraging the mania for mauve: in France, Empress Eugénie, the 'influencer' of her day, decided, asserts Simon Garfield, 'that mauve (the French name for the common mallow plant) was a colour that matched her eyes'.[90] In England, Eugénie's fondness for mauve was first noted by the *Illustrated London News* towards the end of 1857, and it is possible that she influenced Queen Victoria's choice of mauve for the gowns at her daughter's wedding, with the Princess Royal marrying Prince Frederick William in January 1858.[91] 'Mauve mania' did not benefit Perkin at first; the colour originated not from his aniline dye paste but from French supplies of murexide and purple dyes derived from various species of lichens (lichen purple produced primarily in Lyon).[92] Mauve became the rage until 1861 and the crinoline fashions of the time provided wide expanses of fabric displaying the new colour.

Perkin began to receive large orders from abroad, but at the same time his methods were copied. Colour became a determining factor in inspiring new fashion trends. The craze for mauve that lasted a couple of years was followed by successive trends in other colours as aniline became the basis for red, blue, violet and green dyes. At the International Exhibition of 1862 there were twenty-eight other dye-making firms: eight other companies from the UK, twelve from France, seven from Germany and Austria and one from Switzerland.[93] Fuchsine became the latest in fashion: it was initially produced in France and in Britain it became known as solferino and then magenta.[94] With the agency of chemistry, aniline thus opened the path to a new world of colour. Perkin later manufactured alizarin (from anthracene) successfully in the late 1860s and this caused a decrease in the production of red dye from natural madder.[95] Fifty years on from his initial discovery, there were 2,000 artificial colours, all ultimately stemming from Perkin's work.[96] The application of science and chemistry to industry captured the popular imagination and inspired ideas about future possibilities although even in Perkin's time, natural dyes saw something of a revival in those textiles made and worn by followers of the Arts and Crafts and the Aesthetic Movements (Chapters 5 and 6) of the late nineteenth century. Over time aniline dyes have made natural dyes seem less desirable although the latter have made something of a resurgence in the twenty-first-century quest for sustainability.[97] Around the globe history is being repeated as the unregulated disposal of chemical dyes into water systems in the twenty-first century has re-ignited environmental concerns that should have been erased once and for all in Perkin's time (see Chapter 4).

The widespread use of chemical dyes in medicine and pharmacy (in the colouring of pills and mixtures) necessitated a new standardisation of the descriptive names of colours, with new additions to language. By the time such an index was established in the United States in 1939, eighty-three years after the commercial exploitation of mauve, it contained the names of just over 7,500 synthetic colours.[98] It may be impossible to imagine fashion – and, indeed, a whole world – with less colour than we have now and without the many chemical advances that Perkin's discovery inspired (in medicine, perfumery, food, explosives and photography). But that we should have 'reverted' to allowing dyes and effluent to poison our planet and our water supplies – and therefore ultimately us – seems an ecological tragedy and a terrible irony that is beyond comprehension.

Democratisation over time has become a double-edged sword. On the one hand, new technological processes used in the production of clothing, retail practices and scientific discoveries in the field of chemistry have widened access to the availability and colour – in both a literal and a metaphorical sense – of fashion. For people who might not otherwise be able to afford a change of clothing or a pair of shoes, then, this seems like an entirely necessary and 'good' thing. For all classes to have access to a greater choice of material goods of a high quality holds enormous economic and social benefits. But on the other hand, the bane of mass fashion has been its negative impact both on those producing it, and on the environment that supports it if the industry is unregulated and allowed to expand without limits, and for consumers it introduces and encourages uniformity of style and design and pushes out individuality. The following chapter explores philosophical and aesthetic issues in relation to the exponential expansion of fashion as we understand it today and the complexity of what sustainability means in this context.

Sustainability and clothing in context

Before the advent of the far-reaching, social, economic and technological changes described in the previous chapter, clothes were highly valued in ways that today we would find alien. Even among the relatively wealthy, for centuries it was common practice to add a new trimming before you stopped wearing a gown, or you would 'turn' a garment in order to refresh it. But a new and startling change had taken place by the interwar period such as described in Aldous Huxley's novel *Brave New World*, in which protagonist Bernard Marx overhears elementary pupils reciting: 'I do love having new clothes, I do love . . . But old clothes are beastly . . . We always throw away old clothes. Ending is better than mending, ending is better than mending, ending is better.'[1] Having considered the transition from second-hand to ready-made clothing and the contradictions inherent in the democratisation of clothing, in this chapter I set out to explore sustainability in fashion in (historical) context in order to better understand its complexity. Although originating in the past, most of what are now controversial issues around fashion production have been with us for a very long time, but their current seriousness is the result of changing buying habits and increasingly 'comprehensive' wardrobes set alongside a rapidly growing global population: 1 billion in 1800, 7.6 billion in 2017, with the United Nations predicting that it will reach 9.8 billion by 2050.[2] To encourage the drive towards fast and frequent acquisition and disposal – like that of single-use plastics – clothing prices fell dramatically in the 2000s, by 26.2 per cent in Europe and 17.1 per cent in the United States, and consumption boomed.[3] In the UK alone it was estimated (2015) that £1 billion of clothing went to landfill each year.[4]

Meanwhile the relentless emphasis placed by governments on continued growth and GDP (Gross Domestic Product) means that we have reached the point where we must ask whether the fashion industry as it currently operates is, by definition, *unsustainable*. Andrew Brooks posits powerfully that fashion is a practice that 'directly underpins the rapid despoiling of the earth's environmental systems'.[5] Paradoxically, perhaps, study of the past reveals the clothing scarcity and class inequalities before the late eighteenth century that provided the catalyst for the technological development of the textile and clothing industries (discussed in Chapter 2), and facilitated the democratisation of clothing that has shaped concepts of *fashion* as we understand the word today. But at the same time the past reveals the increase in consumption stimulating a faster rate of change and cultural obsolescence in fashion, persuading us that 'enough' is never enough. While it may not be efficacious to use past practices to solve present problems (because contexts have changed so much), by looking to history, we can see more clearly how our current predicament has come about. Revisiting the past takes us out of our blinkered contemporary mindset. We do not need to accept that fashion as we currently experience it is a one-way street, taking us forever forwards into increasingly unsustainable consumption habits. With a more nuanced understanding, we may better evaluate the choices that lie ahead.

The emergence of fashion

One of the first things we can usefully do is to distinguish clothing from fashion and to ask what transforms clothing into 'fashion'? It can legitimately be argued that once an individual's need for warmth and protection – along with the requirement to maintain cultural norms of modesty – is met by an item of clothing, anything other than, or beyond, this can be labelled 'fashion': in other words, trends in style, fabric and colour all have the potential to be 'fashionable' . . . or 'unfashionable'. Fashion is defined by change and stimulated by the desire for novelty or, as some have argued, it is determined by changing economic and/ or political circumstances which impose constraints on what we wear while at the same time offering opportunities for new styles. Dress historian James Laver argued that in the West, it was in the second half of the fourteenth century that clothes for both men and women 'took on new forms, and something emerges which we can already call "fashion"'.[6] One reason why this may have happened at this time was increasing global trade between East and West and the accompanying cross-fertilisation of ideas. In other words, fashion developed out of cultural and commercial exchanges. But there were probably other complex processes at work too and as early as the eighteenth century, historians have noted how fashion filtered down to all classes.[7]

In 1776, the economist Adam Smith wrote of the pressures felt by working-class day labourers to conform, showing how dress was dictated by fashion rather than merely by necessity. In *The Wealth of Nations*, Smith wrote:

> A linen shirt, for example, is strictly speaking, not a necessary of life . . . But in the present times, through the greater part of Europe, a creditable day labourer would be ashamed to appear in public without a linen shirt, the want of which would be supposed to denote that disgraceful degree of poverty which, it is presumed, nobody can well fall into without extreme bad conduct.[8]

The theories of Theodore Veblen (1857–1929) and Georg Simmel (1858–1918) are relevant to an understanding of the emergence of fashion and to the dynamics of fashionable change in relation to the growth of consumerism in the second half of the nineteenth century. In *The Theory of the Leisure Class: An Economic Study in the Evolution of Institutions* (1899), economist and sociologist Theodore Veblen coined the term 'conspicuous consumption': he used fashion to explain the way in which Western cultures display wealth, waste and leisure through material goods, in particular women's clothing. Veblen described the desire to emulate others in unlimited acquisition and his theory helps to explain the motives behind the drive for material goods well beyond what is actually 'needed'. Philosopher and sociologist Georg Simmel, meanwhile, saw fashion as a product of the human desire to imitate but, paradoxically, also as a means of distinguishing oneself from others. (We also see these two apparently opposite behaviours in contemporary fashion.) Simmel described changes in fashion as a process of imitation of social elites by their social 'inferiors', with 'lower' socio-economic groups attempting to acquire status by adopting the clothing of 'higher' ones, thus setting in motion a process of social contagion. Simmel claimed that by the time a style reached the working classes, the upper classes – needing to distinguish themselves once more from those lower down the social scale – had adopted a new style (because the old style had by now lost its appeal). And so, argues, Simmel, the cycle goes on:

> As fashion spreads, it gradually goes to its doom. The distinctiveness which in the early stages of a set fashion assures for it a certain distribution is destroyed as the fashion spreads, and as this element wanes, the fashion also is bound to die . . . The attractions of both poles of the phenomenon meet in fashion, and show also here that they belong together unconditionally, although, or rather because, they are contradictory in their very nature.[9]

While the work of Veblen and Simmel can be considered very much of its time – when the sheer variety and quantity of goods suddenly became widely available

– more recently and as the class system they described has perhaps lessened its grip on Western societies, psychologists and economists have explored the ways in which the consumption of goods along with the quest for novelty goes deeper than mere imitation of one's peers.

Both fashion and *fast fashion* are extremely successful as global industries and one of the reasons for this is that they don't just survive – they *thrive* – at least in part because of specific human psychologies. Alongside the desire for 'emulation' of others, there is our propensity towards 'herd behaviour'.[10] In some respects, human beings are not very different from herds and generally follow social norms: those who eschew these norms in whatever context tend to be in the minority. Herd behaviour is highly contagious and can explain the unpredictability of the next trend that goes 'viral' whether in music, dance or fashion. Indeed, the result of increasing globalisation over the last half a century has led to a greater degree of uniformity around what constitutes fashion at any given time, the internet and social media being highly effective means by which fashion trends and 'norms' are exchanged on sophisticated visual platforms. Add to this the power of advertising: as Philip Smith and Manfred Max-Neef observe, 'the task of cranking up wants belongs in the realm of advertising'.[11] The end result of rapid changes in technology, retailing and marketing practices over the last two centuries and the associated 'democratisation' of clothing and fashion is that the fast-fashion system has come to dominate the culture of high-income economies. At the same time, fast fashion has become far removed from the essential characteristics of clothing per se. In other words and as Andrew Brooks has argued, 'value is socially determined . . . and not derived from the basic usefulness of a thing'.[12] Meanwhile, economist Tim Jackson argues that novelty is seductive because it offers variety and excitement, allowing us to dream and hope: 'And it is precisely because material goods are flawed but somehow plausible proxies for our dreams and aspirations that consumer culture seems on the surface to work so well'.[13] Consumer research conducted by Russell Belk has found that material possessions, through a process of attachment known as 'cathexis', can lead us to think of (and even feel) our homes, cars, bicycles, books and so on, to be part of the 'extended self'.[14] So our clothes may define not only our outward image but also the inner person we are or want to become.

The road to fast fashion

Demands for more sustainable practices for both makers and wearers of fashion have emerged since the end of the twentieth century out of a particular context and in the wake of the destructive growth of fast fashion. Although fashion, by definition, implies change, fast fashion describes exponentially *rapid* change. The potential for swift changes of style in the fashion industry was created at least half a century before the advent of fast fashion as we understand it. While, of course, he didn't invent fashion, in the immediate post–Second World War period, Christian Dior (1905–57) added a new dynamic to the concept of successive change that characterised the fashion industry in Western Europe and the United States. With the introduction of the New Look in 1947 (closely followed by a new silhouette every six months or so), Dior arguably created a desire for women to replace or update their wardrobes each season, thereby establishing the 'traditional' bi-annual change in styles, broadly determined by the sequence of seasons, hence spring–summer followed by autumn–winter. Fashions were 'advertised' on the catwalks in the European, American and, later, Asian fashion capitals of the world and at the trade/fabric fairs such as Première Vision in Paris. Without oversimplifying the process, these trends were often interpreted by high-street retailers, appearing later in stores and sold over the course of most of the ensuing season. However, at the end of the twentieth century, clothing companies accelerated the speed at which they and their suppliers designed, manufactured and delivered clothing to stores: months became a matter of weeks and with this the quality so insisted upon not only by couturiers for their creations but also by retailers such as Marks & Spencer in their early pioneering days dissipated as clothing was produced at increasing speed and at a relatively low price. Andrew Brooks observes that fast fashion therefore encapsulates not only the rapid changes in trends and styles found in the 'Global North' along with the pace of retail sales, but also the speed at which designs can be transmitted around the world and orders turned into garments.[15] This system was subsequently imitated by the majority of mainstream high-street retailers with differing levels of success in order to survive and compete in an environment in which shoppers were constantly tempted with the latest 'must-have' item. In the past, I – and many of my contemporaries no doubt – will remember a feeling of *ennui* by the end of a season as a result of seeing the same garments in store. We may have breathed a sigh of relief when the end-of-season sale cleared out the old and made space for new arrivals, but the unsustainable 'system' that replaced this is open to question and requires urgent review.

The economic context shifted as global trade was encouraged by the abolition of tariffs. Dana Thomas explains how in 1994 NAFTA (North American Free Trade Agreement) eliminated many tariffs between Canada, the United States and Mexico. Significantly, China joined the WTO (World Trade Organisation) in 2001, two years later the World Bank announcing that the elimination of trade subsidies, barriers and tariffs would raise the wages of 320 million workers above the dollar-a-day poverty level by 2015. In 2006, however, it revised that figure: with the offshoring rush to every cheap labour market, only 6 to 12 million, it said, would get the salary bump. In the ten-year period, 2003–13, China's apparel exports to the United States multiplied fivefold. Even though the tariff on clothing was relatively high, 'everyone' along the supply chain still made a profit – everyone, that is, except the thousands of textile and garment workers who make our clothing. It meant that fashion cost little to produce, if, that is, one measures that cost in monetary terms alone.[16] With its emphasis on cheap, disposable goods produced in the main outside the countries where the largest fashion 'corporations' are based, the fast-fashion industry reveals some of the worst features and excesses of the policies of economic neoliberalism that extol free trade, outsourcing (in the name of creating 'jobs' and in order to satiate the 'demand' for cheap goods and promotion of 'healthy' competition on the high street), globalisation ('neo-colonialism' according to Philip Smith and Manfred Max-Neef[17]) and a lack of regulation for the upholding of living wages and decent working conditions for textile and garment workers. At the time, such changes were extolled as a good thing: even though thousands of jobs in long-standing British firms such as Coats Viyella, Courtaulds Textiles, William Baird and Claremont Garments were being shed as companies moved their operations overseas, this meant that companies maintained their profits and increased their profitability and that products would be cheaper for the consumer. Writing for the *Evening Standard*, Ben Leapman pointed out that 'the economics are clear' because wages and benefits for a worker in a Moroccan factory are just one-sixth of those in Britain and workers in China cost just one-twentieth of their British counterparts.[18] Today it strikes us as shocking that these factors were cited as 'advantages'.

Some years prior to the demise of global trade barriers referred to earlier, other developments specific to the fashion production and retailing businesses had already set in train new ways of delivering fashion to the masses. In 1989, the *New York Times* attributed to the company Zara what has become known as the 'Quick Response Model',[19] and with it the phenomenon of fast fashion. In essence this 'model' facilitated frequent delivery of 'cheap' new styles to stores in quick succession and in relatively small quantities, and once a line sold out it would, for the most part, not be replaced. This had a huge impact on supply chains, as well as, significantly, on customer behaviour. Retailers often justify their buying and selling strategies by proclaiming that they are responding to customer demand, but the truth of the matter is that they are, in fact, *creating*, and then continuing to stimulate, that demand. This encourages hyperactivity among customers along with the expectation that there will always be something new whenever they enter the store or go online, which in turn creates an insatiable demand that essentially flies in the face of sustainable acquisition practices. Although not referring to the products of the fashion industry per se, Tim Jackson warns: 'It's telling that our obsession with novelty bears such a key responsibility for undermining sustainability. Because the fundamental point about sustainability is that it's about longevity through time.'[20]

In Shakespeare's *King Lear*, Lear exhorts his family to 'reason not the need'; don't question the desire for more; for better. Aspiration, if not exactly 'necessary', is usually considered desirable and to be part of the human condition: as Carlo Rovelli explains in his account of time and how we experience it, the 'present' fades as soon as we contemplate it and as we anticipate the future.[21] Innate human restlessness embraces change even as we might mourn the past. Desire for novelty is ruthlessly exploited by the capitalist system we live with and the dominant economic imperative of growth and rising GDP at any cost. On one level, the new item of clothing that, at best, remains in our wardrobe for a few months and is worn as many times and gets binned (literally), or put in the charity bag or deposited at the recycling centre and, at worst, never even gets taken out of the non-recyclable plastic packaging in which it was delivered to our homes, can be likened to the mobile phone that is successively 'upgraded' so that the 'old' phone – along with all the valuable metals and parts that it is made from – just sits in a drawer after it has been used for little more than a year perhaps. It still works, just as the clothing that we have discarded can still be worn. But through manipulative marketing and advertising, we believe that it no longer supports the image we are told to have of ourselves. And so, we are trapped on 'a treadmill of consumerism, continually searching for identity, connection and self-transformation through the things that we buy'.[22]

Fashion and phones have become powerful accessories to our Photoshopped images of our exterior lives which we exhibit to others through social media. But this fabricated life is often deeply at odds with our other, inner, spiritual, ecological lives. And the constant rush to upgrade and 'improve' is now a global phenomenon with global implications. The rationale for technology upgrades, we are told, is that the new item is of better quality or that it has more functions. Whether this is true in the case of the new phone, laptop or TV is one thing, but when it comes to the clothing 'upgrade', superior design, skilled workmanship, increased longevity, seem to be the last things on retailers' lists of priorities.

In fact, as Jennifer Farley Gordon and Colleen Hill argue, 'quality and beauty are not important, because fashion changes so rapidly that garments are discarded long before they are worn out'.[23] Perhaps this is what Jean-Paul Gaultier felt when, abandoning ready-to-wear in 2015 in order to focus on haute couture, he said, 'Too many clothes kills clothes'.[24] The history of couture and of the many highly skilled processes of making – often by hand – is a fitting counter to the mass of often badly made, ill-fitting clothes found in the contemporary mass market. As Christian Dior wrote in his 1957 autobiography, 'only precision of design, excellence of cut and quality of workmanship can save us'.[25] It is not that we should return to an overly hierarchical culture in which only a few can afford beautiful clothing but if we could consider our clothes as the objects of value that they are, this would change our focus: consider, for example, the detailed attention given by the authors/curators of the V&A's 'Fashion in Detail' series. (In 1991, the first edition of *Modern Fashion in Detail* by Claire Wilcox and Valerie Mendes was published.) It *is* possible for us all to have fewer, well-made and beautiful pieces: designers working in the sustainable fashion industry have begun to focus on elements of high craftsmanship and individuality as key to creating garments with lasting value.[26] 'In the end', Farley Gordon and Hill observe, 'selecting high-quality pieces over trend-driven items is the greatest bargain, but a change in consumption habits will require an enormous shift of focus within the fashion industry'.[27] Unfortunately, the law of diminishing returns first propounded by William Stanley Jeavons (1835–82) – which proposes that the more of a thing that you consume, the less you will desire still more of it – does not seem to hold fast when it comes to the insatiable demand for more and more 'cheaper' clothing. Instead, economists have noted how material goods in general seem to provide a bridge to our highest ideals but fail, stimulating our appetite for more goods, so that we are left with the paradox that 'consumer culture perpetuates itself precisely because it succeeds so well at failure'.[28]

The backlash against fast fashion

Since the beginning of the twenty-first century and partly in response to increasing awareness of, and research into, climate change – former US vice-president Al Gore's hard-hitting 2006 documentary 'An Inconvenient Truth' punched home the reality and implications of global warming – the fashion industry has been forced to take and give account of its demands on depleting world resources. In 2015 the United Nations defined a series of 'Sustainable

Development Goals' which were agreed by 193 member countries with the commitment to achieve the vast majority of these by 2030.[29] While these goals do not reference the fashion industry specifically, they are directly relevant to how business should be done by clothing manufacturers and retailers. The following are of relevance: Goal 1: No Poverty; Goal 6: Clean Water and Sanitation; Goal 8: Decent Work and Economic Growth; Goal 12: Responsible Consumption and Production; Goal 13: Climate Action. The identification by the United Nations of these aspirations has helped to define what sustainability can and should mean in practice. Even a cursory look at the impact of fast fashion reveals how in many cases these goals have been substantially ignored in that context. However, they can be considered here in terms of the raw materials that make our clothes, including 'natural' cotton and fabrics such as viscose (which in their different ways actually contribute significantly to the depletion of the world's resources), but also in relation to the vast quantities of water used in the manufacture of fabrics such as denim as well as the chemical pollution caused by manufacturing and finishing processes – including dyeing – of both natural and synthetic fabrics (Goal 6, Goal 12, Goal 13). Crucially, we need also to consider conditions of employment and human rights (Goal 1, Goal 8). Added to this are the implications of overproduction and consumption for human satisfaction/ dissatisfaction including on a psychological level. The United Nations Goals identify complex issues that are addressed in this and the following chapter in order to understand better the connection between sustainability and the contribution of the fashion industry to the deepening crisis of climate crisis and depletion of global resources, including the loss of biodiversity.

On a theoretical level, sustainability can be defined as 'an ecological system that is designed to maintain balance, meaning that no more should be taken from the environment than can be renewed'.[30] Thus sustainable *clothing* can be defined as that which takes no more from the environment than can be renewed and 'that is not produced at the cost of the suffering and mistreatment of those who make it'.[31] In this context, Otto Scharmer's warning that 'we currently use *one and a half times* the regeneration capacity of planet earth in our economic activities' is deeply alarming. He argues that what is really needed is 'a deeper shift in consciousness so that we begin to care and act, not just for ourselves and other stakeholders but in the interests of the entire ecosystem in which economic activities take place'.[32] We have to take much less from the environment than we are doing currently and, in the complex process of managing employment and employment conditions, we have to put people, their work experiences and livelihoods before the emptiness of profit and environmental destruction.

And then there is the question of how we treat animals in the production of clothing and fashion. This knowledge and consideration we might describe as 'eco-literacy'. The design of many higher education courses has taken the need for eco-literacy on board, but it needs urgently to be incorporated into the core school curriculum if we are to develop sustainable values and encourage such ways of thinking for the future.

When it comes to thinking about how we maintain 'balance' in relation to the production of clothing – taking no more from the environment than can be renewed – we can learn much from the past. One way of achieving balance is to cease the industrial production of new things and, rather, to use what we already have. The objection from governments and the economic and manufacturing sectors would be that this is out of the question since people's jobs and livelihoods are at stake, but I will return to this objection later: why not make jobs around recycling and remaking from the materials that we already have, rather than keep on making new things destined for landfill? In the past, fabrics and the clothing made from them were valued highly and it was customary to 'turn' garments for example, if they had become stained or faded. I know few examples of this being done nowadays, but *repurposing* is perhaps the contemporary equivalent.

To repurpose is to alter substantially an item of clothing from its original form or even make something completely 'new' from an existing garment or fabric. Similarly, a jumper can be unravelled and the yarn used to knit a repurposed garment. In the past, fabrics represented considerable craft and manufacturing skills, so after the cut and style of an item of clothing had gone out of fashion, it was common practice to reuse the fabric by altering the garment or even completely unpicking it and making it into something else. For example, in the early nineteenth century, dresses were made from Paisley shawls that had been popular in the 1790s. Scraps left over from either this process, or after new fabric had been cut out in order to make a new garment, were often made into cushions or quilts so that nothing was wasted. In the wake of clothing restrictions in the Second World War, clothing discarded for recycling at the London (Oxford Street) department store Bourne & Hollingsworth was 'repurposed' into 'new' clothing (Figure 3.1).

What we now call 'zero waste' therefore has deep historical roots and is part of the sustainable fashion movement, with repurposing having become popular again in recent years: for example, on BBC television's 'Great British Sewing Bee' the 'transformation challenge' tasks contestants with turning an unusual piece of fabric or a variety of garments into something new. However, I find myself asking, what happens to the waste scraps?[33]

Figure 3.1 Fashion model wears outfit created from clothing discarded for recycling at Bourne & Hollingsworth department store, Oxford Street, London, UK, August 1941. Photo by Marshall/Popperfoto/via Getty Images.

Recycling, meanwhile, means that fabrics are reprocessed and converted into new materials, and once again this practice is older than we might think. For example, by the mid-nineteenth century, most fabrics (all of them natural at this time) could be recycled into fabric for clothing or for another end-product (from the sixteenth century linen could be recycled into paper). Rags from cotton and wool and mixtures were shredded and spun into yarn for 'shoddy' cloth, the staple of the growing ready-to-wear clothing industry, which from about 1818 had been located mainly in Batley, Yorkshire, but its manufacture became much more widespread as the century progressed. In the twentieth century, with clothes shortages and rationing during the Second World War, recycling became essential once again and remained relatively straightforward while the majority of clothing was still made from natural fabrics or those made artificially but from natural products such as art silk or rayon. However, recycling synthetic fabrics is more complex and although the trend is for large retailers to make it known that they use recycled polyester, others continue to use 'virgin' polyester. New or recycled, polyester is the bane of the fast-fashion industry (see later). Orsola de Castro describes how in the past mills and factories were run much more effectively and the reuse of old stock and remnants (as well as the mechanical recycling of offcuts and cutting-room floor waste) was integrated into everyday practice. The problem is that we cannot recycle mechanically many fabrics today, in particular those that are mixtures: we can recycle polyester by burning it down (which is how we recycle plastic bottles) and single fibres can be recycled mechanically but chemical recycling remains 'the final frontier'.[34] There is an urgency for the recycling of all fibres (pure and blends) into yarn which would make our unworn clothes the raw material to feed a circular loop of clothing making (Figures 3.2 and 3.3).

Upcycling is a more modern term and is done less for aesthetic or economic reasons but, rather, in the interests of ecology and sustainability. The term was first coined by Reiner Pilz in 1994[35] and popularised by William McDonough and Michael Braungart in their 2002 study *Cradle to Cradle: Remaking the Way We Make Things*.[36] Sandy Black usefully defines upcycling as 'design using reprocessed or waste materials to make a product of equal or higher, not lower, quality'.[37] Upcycling requires time – 'the single most undervalued word in fashion's modern history' – and patience.[38]

Figure 3.2 Manufacture of shoddy (reclaimed woollen rags mixed with new wool), Deffaux's factory, Paris, France. From *La Nature*, Paris, France, 1892. Courtesy of Universal History Archive/UIG/Bridgeman Images.

Figure 3.3 Women sort through old fabric for reuse, Berlin, Germany, 1930–44. SZ Photo/Scherl/Bridgeman Images.

For centuries there has been a market for *second-hand* clothing. Before the huge expansion of the ready-made clothing market in the nineteenth century, and the emergence and later acceptance of the idea that new was superior, second-hand clothing reigned supreme for working-class people, except perhaps when it came to shoes and boots which were expensive and the outlay on a pair represented a major investment. For this reason, shoes were regularly mended and the cobbler's skills were well utilised by village and urban society. It was not until after the mid-nineteenth century (Chapter 2) that clothing and footwear were more routinely made by mass-production methods and so became cheaper. Even so, well into the second half of the twentieth century, many children (myself included) wore second-hand clothing – though ideally not shoes because of the importance of having these fitted correctly for growing feet – until their late teens, although most of us would by then have much rather been able to afford new clothes. Having said that, in the 1960s and 1970s the 'vintage' clothing market made second-hand clothing fashionable, thus casting aside its dowdier and undesirable associations. But there is a negative aspect of the twenty-first century second-hand clothing industry: as a result of overconsumption in the Global North, the sale of second-hand clothing restricts the vibrancy of clothing culture in impoverished communities (mostly African ones).[39] And giving to charity is not necessarily an act of goodwill any longer but increasingly a case of 'dumping our responsibilities along with our unwanted clothes'.[40] Orsola de Castro describes how our clothes, exported to other countries, 'wreak havoc with local economies and infrastructures' and are in part responsible for the demise of local artisanal industries.[41]

We could begin by challenging Aldous Huxley's maxim articulated in *Brave New World* cited earlier by giving ourselves the challenge of making new from the old or 'older' instead of thinking always to buy new. The idea that feeds the ubiquity of fast fashion is that we have constantly to buy new when we simply desire novelty. This is a relatively recent trend. People had new in the past, but as fashions changed, clothes were habitually altered rather than sent to landfill because they were highly valued, for their fabric, their design, the quality of the craft and creative skills that went into making them. The problem with mass-produced clothing – although there are, of course, exceptions – is that it tends to be less highly valued and so is both culturally and literally disposable. As a result, the sense of connection to our clothing is often lost before it is even established. There is at least one school of thought that suggests that the reason for this is that the production process is divorced from the people who end up wearing that clothing and so 'an understanding of how our clothing is made is essential to changing production methods for the better'.[42] Recent research, 'Designing a Sensibility for Sustainable Clothing' funded by the UK's Arts and Humanities Research Council (AHRC), explores how processes of 'making together' in community textiles groups can generate a new ethic, or sensibility, among consumers to help them make more sustainable clothing choices: 'The resultant affective responses ranged from a deeper engagement with the materialities of the clothing industry to an awareness of the amount of time incorporated in the process of making clothes as participants started to re-imagine clothing through the embodied act of re-making.'[43]

The fabric of fashion conundrum

One of the most frequently discussed aspects of the drive towards 'sustainable fashion' and arguably one of its principal challenges is the sourcing and production of fibres/fabric by clothing manufacturers and retailers. The choice of fabric impacts hugely on the whole life cycle of a garment including fibre cultivation/production, manufacture, distribution, consumer laundering, reuse and final disposal.

With man-made fibres comprising almost 60 per cent of all textiles in 2008, representing a 20 per cent increase from 1990,[44] the sustainability debate within the fashion industry has often centred on the relative impact on ecosystems of growing natural fibres such as wool and cotton compared with the production of those used to manufacture man-made and synthetic fibres. It is important here to make a broad distinction between fabrics that are 'man-made' such as viscose – where the fibre is man-made but derived from natural sources such as cellulose from wood pulp – and those that are synthetic – where the fibre is made from a 'synthetic' process derived in the main from petrochemicals as is the case with nylon, acrylic and polyester. For good reason, it is often assumed that 'natural' fibres are kinder to the environment and more sustainable than man-made and synthetic ones but the reality is more complex: for example, fast fashion used (natural) cashmere but by 2017, 70 per cent of Mongolia's grasslands were degraded and desertification was setting in.[45] 'Natural' clearly does not necessarily equal 'sustainable'.

Wool has for centuries been valued as a natural body insulator, regulating the body temperature by keeping it cool when it is hot and warm when it is cold. The English wool industry, for example, provided work and prosperity in many towns from the medieval period. As a fabric it naturally repels dirt, stains and water. However, in the twentieth century pesticides began to be used in sheep baths, in which sheep were dipped or else injected with pesticides to deter parasites. Wool has to be scoured to remove dirt and the by-product, lanolin, is used for cosmetics and soap and often contains residual pesticides. It is not necessarily washable and dry-cleaning uses chemicals.[46] Organic wool means that the fibre has been produced from sheep that have not been subjected to pesticide treatment. But as with organic cotton, it is produced in much smaller quantities, is more expensive to the customer and so tends to be associated with exclusivity.

Increasing availability of cotton to all classes in the Global North can be dated to the late eighteenth century (see Chapter 2). Since the second half of the twentieth century, global population increase combined with the ubiquity of cotton jeans and T-shirts has led to an exponential increase in demand. With the need to produce such huge quantities of cotton came a rise in the use of chemical products to deter pests and weeds and to control soil quality, as traditional cotton crops quickly deplete the soil of nutrients. Cotton growing also uses vast quantities of water and the draining and diversion of water for cotton irrigation has almost completely dried out the Aral Sea, described by the United Nations as 'the greatest man-made environmental disaster of all time'.[47] What is more,

Orsola de Castro cites the use of Genetically Modified Organisms (GMOs) for cotton by the company Monsanto: rather than harvesting seeds from the cotton plants that they have already grown, farmers are required to purchase new seeds each year, discarding those from the previous year's harvest. It is estimated that 95 per cent of all cotton grown in India is genetically modified (GM), and the misery it sows with its seeds includes regular spates of suicides.[48] The alternative is to switch to the production of organic cotton, which is best suited to smaller farms where crop rotation is practised. The disadvantage is that current yields of organic cotton tend to be anything between 20 to 50 per cent lower than those of pesticide-enhanced counterparts.[49] Organic cotton production therefore does not satisfy the current insatiable demands of fast fashion. It should also be noted that although the production of organic cotton avoids the use of pesticides and fertilisers in growing the fibre, it still requires cleaning, scouring and bleaching, all of which processes use chemicals that are usually toxic.

While it is naïve to think that there can be a fabric whose growth and manufacture have zero impact on the environment, some fibres are considered much more 'sustainable' than others. For example, hemp has the advantage of growing very quickly and requires only 20 per cent of the water required to grow cotton. Pesticides are not needed as hemp is naturally resistant to harmful insects and weeds. Likewise, bamboo grows rapidly and requires little irrigation, pesticides or fertilisers; on the other hand, its method of production is commonly adapted from that used for rayon, so there are significant eco-implications as bamboo fabric manufacture is increased.[50]

Rayon is classified as a man-made fibre because it is chemically produced from cellulose derived from the cell walls of plants. Although it is biodegradable (unlike synthetic fibres), the production processes for rayon are highly energy-intensive, especially polluting and laden with chemicals: wood is ground into pulp and spun, a process that requires multiple 'trips' around the rayon factory.[51] By contrast, lyocell (also known by its brand name, Tencel) – a fully biodegradable cellulosic fibre that is derived from easily grown woods such as beech, eucalyptus and pine and was first made commercially available in the late 1980s – has a 'closed loop' manufacturing process as most of the non-toxic chemical solvent and water used are reclaimed and used again.[52] Nevertheless, although waste is thus almost entirely eliminated, the manufacturing processes for lyocell remain energy-intensive.

Synthetic fibres such as nylon, polyester and acrylic are derived from petroleum oil and their manufacture is energy-intensive. Even though nylon does not require ironing (and is therefore more sustainable in respect of its care and maintenance), it generates nitrous oxide, a potent greenhouse gas, which even in small amounts, is a dangerous contributor to global climate change. While nylon production has been in decline since the 1960s, the converse is true of polyester (patented in 1941). Polyester was introduced into Britain soon after government clothing and fabric restrictions were eased in the aftermath of the Second World War, and at retailers such as Marks & Spencer in large quantities from the early 1950s. It was sold variously as Terylene (manufactured by ICI); Dacron (Du Pont); and later as a 'crimped' fabric known as Crimplene (ICI). Heralded as a revolutionary fabric because of its smart appearance and easy-care qualities, it is easy to overlook the huge labour-saving factors that made it so successful in these early days, releasing the housewife from the drudgery of time-consuming laundering and ironing. Initially, polyester was popular for women's dresses and skirts and men's trousers.

By 1968, the volume of production of synthetics surpassed that of cotton, with polyester in greatest demand. In the twenty-first century, the expansion of fast fashion has been greatly assisted by polyester. Relatively cheap and easily available, polyester is now used in about 60 per cent of our clothes. There is a tragic irony that polyester – such a durable and low-maintenance fabric which takes more than 800 years to biodegrade – is used for fast fashion: it is a fabric we should be using more exclusively for coats and outerwear, and garments that can be spot-cleaned or sponged.[53] Like nylon its production is energy-intensive, although it requires less water than the manufacture of cotton. It can be recycled and needs minimum or no ironing. However, its production results in large quantities of hazardous waste.[54] And if we take into account the fossil fuels used in its production, CO_2 emissions for polyester clothing are nearly three times higher than for cotton. Reliance on polyester is one of the reasons why the fashion industry is so polluting, in terms of both its emissions-heavy production and the non-biodegradable waste it leaves behind.

It is a major concern too that polyester releases tiny microfibres every time it is washed (and even into the atmosphere as we wear clothing made from synthetic fibres), and this is the case with both 'virgin' and recycled polyester. As Greenpeace explains:

One piece of clothing can release 700,000 fibres in a single wash. Once our clothes reach a washing machine, the synthetic fabrics release tiny strands: so-called microfibres. These are essentially microscopic pieces of plastic . . . Every time you run your washing machine, hundreds of thousands of microfibres are flushed down the drain. Many reach beaches and oceans where they can remain for hundreds of years. Swallowed by fish and other sea-life, microplastic travels up the food chain, where [it ends] up on our plates.[55]

It is a major concern that approximately 92 per cent of microplastic pollution found in samples from across the Arctic Ocean in 2021 are synthetic fibres, three-quarters of which are polyester and resemble fibres used in clothing and textiles, those particularly common in athleisure cosy fleeces and cheap throwaway synthetic fast fashion: that, says Suna Erdem, is 'basically your entire lockdown wardrobe'.[56] Research has shown that one way of filtering out the microfibres that are released when we wash synthetic clothing is the 'Guppy Bag' (sold online and on the Patagonia website, for example) into which synthetic clothing is inserted before being placed in the washing machine. Alternatively, the 'Cora Ball' is placed in the drum with a whole wash. These simple devices are believed to filter out 87 and 26 per cent of microparticles, respectively.[57]

While the polyester industry is expanding at an alarming rate, few designers ban those materials that have poor eco-credentials. PVC – used in fashion for transparent shoe heels, vinyl raincoats, synthetic patent leather and the flexible tubing inside handbag handles – is a known carcinogen, and when it biodegrades, it releases poisons into the soil and water table. Exceptionally, Stella McCartney has banned PVC in her company. As Jennifer Farley Gordon and Colleen Hill observe, even within the domain of organic textiles production, there is a lack of global standards or systems of garment labelling with comprehensive information about the fabric, which makes it difficult for designers and customers to select fabrics that possess the sustainable qualities they may desire.[58] The problem was addressed by the establishment of the Sustainable Apparel Coalition in 2010.[59] Three years later in 2013 four leading US textile manufacturers organised an association called the Sustainable Textiles Coalition.[60] The two groups set out to work together in order to develop an 'environmental index' and to promote transparency regarding all the details relating to fabric and garment production.

Transparency on the label

Notwithstanding such initiatives, the fashion industry is not regulated as other industries are, such as in the case of food and pharmaceuticals, which means that transparency, public disclosure and traceability of products from raw materials to manufacturing are not mandatory. Orsola de Castro points out: 'This in turn means there are no legal obligations for brands to give us credible and comparable information on the products we buy, where they were made, by whom, utilising what materials and under what circumstances.'[61] It might be argued that few people are used to examining a garment label prior to purchase, but perhaps if we were encouraged to do so we would demand more information and arguably the product would come to mean more to its owner if we knew who made a garment and where. The fact of the matter is that provenance and, therefore, comprehensive labelling have become extremely complex. Until the end of the twentieth century, if a label on an item of clothing said 'Made in the USA' or 'Made in England' this meant that the item was likely to have been both manufactured and packaged there, even if the fibre/fabric may have come from elsewhere. But as Dana Thomas observes, 'Made in the USA' does not automatically confer authenticity or integrity of production.[62] In the past, labels could be highly specific, pointing to the precise location where the item was made. For example, a 1970s Laura Ashley dress I bought on eBay has a back-neck label stating 'Made in Carno, Wales' and because we know from other sources when Laura Ashley was making clothing in her Carno factory, we can date the garment with accuracy and thus feel connected to its provenance. However, with the globalisation of the fashion industry and outsourcing of clothing by North American and European chains, the supply chain has become so complicated that it can be impossible to locate each separate stage of manufacture and production. The situation is made more complex because of different laws for different countries in respect of 'country of origin' on garment labels (Figure 3.4).[63]

For example, in the United States, the Federal Trade Commission (FTC) requires that all clothing labels disclose the country where the clothing was created. A textile product can be labelled 'Made in USA' only if it was manufactured in the United States of America and is made from materials that were manufactured in the United States. If a garment was made in the United States from materials that were created in a different country, its label must state 'Made in the USA of Imported Materials'. There are also regulations concerning the identification of the manufacturer. This aspect of the FTC's garment labelling code also helps retailers market their brand(s). A garment label on a textile product sold in the United States of America must feature the 'registered identification number' (RN) of the manufacturer, importer or corporate entity handling the sale of the product. All domestic textile companies and importers are required to have RNs. This number establishes dealer identity, and brand identity can be reinforced by including the name of the manufacturer on the garment label.

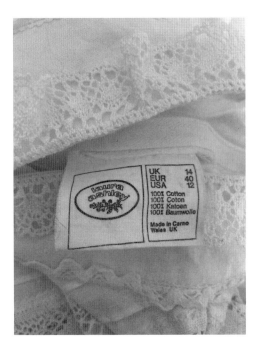

Figure 3.4 Laura Ashley dress, 'Made in Carno, Wales' label. Photo by Rachel Worth.

However, at the time of writing, comprehensive information relating to country of origin is not compulsory in garment production in the UK. Although it is essential as part of trading regulations – so that brands do not mislead customers about where the item was created – to state the country in which the product was 'made' (e.g. if clothing is designed in the UK but manufactured in China, 'Made in China' has to be clearly displayed), the label does not have to state the origin of the fabric or where the garment was packaged and dispatched. In other words, as customers we are given very selective and incomplete information and are therefore mostly ignorant of the 'clothing miles' that have been travelled by fibre, fabric and garment in order for a finished article to reach the customer. Meanwhile, within the European Union, legislation regarding declaration of country of origin is not harmonised. Certain member nations may require this type of labelling, but others may not. In this important respect, the 'early' life of clothing remains hidden and opaque. One shocking aspect of the lack of transparency meant that in the wake of the Rana Plaza factory disaster, it was nearly impossible to know for sure exactly which brands had been using the facility. The Clean Clothes Campaign, a global garment-worker-rights NGO, and its UK partner, Labour Behind the Label, ultimately identified twenty-nine global brands that had recent or current orders with at least one of the five garment factories in the Rana Plaza building. In terms of the range and brands of clothing produced at the Rana Plaza factory at the time of the disaster (see Chapter 4), shockingly, 'the list', says Orsola de Castro, 'leaves almost no Western consumer untouched (or unclothed)'.[64]

The use of fur and feathers

The use of animal skins and fur in fashion has a long and complex history. Wearing them received powerful 'endorsements': in the Authorised Version of the Bible, 'unto Adam also and to his wife did the Lord God make coats of skins, and clothed them' (Gen. 3.21). Left over after the meat was eaten by hunter-gatherers, animal skins were worn over thousands of years by our distant ancestors, for warmth and protection and to overwhelm enemies by the sheer impact of an (animal-like) appearance.[65] Thorns and, later, thongs were used to attach skins across the body, both as fixing and to give shape. Some of the bone needles found in caves are thought to be some 40,000 years old with the earliest reference to the wearing of furs in Britain (Caesar's *De Bello Gallico*) stating that the inland Britons of the time, *c.* 55 BCE, were 'clothed in skins' (*pellibus vesti*) which included those of sheep, oxen, bears and other wild animals, unlike the dwellers of the Kentish coast, who had adopted European dress made of woven fabrics.[66] What is thought to be the oldest extant fur coat in the world (dating from the first century BCE) is in the State Hermitage Museum in St Petersburg.[67]

Armenia was one of the first international centres of the trade in fur: from the Armenian rat came 'ermine', for centuries one of the most prized of furs worn by royalty and nobility. Ermine was used on formal robes in their white winter coat, often dotted with the tails which remain black all year. The Hanseatic League (in its heyday a federation of about 100 towns, centred at first on Lübeck, Wisby, Rostock and Hamburg) was founded in the thirteenth century to protect the carrying trade of the Baltic and the North Sea. It was the leading force in the fur trade until the City of London began to build its own trading structure in the fourteenth century and was the main outlet to Britain and Western Europe for the vast supplies of furs from the north, where Siberia, the eastern regions of Russia and the Baltic countries had almost inexhaustible resources of fur-bearing animals.[68] Fur was worn as a lining, or facing the body: '*furred* with miniver', for example, meant lined.[69] Given that homes of all classes in the Middle Ages were cold with inadequate fires and glassless or imperfectly glazed windows, clothing offered what was essential protection, and fur-lined garments, fur hats, gloves and shoes were ubiquitous as were fur bedspreads, pillows and curtains. Fur was deemed a necessity and, depending on the kind used, not just a luxury.[70] While noblemen provided fur liveries for their vast retinues of servants, long and short fur gowns were worn in the Middle Ages by both men and women: sheepskin (the roughest of furs), goat or wolf for the poorer, humbler classes and squirrel, sable, lynx, marten, for example, for those of wealth and rank.[71]

From the fourteenth to the late sixteenth centuries, the passing of sumptuary legislation in many European countries – laying down who could wear furs and, depending on a person's rank, which varieties – indicated the extent to which fur was associated with status. In England the first of such laws was passed in 1337: it forbade the wearing of all furs except by the highest classes – royalty, nobility, privileged members of the higher clergy and judiciary.[72] William Langland in his late-fourteenth-century narrative poem, *Piers Plowman*, inveighed against fur which he saw as the epitome of depraved luxury,[73] and the use of luxurious furs by the clergy was attacked by moralists and satirists. Famously, Chaucer's monk in the *Prologue to the Canterbury Tales* is a case in point: living luxuriously in blatant denial of the spirit of his vows, he wears 'grys' or squirrel fur on his sleeves.[74]

By the reign of Elizabeth I, fashion was changing, with furs ceasing to be the principal symbol of rank and wealth.[75] In the first half of the sixteenth century, however, fur became popular as tippets or scarves as well as muffs.[76] Even taking into account the fact that portraitists did not generally depict sitters in outdoor wear – thus the 'decline' in the wearing of fur at this period should be seen in this light – women of high rank increasingly dressed in sumptuous fabrics (including velvets, satins and brocades), embellished with lavish embroidery, precious stones and elaborate lace.[77] For men, beaver hats – originally made of beaver skin and later of felted beaver[78] – became popular. Later mentioned by Samuel Pepys in 1661, Mr Holder sends Pepys a 'bever [sic], costing £4 5s.'.[79] Notwithstanding the slow decline of its use in dress by the richest in society, by the seventeenth century, fur was slowly being democratised and increasingly worn by the middle classes: women are depicted in fur-trimmed jackets in the paintings of Johannes Vermeer (1632–75), for example. Meanwhile, the retention of some fur in ceremonial and occupational attire is evidence of its longevity and the extent to which certain occupations eschew fashion – as seen in the clothing of high-ranking churchmen, and in the richness and formality of legal robes (which can be traced back to the eleventh century), symbolising the might of the law.[80]

The discovery of huge supplies of fur in North America and Canada took place just as European resources were becoming scarcer and, despite its decline over time, fur stayed in fashion, with the English fur trade taking on a new lease of life. In 1689 the ship *Nonsuch* returned from Hudson Bay to England with the first batch of Hudson Bay furs, including North American beaver, which featured on the coat of arms for the Hudson Bay Company.[81] In 1677, what is generally accepted as the earliest specific reference to the use of fur in the modern British army is found in the account of the formation of the Grenadier Guards, who were to become famous for their headgear.[82] Beaver was the fur in greatest demand from the seventeenth century, used for the splendid Cavalier hats that were decorated with feathers while the tall hats worn by Quakers from the end of the seventeenth century were also often made of beaver. Interestingly, the best beaver for hats was considered to be older, worn pelts because unless the beaver was greasy and dirty it would not felt properly.[83] Beaver hats declined in popularity by the late eighteenth century when men began to favour silk hats or those made of shiny plush.[84]

Fur featured as high fashion in the plates of *La Belle Assemblée* (first published 1806) and *Ackermann's Repository of Arts, Literature, Commerce, Manufactures, Fashions and Politics* (published 1809–29), where it can be seen used for linings as well as for deep hems of gowns and as enormous muffs.[85] At the Great Exhibition of 1851, the Hudson Bay Company exhibited a large variety of furs including racoon, beaver, chinchilla, bear, fisher, fox (red, cross, silver, white and grey), lynx, marten, mink, musquash, otter, fur seal, wolf (all from Canada). European marten, squirrel, fitch, kolinski and ermine also featured.[86] While the fur coat in its modern form was a Victorian invention, the peak of its popularity was in the twentieth century.[87] Sealskin was used extensively for coats, the sealskin jacket popular in the nineteenth century and continuing to be in demand until well into the twentieth.[88]

In the 1890s the appalling fashion of using the head and tail of the animal on muffs appeared. Meanwhile, 'celebrities' such as the actor Sarah Bernhardt famously wore fur and contributed to its popularity.[89] In 1900 fashion appeared for the first time in a major international exhibition, the Paris Exposition Universelle: the fashion section, under the couturier Madame Paquin, included fur coats, one of which was a Princess-style coat in Canadian mink said to have used 300 skins, the cutting taking 100 hours and the sewing 1,000 hours.[90] In the years leading up to the First World War, furs such as skunk, grey squirrel, moleskin and various martens came to the fore and became part of more popularly priced fur coats and accessories sold in department stores across Britain. In the interwar period, fur became relatively inexpensive, with large-scale production of coats and jackets of fur of many kinds, including coney (rabbit) and musquash, although silver fox was the hallmark of the fashion in fur in the 1920s and 1930s.[91] Responsible for clothes rationing, the Board of Trade encouraged the purchase of fur by civilians in order to save wool, which was in demand by the armed services. The Irvin sheepskin jacket – often with a large fur collar – and trousers made of glazed sheepskin and thermally insulated evolved at this time and were worn for their warmth by bomber crews during the Second World War.[92]

Disturbingly, albeit with some exceptions, fur had evolved in the main as a means of display and for the embellishment of an outfit rather than for warmth or protection. In the period after the Second World War, the formality of 'traditional' furs gave way to 'fun furs', a short-lived fashion in the 1960s followed by the young who could afford inexpensive fur such as various kinds of coney.[93] But if there were any practical reasons (e.g. for warmth) for furs being worn in climates such as Britain's relatively mild one, these mostly disappeared with ubiquitous car ownership and central heating. However, even in 1981 Elizabeth Ewing could write that London was still 'the greatest fur centre in the world' with furs being imported from all over the world.[94]

Alongside the evolution of the fashion for real fur was that for fake or imitation fur. In 1879 Spencer & Co. of St Paul's Churchyard produced a cloth that imitated fur while 'sealskin cloth' was thought closely to resemble real seal.[95] In the early twentieth century, a plush that also looked like sealskin was used, mainly in grey or tan, for warm, light and comfortable 'Teddy Bear coats' which became popular for men and women on both sides of the Atlantic. Imitation furs really took off in the 1950s and 1960s with pile fabric weaving and in 1970 Paris and Italian couture houses began to use pile fabrics and simulated furs in their collections. But synthetic fur, not only because it is made from non-renewable resources (petrochemicals), but also because of the intensive processes incurred in its manufacture, as well as its suggestion of real fur, was from the outset held up to scrutiny.

Some of the first fur farms were for Arctic fox (farmed in Alaska as early as 1865), but by the 1950s mink had become the most prized fashion fur. In the first three decades of the twentieth century, the number of fur farms in the United States and Canada grew significantly, such that by 1926, there were 15,000 fur farmers in the United States and the same number in Canada;[96] at this time the silver fox was the staple – and most valuable – fur of the industry. Public awareness of fur-trapping practices (animals whose fur can be obtained only by trapping are musquash and beaver) as well as of fur-farming led to growing outrage over the wearing of fur, especially from the 1920s. One of the most hard-hitting indictments of the cruelty of making fur garments – which also implicates those wearing fur – is Thomas Hardy's poem 'The Lady in the Furs' (1925). With characteristic irony, Hardy describes 'a lofty lovely woman' who through 'the glance she throws around her / On the poorer dames and sirs' seems to draw attention to her fur 'robe' costing 'three figures'. In the second stanza the woman refers to the fact that her husband's money bought this apparel and that it was acquired at the expense of the murder of 'things feeble and afraid'. It therefore has no real connection with the woman because she has not contributed to its design, making or fit; rather, its production has relied on the exploitation of others:

> True, my hands, too, did not shape it
> To the pretty cut you see,
> But the hands of midnight workers
> Who are strangers quite to me:
> It was fitted, too, by dressers
> Ranged around me toilsomely.[97]

In the final stanza, Hardy contrasts brilliantly the woman's perception of herself as 'a lovely lady' with that of critics (including Hardy himself) who view the wearing of fur garments as constituting robbery from 'Nature's children'. The poem finishes with the woman's own perception that 'sneerers' see her in a sinister light, as 'but a broom-stick / Like a scarecrow's wooden spine'. The implication is that, despite such knowledge, the woman will continue to wear fur.

The revolt against fur gained momentum, and in 1976, the Endangered Species (Import and Export) Act was passed in Britain, following the 1973 Washington Convention (or Convention on International Trade in Endangered Species of Wild Fauna and Flora). Meanwhile in 1977 the RSPCA denounced the fur trade: 'There is no excuse for the continued wearing of furs from wild animals, with their attendant suffering.'[98] More recently, some of the most shocking practices have been in relation to the culling of baby harp seals, hunted primarily for their fur.[99] PETA (People for the Ethical Treatment of Animals[100]) was founded in 1980, and soon established itself as one of the most outspoken champions of animal rights. Celebrity models began to support the anti-fur campaign spearheaded by PETA with some of the world's top supermodels posing naked for a series of anti-fur advertisements that became some of the most iconic images of the 1990s with Kate Moss, Naomi Campbell, Christy Turlington, Cindy Crawford and Elle McPherson photographed under the slogan 'We'd Rather Go Naked Than Wear Fur'. As I write, PETA is campaigning to ban the import of fur into the UK (even though fur-farming is illegal in the UK, the import of furs is not) and to pressurise the Italian government to ban fur-farming in Italy.

Growing transparency around the condition in which animals are kept and slaughtered has increased public awareness of the negative impact of meat production and the dairy industry on the environment, along with veganism as an increasingly influential public 'movement' and lifestyle choice. The age-old assumption that it is ethically acceptable to use for fashion products leather that is a by-product of the meat industry has also been called into question. Vegan 'leather' is used extensively by Stella McCartney in her ranges. For the increasing number of people who are ethically and sustainably conscious, products that are 'cruelty-free' are in demand: materials whose harvesting and manufacture do not harm animals. In other words, this describes all synthetic fibres and organic cotton as well as 'tusaah' or wild silk and organic wool. But the dilemma is that, as we have seen, synthetic fibres, although they do not incur cruelty to animals, are disastrous for the environment, making customer choices far from simple. Thus, products that are vegan are not necessarily sustainable. In 2020, Zoe Wood reported in *The Guardian* new guidelines for producing vegan fashion (drawn up by the British Retail Consortium) for the retail industry to ensure that vegan fashions are 100 per cent cruelty-free and environment-friendly. The process for producing vegan fashion is more complex than just eliminating materials such as leather, suede and wool; businesses must examine every material used in a product including the ingredients of the glues, dyes and waxes.[101]

In contrast to the relatively late outcry against the use of fur in fashion was that against feathers, a focus of controversy in the late nineteenth century. In the UK, the Royal Society for the Protection of Birds was formed to counter the trade in plumes for women's hats, a fashion which accounted for the destruction of many thousands of egrets, birds of paradise and other species whose plumes had become fashionable in the late Victorian period. Founded by Emily Williamson at her home in Manchester in 1889, the organisation started life as the Society for the Protection of Birds (SPB). The group quickly gained popularity and in 1891 it merged with the Fur, Fin and Feather Folk, to form a larger and stronger SPB, based in London. In its earliest days the society consisted entirely of women and members who set out to discourage the wanton destruction of birds and interest themselves generally in their protection, while refraining from wearing the feathers of any bird not killed for purposes of food, the ostrich only excepted. Leading ornithologist of the day, Professor Alfred Newton, lent support to the cause, which gained widespread publicity, leading to rapid growth in the society's membership and a widening of its aims. So successful was the fledgling society that, just fifteen years after being founded, it was granted its Royal Charter in 1904. In 1921, the Importation of Plumage (Prohibition) Act was passed, forbidding plumage from being imported to Britain.[102] With changing fashions, the wearing of plumes waned and, from the 1950s onwards, there was a more general decline in the wearing of hats except for special occasions such as weddings.

This chapter has explored significant aspects of sustainability in relation to fashion in its historical context. The trade in fur and feathers raises issues not only in connection with sustainability but also as it affects the relation between humans and the natural world including other sentient beings. It thus makes clear that fashion should answer to a rigorous ethical framework: nowhere is this more relevant than with regard to human rights and our own direct relationships with clothing, its making and wearing – the focus of the next chapter.

The human factor

Clothing, growth and alternative economic paradigms

'The fashionable trainer', wrote Ben Fine, 'does not display the child labour upon which it depends'.[1] In their thought-provoking book *Economics Unmasked: From Power and Greed to Compassion and the Common Good*, Philip Smith and Manfred Max-Neef cite the $20 million reportedly received by the basketball star Michael Jordan in 1992 for promoting Nike shoes, a figure which exceeded the entire annual payroll of the Indonesian factories that made them.[2] Their book offers a critique of the 'dominant economic paradigm' which postulates that 'ecosystems are invulnerable to damage at the hand of humankind', the authors arguing that a socio-economic system based on the growth paradigm can never be sustainable.[3] This economist and physicist team are damning in their indictment of the economic system in which we live and which, they argue, forces the great majority of humanity to live in indignity and poverty, threatening all forms of life, indeed life itself. The 'merciless onslaught' on the life-sustaining capacity of ecosystems brought about by the ten- to hundred-fold increase in production (in general) and the consequent poisoning and depletion of reserves, rather than being a 'chance property of the system', is, in fact, 'inherent in the system itself': 'It is a direct consequence of the view of life, human and non-human, fostered by neo-liberal economic thinking – which, as a corollary of its fundamental *raison d'être*, the enrichment of the few, can recognize value only in material things.'[4] Neither, Smith and Max-Neef argue, does social justice play any part in the thinking of mainstream economics,[5] while in the dominant world view the real goal of a 'well-functioning economic system' is to protect the wealth and power of the rich',[6] in other words an inequitable status quo.[7]

The discussion in Chapter 3 touched briefly on the cruelty of the fashion system in its treatment of animals and also in its treatment of humans. How can the profits of clothing manufacturers and retailers along with our access to 'cheaper' clothes ever be justified if the fashion system assists in destruction not only of the planet but also of the livelihoods of the people who make them? While the shift to overseas production resulted in many cases in rock-bottom prices paid by retailers for clothing, those low prices may be passed on (or not) to the customer. Such low prices can often be at the expense of the quality of merchandise. However, the most insidious consequence is the exploitation of a poorly treated, drastically underpaid workforce. In the UK, the move towards outsourcing of production overseas gained momentum in the 1990s; while domestic factory and employment conditions were far from perfect at that time, there was, nevertheless, well over a hundred years of history in terms of establishing higher working standards following the abolition of the worst abuses by successive Factory Acts passed over the course of the nineteenth century.

Meanwhile, the establishment of trade boards and unionisation of the textile industries put pay and conditions firmly on the agenda. But keeping control of such regulations when clothing is contracted out and mass-produced far away from a retailer's main centre of operations and buying makes it easier to be distanced from the human factors of health and well-being among workers. This chapter considers the human factors in relation to fast fashion in the historical context of the history of sweating in Britain. It then moves into the contemporary arena by problematising the ways in which fashion, though rarely discussed in this way, can be implicated when it comes to dominant business models and economic paradigms privileging growth and profit that have paved the way for ever-increasing and ultimately unsustainable levels of production. Meanwhile, terrible working conditions for textile and garment workers – which should have been eradicated once and for all in the past – have persisted. Finally, it suggests alternative paradigms put forward by enlightened economists.

'Sweating' and the fight for a minimum wage

The history of 'sweating' offers some perspective on contemporary issues around 'modern slavery', which term encompasses the exploitation of human beings through poor working conditions and execrable wages. In the nineteenth century and into the twentieth, 'sweating' implied earnings that were barely sufficient to sustain existence, hours of labour such as to make the lives of workers periods of ceaseless toil, and sanitary conditions injurious to the health of those employed and dangerous to the public.[8] In her pioneering research on sweating and minimum wage legislation, Sheila Blackburn identifies the

1909 Trade Boards Act as the state's first attempt in nearly one hundred years (following the abandonment of paternalistic wage-fixing in the late eighteenth and early nineteenth centuries) to regulate pay in Britain. It was applied initially to tailoring, paper-box-making, lace-making and chain-making with legislation encompassing some 250,000 sweated workers. However, historians are still uncertain about what specific forms sweating took, how many sweated labourers existed, why it grew and where it was mostly located. Not confined to home workers, it was also rife in factories.[9]

The factory system that evolved in the early nineteenth century brought to centre stage public awareness of employment abuse; the fight against that abuse began with the 1833 Factory Act, which restricted the hours of young people aged thirteen to eighteen to twelve per day and prohibited night working for those under eighteen. It was applied to virtually all textile factories but excluded lace-making, and its administration was overseen by a salaried inspectorate. Lord Ashley's request for an enquiry into the working of the 1833 Act led to the establishment of the Children's Employment Commission. The Commission's 1843 report revealed gross exploitation of girl apprentices in millinery and dressmaking.[10] Nearly thirty years later, in the wake of the 1870 Education Act, children were still subject to sweated labour, with sweating particularly common in the textile and clothing trades, with companies such as Barrans (albeit forward-looking in terms of its contribution to the developing ready-made clothing industry), notorious for its employment of workers at low rates.[11] Technical innovation is so often at odds with supporting human rights and the dignity of labour, with women and children often the most grossly exploited, just as they are in the contemporary fast-fashion industry (Figure 4.1).[12]

In 1843, Thomas Hood's 'Song of the Shirt', the lament of a poor seamstress who wears herself out by working incessantly for starvation wages, appeared anonymously in the Christmas edition of *Punch*. The poem, arguably more than any factual 'document', captured the conscience of the nation, even if it didn't advocate reform. Shortly after this, the writer, social commentator and former editor of *Punch*, Henry Mayhew, published a series of letters on sweating in the *Morning Chronicle*. Mayhew believed (mistakenly) that sweating was exclusively bound up with small masters, domestic pieceworkers and subcontracting, although the worst cases, in fact, had little to do with subcontracting.[13] The social reformer and novelist Charles Kingsley under the pseudonym 'Parson Lot' delivered a tract entitled 'Cheap Clothes and Nasty' (1850) which, influenced as he was by Mayhew's letters, made references to the need for emancipation of white 'slaves' in the wake of emancipation of black slaves. Kingsley was a founder

Figure 4.1 Cotton spinning, *c.* 1835. Photo by Ann Ronan Pictures/Print Collector/ Hulton Archive/via Getty Images.

of the Christian Socialist movement in 1848 which sought to address the evils of industrialism through measures based on Christian ethics: his second novel *Alton Locke* (1850) is the compelling story (told in the form of an autobiography) of a tailor and poet who rebels against the ignominy of sweated labour and becomes a leader of the Chartist movement. Reading Locke's descriptions of working people making clothes in the nineteenth century – their appalling working conditions and the constant drive by employers towards lower pay for increased productivity – is a stark awakening that, more than a century and a half later, competition among retailers to capture the market for 'cheap' clothing and subcontracting of work are (still) the principal features of the (fast) fashion system. In 'Cheap Clothes and Nasty', Kingsley writes of the aristocracy, clergy and gentry who buy such clothes: 'If these men know how their clothes are made, they are past contempt' (Figure 4.2).[14]

Following the deprivations of the 'Hungry Forties', the end of cholera outbreaks and some return to economic prosperity, there was a diminution of interest in sweating until the 1870s and 1880s when the medical journal *The Lancet* appointed a commission to report on the spread of infectious diseases through garments made in unsanitary London tenements.[15] One of the darker

Figure 4.2 *Needle Money* by John Leech (1817–64), *Punch*, 1849. Photo by Universal History Archive/Universal Images Group/via Getty Images.

aspects of the debate was the racial stereotyping of Jewish immigrants who were frequently blamed for the continuation of sweating. Also sinister were the economic arguments levied *against* state intervention for wage levels. Socialists Beatrice (née Potter) and Sidney Webb added a new dimension to sweating: the insistence on a living wage.[16] By 1890 Beatrice had begun to formulate her thesis that under capitalism employers should be directly responsible for their employees' welfare: this represented a huge change in economic thinking.

In 1906 the entrepreneur and social reformer George Cadbury financed a sensational sweated industries exhibition in which viewers could scrutinise all the details of sweated labour. Visitors to the exhibition were dismayed when they discovered that even expensive garments were often completed in disease-ridden slums.[17] The work of the Independent Labour Party in the 1920s and that of the economist John A. Hobson (1858–1940) focused on establishing a living wage; the movement was informed partly, though not uncritically, by the ideas of Thomas Carlyle and John Ruskin. Hobson's enlightened argument was that if an industry could not afford to pay its workforce a decent wage, then such a trade or industry should not exist in a civilised society and, furthermore, that higher wages and shorter hours would, in fact, improve the quality of products.[18]

How can that which should be so startlingly obvious a fact have been forgotten in the twenty-first century?

Given that the Factory Acts did not regulate pay, the Trade Boards Act of 1909 – as far as legislation in relation to pay was concerned – was a breakthrough: boards were empowered to fix a minimum time rate on which piece rates could be based. Significantly, this Act applied both to factory workers and women homeworkers and some have made a direct link between the passing of the Trade Boards Act and Thomas Hood's 'Song of the Shirt'.[19] Although it was eulogised by the historian R. H. Tawney, in reality the Act was limited and defective in a number of ways.[20] Its application to the tailoring industry – a complex industry employing numerous outworkers across Britain as a whole – was confined to the wholesale, bespoke and ready-made sections of the industry. It catered for clothing worn entirely by men and left untouched the whole field of women's tailoring.[21] In 1913 the Trade Boards system was extended to five more industries with the National Miners' strike of 1912 prompting further interest in a living wage.[22]

Conventional capitalist/'economic' arguments held out while even such enlightened Liberals and philanthropists such as Joseph Rowntree (1836–1925) – who advocated the general principle of a subsistence wage for every worker and the extension of wages boards to agriculture – believed that there were limits beyond which wages could not be increased without creating unemployment.[23] Objections were also made by economists who refused to countenance the idea of a living wage: for them the only solution to Britain's economic problems was the introduction of wage *cuts* leading to lower production costs and to more competitive exports.[24] This fallacious argument seems to have been tacitly accepted and perpetuated as British and other retailers outsourced production from the 1990s.

Trade boards continued their work well into the twentieth century. In 1945 they were renamed 'wages councils' in order to rid the system of the old stigma associated with 'sweating', the number of workers covered by legal wage-regulating machinery having increased to approximately 3.5 million. (This number excluded approximately 750,000 workers who were protected by the Agricultural Wages Boards). The Wages Councils Act was considered a personal achievement for the then Minister of Labour Ernest Bevin and by the time of his death in 1951, the number of wages councils had been increased to sixty.[25] Bevin's second reading of the Wages Councils Bill in 1945 is enlightening:

> The first purpose of the Bill is to bring the Trade Boards Acts up to date and to rename the trade boards 'wages councils'. Many people might ask what is in a

name, but as the purpose of the Bill is unfolded it will be seen that the change in the name not only widens trade boards legislation but is a declaration by Parliament that the conception of what was known as sweated industry is past. The Bill also proposes to provide additional powers for establishing the councils where voluntary machinery is inadequate or is likely to become inadequate, and reasonable standards of remuneration are not being, or are not likely to be, maintained.[26]

In 1953 discussions around a minimum wage resurfaced at the annual Trades Union Congress (TUC) but the idea was resoundingly rejected on the General Council's advice by a margin of almost two million votes. Some trade union leaders believed that wages councils institutionalised low pay and discouraged the labour force from seeking union membership.[27] In 1986 Margaret Thatcher's Wages Act repealed the 1945 Act. Young workers were removed from wages council protection although wages councils held out until 1993 when they were abolished by John Major's government. A national minimum wage was finally introduced in 1999, set at £3.60 per hour for adults and £3.00 for those aged between eighteen and twenty-one.[28]

In retrospect, the significance of the 1909 Act was that it heralded a break in economic and social thought rather than practically combating sweating. When wages councils were abolished in 1993, they covered 2.5 million employees, which represented only some ten per cent of the workforce. 'Taking the long view', Sheila Blackburn points out, 'the history of minimum wage legislation in Britain is one of continuity, discontinuity and tergiversation' while 'new theories had to be fashioned in order to dethrone orthodox economic thinking that state intervention in the wages contract would be ruinous for the British economy'.[29] Thought-provokingly, some hold that if Britain is to finally end its historic tradition of low pay, it must be prepared for the institution of maximum income limits as well as minimum wages.[30]

The move to outsourcing

When the UK, European countries and the United States began a concerted outsourcing movement, no history either of minimum pay or legal working conditions existed in many of the factories located overseas that were contracted to produce clothing. The 'corporate social responsibility' departments of large UK retailers set up systems and 'codes of conduct' in the 1990s intended to ensure that standards in overseas factories were regulated in response to the growing backlash against accusations of sweatshop exploitation; however, we know from tragedies such as the Rana Plaza catastrophe (see later) and many other less well-known cases that once you locate a factory thousands of miles away, it is much harder to monitor and enforce pay and factory conditions. Not only that, but those 'conditions' are, crucially, 'often easier for consumers to ignore'.[31]

Lack of transparency of operations is compounded if a brand contracts to a manufacturing company, which in turn farms out a proportion of its production to another factory/manufacturer, making the chain more convoluted and harder to monitor. Outsourcing has encouraged subcontracting which is now endemic in the clothing/apparel industry, creating a fractured supply chain in which workers are easily put in jeopardy.[32] When I was a selector (buyer) at Marks & Spencer in the early 1990s, the regular visits we made to UK manufacturers meant that the quality of garment production could be monitored directly but also that labour abuses were less likely to occur because of the close (although not always harmonious) relationships between factory/manufacturer and retailer and as a result of transparency of operations from design of clothing ranges through to final fit and manufacture.

Directed by Andrew Morgan, the documentary film *The True Cost* (2015) provides a shocking indictment of the impact of fast fashion; its many disastrous impacts on the environment along with the consequences of large retailers outsourcing their supply to developing countries where slave labour in 'Victorian' working conditions with appalling treatment of textile and garment workers and basic human rights abuses are the norm and are accepted as the necessary cost of profit and economic growth. Much of our clothing in the early twenty-first century is sewn, processed and dyed in countries where regulations may be insufficient and enforcement lax. It can legitimately be argued that many of the problems associated with the technological development of the textile and garment industries in the UK and Europe in the late eighteenth and nineteenth centuries have effectively been 'exported' with the outsourcing of production but without the 'solutions' in terms of factory legislation, minimum wage levels and so on discussed earlier. The worst of history is thus replicated overseas. More recently, however, there is a worrying increase in citing of concerns about the emergence and growth of 'modern slavery' in the UK.

Philip Smith and Manfred Max-Neef point out that there are more 'slaves' in the twenty-first century than there were before the abolition of slavery in the nineteenth century and that at least two-thirds of these are children.[33] Although they do not discuss fashion per se, they compare the outsourcing aspect of globalisation to 'old-fashioned colonialism'[34] since the 'host' countries to whom the industry is outsourced provide cheap labour, agricultural products and raw materials for the benefit of the 'metropolis' and simultaneously provide markets for these manufactured goods.[35] They point out that the World Trade Organization (WTO), which supports free trade, has no rules whatsoever about child labour or workers' rights and that its policies serve the 'corporations' which are bent on making profits.[36] Any corporation that outsources its production according to WTO principles 'produces unemployment in its place of origin and under-employment in the place where the work is carried out'.[37] The argument that such outsourcing assists 'industrialisation' in developing countries is challenged by the authors, who point out that 'industrialization takes place only when native control is maintained over (technical) education, infrastructure and the technologies necessary for industry'.[38]

A similar pattern of 'neocolonialism' has emerged in the fast-fashion industry, which relies on cheap labour in industrialising countries to whom Western and American brands have outsourced their supply chain. It can be argued that very little has changed or progressed since the nineteenth century when clothing production moved into factories in industrialising countries; in the twenty-first century, the 'historical' pattern of exploitation of women working long hours and paid a pittance has been outsourced to China and Bangladesh, for example. Writing for *The Guardian* in August 2020 in the wake of the Covid-19 pandemic, Meg Lewis, a senior campaigner at Labour Behind the Label, discusses the announcement by the UK's Department for International Development (DfID) of the decision to direct £4.85m of taxpayers' money towards the work of large retailers including Marks & Spencer, Tesco and Primark. By supporting large companies in fixing vulnerable supply chains, the funding was intended to ensure that 'people in Britain can continue to buy affordable, high-quality goods from around the world'. Lewis writes: 'These aims, along with the fact that UK brands have been entrusted to deliver them, set off alarm bells for labour rights campaigners like myself, who advocate for better working conditions in the global garment industry':

> Given that many of the supply chains that brands have built and reap huge profits from, are eroding and undermining workers' rights, it is absurd that the government is entrusting and subsidising retailers to 'fix' the problem. The fashion industry regularly churns out billionaire CEOs, while garment workers are paid poverty wages.

Lewis continues:

> DfID does not attempt to conceal the prioritisation of British consumers, and
> their need to buy 'affordable' goods, rather than support exploited workers.
> Instead of ensuring a steady flow of cheap goods at unrealistic prices that
> barely cover wages and materials, the UK government should be ensuring that
> consumers pay a fair price for their goods. To do otherwise effectively subsidises
> the exploitative and systemically unfair model.[39]

The onset of the Covid-19 crisis and subsequent lockdowns saw brands rushing
to protect their profit margins, exploiting loopholes in supply chains that are
built to limit their obligations to suppliers, with devastating effects for workers.
The Clean Clothes Campaign estimated that garment workers were owed
approximately $5.8bn (£4.4bn) in unpaid wages from the first three months of the
pandemic alone. Lewis points out that 'the structure of supply chains is by design
– not by accident – and brands are the lead architects', with the latter abandoning
production in countries where supply chains are strengthened in favour of
workers. The garment industry, she says, echoes and perpetuates 'colonial
structures that extract labour and resources from countries in the Global South,
maximising profits for wealthy (mostly white) Western bosses' and the DfID
funding is playing into 'this archaic structure, by injecting funding for solutions
at the top of supply chains, rather than listening and supporting worker-led
solutions and initiatives to create secure, safe and dignified employment'. She
calls for 'real systemic change' and for the UK government to use its influence to
strengthen 'mandatory due diligence and bolster enforcement of human rights
protections in supply chains' with the DfID ensuring that workers receive living
wages that cover food, housing and education.[40]

As if the neglect of payment of fair wages is not a damning enough indictment
of the outsourcing of supply chains, there is also the damage that unregulated
fashion manufacture is doing to the environment (and by extension to health and
livelihoods) in which so many poor people around the world live. According to
Greenpeace, waterways worldwide have become a dumping ground for all types
of wastes, with textile dyeing a case in point. Without proper regulation and a
safe system of effluent disposal, chemical dyes on which the fashion industry
now largely depends opened the way for pollution of rivers and water courses.
The history of the dyeing industry reveals that the resultant river pollution is
not a 'new' problem. Charles Dickens in his novel *Hard Times* (1854) famously
described 'Coketown' (named after the coal used to provide power in steam-

driven factories) and the social and environmental devastation caused by early industrialisation:

> It was a town of red brick, or of brick that would have been red if the smoke and ashes had allowed it; but, as matters stood, it was a town of unnatural red and black like the painted face of a savage. It was a town of machinery and tall chimneys, out of which interminable serpents of smoke trailed themselves for ever and ever, and never got uncoiled. It had a black canal in it, and a river that ran purple with ill-smelling dye.[41]

In England in 1856, William Perkin (1838–1907) produced the first commercially successful synthetic or aniline fabric dye derived from coal tar to give a vibrant mauve (see Chapter 2), Perkin's work paving the way for new chemically produced colours, and with these were introduced new problems of safe disposal of waste. Up until this time, dyes were derived from natural sources (red from cochineal beetles and madder, blue from the indigo plant and so on) and the waste produced was less harmful to the environment. In 1857 Perkin had found a site for his dyeworks at Greenford Green near Harrow, Middlesex, a meadow close to the banks of the Grand Junction Canal which he managed until the sale of the works was agreed in 1873. Of Perkin's Greenford manufactory, it was said that it was polluting the canals and local waterways in the area and that the Grand Junction Canal turned a different colour each week. The site of Perkin's dyeworks had two great defects, an inadequate water supply and the absence of suitable drainage: it sloped from north to south and was heavily waterlogged from the canal. Multicoloured waste regularly found its way back into the canal, the nearby brook and River Brent (Figure 4.3).[42]

Aside from the environmental impact of the rapid development and expansion of the aniline dye industry was the harm to human health as a result of the manufacture and wearing of the new dyes. For example, the French dye company La Fuchsine ceased producing its red dye following several claims that its arsenic acid process was poisoning the locals. A post-mortem of the wife of a signalman who died very close to one of the company's factories established that there was arsenic present in her organs. The same type of arsenic was detected in the well from which she drew her drinking water and in all the wells and subsoil within 200 yards of the fuchsine factory.[43] Alongside a plethora of documented cases across Europe of arsenic poisoning from contaminated water from wells, the gathering health debate centred on alleged skin inflammations in people wearing the fabrics dyed with the new aniline colours. While dry fabric was considered safe,

Figure 4.3 View of the Perkin & Sons dyestuff factory, Greenford Green, Middlesex, UK, *c.* 1870. Photo by Science and Society Picture Library/via Getty Images.

in 1884 the issues discussed in the pages of *The Times* and a number of medical journals were concerned mainly with colour fastness and the fugitive nature of some of the cheaper dyes: substantial traces of arsenic were found in water after the first wash of fabrics, such that they were deemed to pose a substantial risk when exposed to rain or perspiration.[44] Coal tar dyes had democratised access to colour; poorer people could now add colour to their lives, but at what cost? The *British Medical Journal* noted that the problem largely affected the working class, advising against the cheaper magenta and scarlet fabrics that were much sought after for underclothing, stockings and trimmings.[45]

This 'historical' problem is now replicated abroad and around the globe as the unregulated disposal of chemical dyes into water systems in the twenty-first century has re-ignited environmental concerns that should have been erased once and for all. Just as in Perkin's day, in the twenty-first century, not only is this an environmental problem but it is also a human rights issue, because it deprives millions of people access to safe drinking and bathing water. It is execrable that the 'environmental' problems associated with the evolving textile/clothing industry in the UK and Europe have resurfaced almost two centuries later in South-East Asia and the Indian subcontinent (Figure 4.4).

Figure 4.4 Garment factory waste dump in canal in Savar, Dhaka, Bangladesh, February 2022. Courtesy of STORYPLUS/Moment/via Getty Images.

Co-directed by David McIlride and Roger Williams, and produced by Lisa Mazzotto, the sobering documentary film *RiverBlue* was premiered in March 2017 in the United States at the twenty-fifth Annual Environmental Film Festival in Washington DC.[46] In China, it is estimated that 70 per cent of the rivers and lakes are contaminated by billions of gallons of wastewater produced by the textile and fast-fashion industry. In the opening scene, deep magenta wastewater spills into a river in China as the voice of fashion designer and activist Orsola de Castro can be heard saying, 'there is a joke in China that you can tell the "it" colour of the season by looking at the colour of the rivers'. The film examines the destruction of rivers in Asia caused by the largely unregulated textile industry and follows river conservationist Mark Angelo as he paddles the rivers devastated by a brew of toxic chemical waste, which includes mercury, cadmium and lead fabric dyes from the denim and leather industries, for example. Angelo explains that such is the level of pollution, these waterways in China, India and Bangladesh are devoid of life even as local communities rely on them for drinking and bathing. The water in these rivers has become a public health scandal with a high incidence of cancer and gastric and skin issues afflicting those who work in the industry or live nearby.

The widespread use of dyes in medicine and pharmacy (in the colouring of pills and mixtures) necessitated a new standardisation of the descriptive names of colours, new additions to language no less. By the time such an index was established in the United States in 1939, eighty-three years after the commercial exploitation of mauve, it contained the names of just over 7,500 synthetic colours.[47] It may be impossible to imagine both fashion – and, indeed, a whole world – with less colour than we have now and without the many chemical advances that Perkin's discovery inspired (in medicine, perfumery, food, explosives and photography) but that we should have 'reverted' to allowing dyes and effluent to poison our planet and our water supplies – and therefore ultimately us – is a terrible irony and tragedy that beggars comprehension.

While environmental pollution affects water supplies adversely with the impact on health and well-being potentially fatal, other casualties of the fast-fashion industry are those who have died tragically as a result of the lack of building/factory safety. On 24 April 2013, an eight-storey garment factory, known as the Rana Plaza, in Dhaka, Bangladesh, collapsed, killing 1,134 people and injuring around 2,500 more, many of whom were primarily garment workers. The collapse of the building, due to a structural failure, has been described as 'the deadliest garment-factory accident in history'.[48] One of the outcomes of the disaster was exposure of the practice of subcontracting out of retailers' orders and the lack of transparency in the supply chain. This caused well-known global brands, including several department stores, clothing specialists and fast-fashion brands, such as Benetton, Bonmarché, the Children's Place, Joe Fresh, Mango, Matalan, Primark and Walmart to be identified as companies using garment factories in Rana Plaza as suppliers, in addition to other factories that employed sweatshop conditions. In a case study of H&M, which considers the measures that the company have put in place to prevent such a tragedy occurring again, alongside ways of managing brand communication about ethics to the increasingly aware and conscious consumer, David and Helen Waller have asked the pertinent question as to whether it is, in fact, possible for fast fashion to be 'ethical' (Figure 4.5).[49]

There is yet another aspect of the consequences of switching to offshore manufacturing. While this may lead to cheaper products for consumers and job creation overseas, it can also result in domestic job losses, one of the paradoxical and damaging features already referred to by Smith and Max-Neef. Kate Raworth observes, 'cross-border flows are always double-edged and so need to be managed'.[50] When Burberry closed its polo-shirt-making plant in Treorchy, South Wales, in 2007 with more than 300 local jobs lost as these were outsourced to China, a whole community was decimated. In 2009 a further 170 jobs were lost at the Rotherham (Yorkshire) plant.[51] One response to the

Figure 4.5 Protest marking the sixth anniversary of the Rana Plaza disaster, Dhaka, Bangladesh, April 2019. Photo by Mamunur Rashid/NurPhoto/via Getty Images.

trend towards outsourcing and all its allied problems has been the positive move towards 'reshoring', in order to bring back the manufacturing that went offshore during the post-NAFTA globalisation boom described previously. In Britain, apparel production jobs jumped 9 per cent from 2011 to 2016 to a total of 100,000 and another 20,000 were expected to be added by 2020. Dana Thomas describes this trend as a 'reversal' of globalisation as we've known it, citing Paul Donovan, global chief economist at UBS Wealth Management, who predicts that global trade of goods such as apparel will 'revert to something like the old "imperial model" of importing raw materials and then processing it close to the consumer'.[52] However, at the time of writing, with some notable exceptions, this does not appear to be a dominant trend.

The 'economics' of fast fashion

Although they do not specifically discuss the fashion industry, a new wave of economists question the way in which governments, led by the discipline of economics, focus relentlessly on the paradigm of economic growth (GDP) as the only way forward and as a panacea for many social, economic and political ailments. Economist Diane Coyle advocates that GDP – a construct that came about in the specific circumstances of the Second World War when the US and UK governments wanted to understand what resources they had available for wartime production – is very limited because it only accounts for 'productive' (paid for) work in the economy and not for unpaid work or things without a market value.[53] Subsequently, this obsession with growth is based partly on a belief that Okun's Law (named after Arthur Okun's 1962 analysis) is gospel. Okun argued that an annual 2 per cent growth in US national output corresponded to a 1 per cent fall in unemployment. The result, Kate Raworth argues, is that 'in the twentieth century economics lost the desire to articulate its goals: in their absence, the economic nest got hijacked by the cuckoo goal of GDP growth'.[54] Citing the work of George Lakoff and Mark Johnson, she shows how orientational metaphors such as 'good is up' and 'good is forward' in opposition to phrases such as 'all-time low' or the tendency to refer to a person as 'low' in mood or 'down' are embedded in Western culture, 'shaping how we think and speak'.[55] In his 1960 publication, *The Stages of Economic Growth*, Walt W. Rostow (at the time about to become US presidential adviser) laid out his theory in which he argued that every country must pass through five stages of growth as follows: the traditional society, the preconditions of take-off, the take-off, the drive to maturity and the age of high mass-consumption. Early economists acknowledged what most of their successors have since ignored: that economic growth must eventually reach a limit. But to continue the flight metaphor, while Rostow's plane never lands (in other words continues forever on a course of 'high mass-consumption'), Raworth significantly amends the model by substituting the fifth stage with 'preparation for landing' and, in addition, adds a sixth stage: 'arrival'.[56] If we apply this model to fast fashion – an important aspect of economic growth overall – then it must have a *limit* because endless growth runs completely counter to sustainability.

When Theodore Veblen described the tendency for human beings to emulate their class or the class above them by displaying affluent clothing and making their consumption habits 'conspicuous' to others, he was alluding to the herd instinct for social and material emulation already referred to in Chapter 3. The democratisation of fashion (discussed in Chapter 2) has the potential to bring about a degree of social and economic levelling: as clothing becomes cheaper and more widely available, a 'virtuous' cycle allows more people to have access to increasingly more, along with more choice. However, there is a paradox here. Even with the advent of cheaper clothing, the fast-fashion phenomenon does not work against inequality more generally. In 2015, the world's richest 1 per cent owned more wealth than all the other 99 per cent put together.[57] High levels of inequality both between and within countries can mean that those people outside the top 1 per cent increasingly live beyond their means.[58] In 2013, in the United States, 400 people had more wealth than 155 million people combined.[59] Virtuous cycles of wealth and vicious cycles of poverty can send otherwise similar people spiralling to opposite ends of the income-distribution spectrum.[60] In the two decades between 1988 and 2008 a majority of countries worldwide saw rising inequality within their borders. While global inequality fell slightly, over 50 per cent of the total increase in global income in this period was captured by the richest 5 per cent of the world's population, while the poorest 50 per cent of people gained only 11 per cent of it. Furthermore, in high-income countries the gap between rich and poor is now at its highest level in 30 years.[61] The impact of the Covid-19 pandemic, the war in Ukraine from 2022 and high inflation will exacerbate these disparities.

Such inequalities have to an extent been 'justified' once again by economics. The Kuznets Curve propounded the theory that as countries grow richer, inequality increases for a time before falling. Although this theory has largely been debunked, it has, however, been 'mirrored' by the 'Environmental Kuznets Curve', which suggests that growth will eventually fix the environmental problems that it creates, with mainstream economists mocking what they called the 'alarmist cries' of environmental critics.[62] While climate crisis – along with the particular impact of the fast-fashion system on the depletion and despoliation of environmental resources – is now beyond any doubt, the *economic* conundrum is this: 'No country', says Raworth, 'has ever ended human deprivation without a growing economy. And no country has ever ended ecological degradation with one'.[63] Philip Smith and Manfred Max-Neef make this point in another way: because the economy is a sub-system of a larger and finer system – the biosphere – permanent growth is therefore impossible.[64] They posit a particularly powerful counter to the fixation with economic growth, which they refer to as 'the 'beckoning buoy to which all humankind must sail'.[65] They make the distinction between growth and development,[66] stressing that development is about people and not objects.[67] GDP has the following shortcomings: with GDP everything is added whether the impacts are positive or negative, for example, the costs of traffic accidents and diseases are counted along with investments and education. Moreover, GDP does not include the value of unpaid work, so discriminating against household and voluntary work. In summary, it only expresses that which can be expressed in monetary terms and, significantly, nature and ecosystems are not given any value.[68]

Clothing producers and retailers might counter an accusation of the negative effects of democratisation by arguing that through mass production and outsourcing, prices have been reduced, thus 'evening out' inequalities. Meanwhile, others have stressed the elitist nature of couture notwithstanding the observation that couture 'functions as a laboratory of ideas, a place where designers can allow their creativity to be expressed to the full.'[69] But, in fact, the strength of brand marketing that encourages 'repeat' and/or multiple buying of a product (trainers for example), leads not only to overconsumption and the resultant tendency to devalue clothing but also to the abuse of rights in terms of low pay and execrable working conditions for those employed in the manufacturing of fashion. The large brands and retailers, meanwhile, come out on top. In other words, democratisation encourages overconsumption, which in turn can create *increased inequalities* between rich and poor. And aside from the pressing need to counter inequality, we need urgently to find an alternative to the current paradigm of 'degenerative industrial design', the cradle-to-grave manufacturing supply chain of take, make, use, lose, in which humans extract the Earth's minerals, metals, biomass and fossil fuels, manufacture them into products and sell them on to consumers who, probably sooner rather than later, will throw them away. This system is fundamentally flawed because it runs counter to the living world, which thrives by continually recycling life's building blocks such as carbon, oxygen, water, nitrogen and phosphorus.[70] The challenge is to create economies that make us thrive, whether or not they grow. Raworth concludes that we need to be 'agnostic' about growth and to transform the financial, political and social structures that have made our economies and societies come to expect, demand and depend upon it.[71] Likewise, Tim Jackson emphasises the importance of 'governmentality' – the set of organised practices and structures through which subjects are governed – arguing that these need to be different from current governmentality, in which 'the institutions of consumer society are designed to favour a particularly materialistic individualism and to encourage the relentless pursuit of consumer novelty'.[72]

Moreover, there is a strong counterclaim to that which simplistically assumes that higher levels of wealth and the means to consume necessarily bring happiness. The Easterlin Paradox put forward in the 1970s (named after US economist Richard Easterlin) states that 'at a point in time happiness varies directly with income both among and within nations, but over time happiness does not trend upward as income continues to grow'.[73] So if the paradigm of economic growth – of which one implication is continued, relentless overconsumption of fashion – is no longer fit for purpose in the context of world population growth, the diminution of resources, environmental destruction and climate crisis, then we need alternative models and essentially a 'vibrant new economic paradigm that measures economic value in totally new ways'. There is evidence that the 'sharing economy' is growing, in which the culture of ownership is giving way to a culture of access, for example, renting cars by the hour, and, rather than going shopping for new clothes, books and so on, a growing number of people are swapping or 'swishing' them with friends or neighbours.[74] Tim Jackson argues persuasively that we should escape from 'the iron-grip of consumerism', advocating a service-based 'circular economy' founded on 'care, craft and creativity'.[75] There are, he says, 'swiftly diminishing returns of growth beyond a certain income; the huge advantages of income growth below that point; and the remarkable performance of some poorer countries who are able to enjoy levels of human wellbeing on a par with the richest nations on earth on a fraction of the income'. He adds that 'all of these lessons are vital in our ability to understand the complex relationship between GDP growth and prosperity'.[76]

Just as research shows that after a certain point, additional income provides correspondingly less additional satisfaction (known in economics speak as 'diminishing marginal utility'), so the same is thought to be true of additional goods, including clothing. In other words, beyond a certain level, the more we have, the less we seem to be satisfied.[77] A core element of neural design is that a pulse of dopamine is delivered to key areas of the brain whenever we obtain what at any given moment we desire the most. 'We experience this pulse of chemicals as a pulse of satisfaction', neuroscientist Peter Sterling points out. He explains: 'The pulse soon fades, so to obtain another, we repeat the behaviour.'[78] This in part explains the addictive, compulsive behaviour that leads to multiple and frequent clothing purchases that feed the fast-fashion industry. How many times do we hear accounts of people with full wardrobes with 'nothing to wear' or of the addiction to shopping for clothing that is never taken out of its packaging, let alone worn? So when it comes to our clothes, how can we replicate a sense of satisfaction by acquiring less, and feel fulfilled by both the quality of what we have and our sense of attachment to it rather than its quantity? These important questions will provide the backdrop to the discussions that follow.

Clothing, nature and the environment

Elsewhere I have reflected upon how the clothing of the rural working classes was represented (in painting, photography, fictional literature and in the very items of clothing that have survived and been collected by museums) as a result of social and economic change and the ways in which clothing intersects with history in unexpected ways.[1] Here, however, I want to consider the ways in which narratives have been woven around the colours and textures of cloth and the crafting of clothing in order to throw light on our changing relationship with the natural world. Given that early industrialisation in Britain and the United States was spearheaded by the expansion and development of the cotton industry and the clothing trade, it is not altogether surprising that such developments should have provoked a response in which 'fashion' became the focus of a backlash against the drive towards consumerism and the commodification of 'stuff' along with retailing/shopping. As early as the late eighteenth century, the poetry of John Clare (1793–1864) presages economic and social change in rural districts while later, writers from Thomas Hardy (1840–1928) to D. H. Lawrence (1885–1930) acknowledge and often lament the breakup of old agricultural practices and communities as a result of industrialisation. F. R. Leavis puts it well when he says: 'Lawrence knew every day of his life in intimate experience the confrontation, the interpenetration, of the old agricultural England with the industrial; the contrast of the organic forms and rhythms and the old beauty of humane adaptation with what has supervened.'[2] Here we are offered insights into a culture that came to extol nature and the environment and that has long been a thread in cultural history that is, however, often difficult to unpick. In the nineteenth century we see a variety of responses in the work of writers such as Henry David Thoreau (1817–62) and W. H. Hudson (1841–1922), while some of the most trenchant objections to both fashion and to the processes of mass production that produced it were voiced in the cause of 'nature' and are exemplified by the work of designer William Morris (1834–96) and his daughter

May (1862–1938) along with adherents of the Arts and Crafts Movement. Out of this emerged what, in Chapter 6, I call 'philosophies' of dress encountered in the views expressed by exponents of the Aesthetic Dress Movement, specifically those of the poet and playwright Oscar Wilde (1854–1900); writer and women's rights supporter Mary Eliza Haweis (1848–98) and, finally, in the lesser-known writing of the controversial sculptor Eric Gill (1882–1940). Together, these narratives reflect the enormity of industrial change in the nineteenth and twentieth centuries and its impact over time on our relationship with our clothes.

Clothing in pastoral narratives

One set of reactions to the changes brought about by industrialisation and the mass production of textiles and clothing and increasing urbanisation might be described as a quest to 'return to nature'. This, of course, can mean different things in different contexts, but to see that 'return to nature' in metaphorical terms by relating fabrics and clothes to the countryside in some way, or perhaps more simply, to compare fabrics with the colours and textures of nature, is a theme to which writers and designers have frequently returned. Clare Hunter points out that until the invention of aniline dyes in the mid-nineteenth century (discussed in Chapter 2), all the colours for cloth and thread were coaxed from nature. It was not only their hue that was harvested; many of the plants used for dyes were chosen for their additional medicinal and spiritual qualities.[3] We should not underestimate how such changes must have changed people's view of the world.

John Clare is sometimes described as the greatest of all poets of the natural world. The few physical descriptions we have of him, including his clothes and also the clothes of those who people his poems, place him firmly in a world poised on the brink of significant change brought about by enclosure and agricultural 'improvement': increases and efficiencies in food production were sought while Britain's population grew and with industrial development, people began the mass exodus from villages into towns. In one sense, Clare's poetry takes us away from objective, grand narratives of historical discourse into a narrower domain. Geographically, his world was that of the area known as the Peterborough Soke in Northamptonshire, bounded to the south by the River Nene along the Huntingdonshire border and to the southeast by Cambridgeshire, and, in the north, by the River Welland adjacent to Lincolnshire. In the twenty-first century the area is dominated by the urban sprawl of Peterborough, but it also contains large areas of relatively flat farmland encompassing ancient rural parishes such as Clare's own birth village, Helpston (Helpstone in Clare's own time). Although in a physical sense intensely local, it is also, perhaps, a world which for William Blake (1757–1827) might hold within it intimations of the universal and eternal. The first well-known lines of Blake's beautiful 'Auguries of Innocence' (probably written *c.* 1803 but not published until 1863), run in the form of a quatrain (rhyming scheme ABAB) thus:

> To see a World in a Grain of Sand
> And a Heaven in a Wild Flower
> Hold Infinity in the palm of your hand
> And Eternity in an hour.

Clare's biographer Jonathan Bate points out that as Clare matured his poems became more *local*: 'Paradoxically, it is through the very quality of locality that he achieves his universality.'[4] But place is never static, and, as Iain Sinclair says in his exploration of Clare's 'Journey Out of Essex' (attempting to follow the route out of Epping Forest taken by Clare when he ran away from the first asylum to which he was committed), 'place expresses itself through the person you choose as guide'.[5] And, of course, we take what we need and want from the words and spirit of a poet. Iain Sinclair again: 'The Clare I found will not be your John Clare . . . The track we travelled, coming from London, is no longer Clare's Great North Road. Through error, perhaps, we arrive at a richer truth: in the telling is the tale.'[6]

The colour of Clare's world is, of course, one before aniline dyes and fashion more generally had spread their influence among those working-class people who, like Clare, and his father before him, worked in predominantly rural occupations including as day labourers, digging and planting the heavy clay fields roundabout. Indeed, as Bate observes, 'hard labour on the land was written into the very name of the family: *Clare* derives from *clayer*, one who manures or marls agricultural land'.[7] Like the 'clothing' of the land, working-class clothes are, above all, functional (though often inadequate given their long wear and threadbare condition), but of high relative value and also of symbolic and elemental significance. We see glimpses of Clare's appearance – and of his world – through scanty descriptions of his clothes, such as when he goes for an 'interview' for possible employment with an uncle who worked as a footman to a counsellor-at-law in Wisbech. Clare was kitted out by his mother in his Sunday best: a white neck cloth and a pair of gloves to hide the hands that were coarse from labour and, because she could not afford a new one, a coat that was far too small with sleeves extending barely beyond his elbows.[8]

Dress plays an important part in courtship and display, such as in a poem about Bessy, who is 'the top wench that walks on a Sunday / To seek for a sweetheart or show a new dress', or, more erotically but also comically, in a ballad on the relative merits of indoor and outdoor courtship:

> How can I kiss my love
> Muffled i' hat and glove . . .
> Lay by thy woollen vest
> Rap no cloak o'er thy breast
> There my hand oft hath prest
> Pin nothing there
> There my head drops to rest
> Leave its bed bare.[9]

In his poem 'July', Clare describes the 'maidens' dragging the rake behind the haymaker's cart 'Wi light dress shaping to the wind / And trembling locks of curly hair'.[10]

We know a limited amount about Clare's personal appearance including his clothes. In the description of Clare's dress, notions of class are played out: for the 'peasant poet', seeking patronage from aristocratic benefactors necessitated a careful balancing act between Clare dressing according to his 'station' (and not above it!) but also not overly indicating his poverty. On a visit to Milton Hall to deliver to Lord Milton ten copies of Clare's first book (*Poems, Descriptive of Rural Life and Scenery. By John Clare, a Northamptonshire Peasant*, published in January 1820), Edward Drury (a local bookseller who first supported Clare in getting his work into print) advised Clare not to wear his Sunday best. The important thing was to have a 'clear clean shirt, clean stockings and shoes'. He sent a shirt of his own, suggesting that Clare should tuck in 'the frippery of the frill' under his clean waistcoat. 'A nice silk handkerchief will also be useful', he added.[11] In deliberating whether or not to call on the Marquess at Burghley House (Stamford, Lincolnshire), Clare postponed his visit because of snow and because he did not want his one pair of shoes to 'be in a dirty condition for so fine a place'.[12] Clare had vivid memories of the inconvenient noise made by his 'hard-nailed shoes' on the marble and boarded floors and during the interview with the Marquess, he recalls 'eyeing the door and now and then looking at my dirty shoes and wishing myself out of the danger of soiling such grandeur'.[13] In fact, it was conjectured that one reason for Clare's reluctance to show himself in company was his poor wardrobe. However, even when Clare was offered clothes, he is said to have refused to accept with the exception of an ancient overcoat which was too large for him, but which was useful for hiding his whole figure from head to toe and which he apparently refused to take off even at dinner and in hot rooms.[14] One item of clothing he did accept was a fine silk cravat which he wore when sitting for his portrait. Of the portrait, Jonathan Bate says of Clare: 'He looks hot and uncomfortable in wing-collar, carefully folded neckerchief and tightly-buttoned yellow waistcoat'.[15] Elsewhere, the artist Henry (Harry) Behnes, who specialised in the sculpting of portrait busts, described the poet after a visit he had made to Clare in Helpston in July 1827 in his '*delightfully* rustic attire'.[16] Clare's aristocratic friend Eliza Emmerson sent her usual Christmas gifts to the Clare family in 1827: a box of books, a waistcoat piece for Clare's wife Patty to make up, two neckerchiefs of Indian silk (one in yellow and both 'of the *newest fashion*'), money for school fees for the children and a guinea for roast beef and plum pudding.[17] After Clare was admitted to Northampton Asylum, fellow patients William Jerome and G. D. Berry left some accounts and sketches, according to which Clare was bald on top, his remaining hair light flaxen at the time of his commitment to the asylum. It turned to silvery white and in his last years he wore it long over his shoulders. He usually walked about in a light fustian coat or jacket, his deep outer pockets stuffed with books, newspapers and notebook. Beneath the outer coat he wore a double-breasted waistcoat, favouring dark olive for colour: 'Also Kerseymere breeches with gaiters, shoes with one tie (he had very handsome feet and hands).' Apparently, he wore a better suit on Sundays. In later asylum days Clare often wore a black 'sur-tout' coat with breeches and in his last years he took to wearing very fashionable trousers (Figure 5.1).[18]

The inadequacy of Clare's clothing is often hinted at. In April 1820, having paid a courtesy visit to one of his early supporters, he collapsed on the way home in what is thought to have been a quasi-epileptic fit: 'Whether I lay down or fell down I cant [*sic*] tell but when I came to my self my hat was lying at a distance from me and my coat was rather dirtied'.[19] The fact that he was afflicted with 'shiverings' for the next few weeks in all likelihood indicates that he had caught a terrible chill, and one can surely put this down in part to the inadequacy of his clothing. In 1827 Clare's illness was thought in part to be rheumatism, Marianne Marsh suggesting that Patty should make some flannel shirts (presumably for warmth).[20] Nevertheless, when he heard of the delay in the publication of the two volumes of his second collection of poetry, he grimly joked to his publisher that he would wear his black waistcoat in mourning 'for the last twin children

Figure 5.1 Portrait of John Clare, by William Hilton (1786–1839), 1820–1. Oil on canvas. National Portrait Gallery, London, UK. © National Portrait Gallery, London.

[which referred to the two volumes of poems] which I fancy are still born and gone hom agen', that last phrase being the one he had used only a few weeks before on the actual death of his first baby son.[21]

In the (probably) autobiographical poem 'The Village Minstrel', Clare describes young Lubin in his worn clothing, which others tried to keep neat and clean for him, despite the fact that it was patched:

> It might be curious here to hint the lad,
> How in his earliest days he did appear;
> Mean was the dress in which the boy was clad,
> His friends so poor, and clothes excessive dear,
> They oft were foil'd to rig him once a year;
> And housewife's care in many a patch was seen;
> Much industry 'gainst want did persevere:
> His friends tried all to keep him neat and clean,
> Though care has often fail'd, and shatter'd he has been.[22]

Thomas Hood, literary editor of the *London*, described Clare in his *Literary Reminiscences* as 'our Green Man', with his 'bright, grass-coloured coat and yellow waistcoat'.[23] Unsurprisingly, Clare himself was an astute observer, describing Thomas De Quincey as 'a little artless simple-seeming body, something of a child overgrown, in a blue coat and black neckerchief – for his dress is singular – with his hat in his hand, [who] steals gently among the company with a smile, turning timidly round the room'.[24]

It seems likely that Clare suffered from alternate bouts of mania and depression; a characteristic of the former was possibly binge-spending, including on books that he could ill afford. Among the fragments in his manuscripts is a note of 'little expenses occurred' including a guinea for a new hat, and thirteen shillings and five pence for 'washing'. Bate suggests that we imagine the marital exchange:

> Patty accuses him of spending money they haven't got on his new hat and the constant stream of books, while she slaves away at the household chores. Washing would have involved fetching water from the parish pump, heating it over the fire, soaking clothes and linens in a tub by the back door and scrubbing by hand with poor-quality yellow soap. So he makes it up to her by spending more money they haven't got sending everything out to a washerwoman.[25]

We see in George Morland's paintings (before 1790), the 'Comforts of Industry' and its companion the 'Miseries of Idleness' (National Galleries of Scotland, Scottish National Gallery), a comment on the profligacy of poor, working-class people who indulged in what was considered an unnecessary expense by obtaining a fashionable hat and thus we can surmise that Clare's putting the acquisition of clothing and books before the immediate needs of his family would have been frowned upon even among his nearest relations.

In fact, hats feature regularly in Clare's life. Before walking away from the private asylum in Epping Forest to make the journey back to Helpston by foot, he picks up an old wideawake left by some gypsies with whom he had been conversing, thinking it might come in handy.[26] Later, when he actually embarks on the journey from Essex, he is cautioned by a gypsy girl he meets to put something in his hat (this, presumably, says Jonathan Bate, is the gypsy hat that he had earlier found in Epping Forest) 'to keep the crown up', otherwise he would be noticed. The hat was, presumably, too big for him. Or it could have been that he wore the crown down and it looked as if he was trying to go about in disguise, which perhaps drew unnecessary attention to him.

Clare links fashion to sexual mores and 'whoring' as in the poem 'Don Juan':

> Poets are born – and so are whores – the trade is
> Grown universal – in these canting days
> Women of fashion must of course be ladies

And whoreing is the business – that still pays
Playhouses Ball rooms – there the masquerade is[27]

Clare was not alone in associating fashion with vanity and corrupt morals. Perhaps more subtly, poet and novelist Thomas Hardy later draws together landscape and clothing, arguing that 'civilization', fashion and the 'modern' are the antithesis of the 'antique' and 'primitive'. One of the finest pieces of writing on this theme is Thomas Hardy's memorable description of Egdon Heath in his novel *The Return of the Native* (1878). Hardy's Egdon refers to a now much-reduced area of heathland that borders his birthplace in Higher Bockhampton near the county town of Dorset, Dorchester, and which Hardy knew intimately:

> Civilization was its enemy; and ever since the beginning of vegetation its soil had worn the same antique brown dress, the natural and invariable garment of the particular formation. In its venerable one coat lay a certain vein of satire on human vanity in clothes. A person on a heath in raiment of modern cut and colours has more or less an anomalous look. We seem to want the oldest and simplest human clothing where the clothing of the earth is so primitive.[28]

I have written elsewhere of the role of clothing in Hardy's writing and of his response to change expressed through the dress of his characters and of the values that attached themselves to particular items of clothing such as the cotton sunbonnet (Figure 5.2).

Hardy's reactions are usefully seen in the context of the transition in Britain from an agricultural to a rapidly urbanising population in the 1840s and post-1850 which, with the exception of *The Trumpet-Major*, is the period during which Hardy's novels are set.[29] W. J. Keith in *The Rural Tradition* notes the extent to which the 'rural tradition in literature' (he includes a predominantly 'male' list of Izaac Walton; Gilbert White; William Cobbett; Mary Russell Mitford; George Borrow; Richard Jefferies; George Sturt, known as 'George Bourne'; W. H. Hudson; Edward Thomas; Henry Williamson; and H. J. Massingham) was 'stimulated by the effects of the Industrial Revolution . . . that it was a literature created in the main for urban consumption.'[30] While the clothing metaphor in *The Return of the Native* cited earlier was inspired by Thomas Carlyle – who had very clear views on the disaster of industrialisation and its deleterious effect on most aspects of Victorian society – Hardy's philosophy is very much his own: the haunted and haunting voice of someone who believed that the individual's outward appearance was an expression of their actual selves, which was in turn intimately connected to their environment. Thus clothing becomes a kind of second skin, which imbibes the character and experiences of its wearer. In his

Figure 5.2 Cotton sunbonnet, *c.* 1850–80. Collection of Rachel Worth. Photo by Rachel Worth.

historical novel set in the period of the Napoleonic Wars, *The Trumpet-Major* (1880), Hardy takes up this theme, describing brilliantly the deceased miller's clothing:

> They moved what had never been moved before – the oak coffer, containing the miller's wardrobe – a tremendous weight, what with its locks, hinges, nails, dust, framework, and the hard stratification of old jackets, waistcoats, and knee-breeches at the bottom, never disturbed since the miller's wife died, and half-pulverized by the moths, whose flattened skeletons lay amid the mass in thousands.[31]

Very much of its time, Hardy's description here refers to what must have been a common occurrence: the storing of the clothes of deceased loved ones for so many years that they are eventually forgotten about as they fall into decay. The perception that clothes, as a result of long wear, become, over time, as one with the person who owns and wears them is not something that would resonate with us in an age of fast fashion, but it is likely to have been a common trope before mass-produced clothing dominated the market.

In the United States, where, significantly, the ready-made clothing industry had been expanding since the beginning of the nineteenth century at least, reactions to increased consumption and the democratisation of clothing reveal some parallels to reactions in Britain. In particular, Henry David Thoreau was highly critical of the factory system (which he compared to that in England), noting the (poor) 'condition of the operatives' and questioning whether it could be the 'best mode by which men may get clothing', commenting with justifiable cynicism that 'the principal object is, not that mankind may be well and honestly clad, but, unquestionably, that corporations may be enriched'.[32] In his autobiographical work *Walden* (first published in 1854 as *Walden; or, Life in the Woods*) he reflects on his daily life while living in natural surroundings in solitude on the banks of Walden Pond. He recounts his visit to the house of an Irishman, Hugh Quoil, after the latter's death, describing him as 'the last inhabitant of these woods before me'. He likens the man to his clothes and vice versa, so much so that they are almost one and the same: 'There lay his old clothes curled up by use, as if they were himself, upon his raised plank bed.'[33] More than half a century later, the poet Edward Thomas (killed in action at the Battle of Arras in 1917 soon after he arrived in France) wrote poignantly in his verse and prose of the English countryside at a time of social and economic transition. In *In Pursuit of Spring*, Thomas walks from his home in London, documenting the changing season and his experiences of the southern countryside. In so doing he comes across a road-mender in the Somerset Quantocks: 'The only people on the road were road-menders working with a steamroller; the corduroys of one were stained so thoroughly by the red mud of the Quantocks, and shaped so excellently by wear to his tall, spare figure, that they seemed to be one with the man.'[34] Hardy had made similar inferences about the relationship between clothing and the wearer, for example in his reference to the mason in *Under the Greenwood Tree* (1872) whose sleeves of his fustian jacket are creased permanently due to wear, the creases produced over long years by the bending of his arms and the dust captured in the hollows as a kind of legacy of his trade:

> He also wore a very stiff fustian coat, having folds at the elbows and shoulders as unvarying in their arrangement as those in a pair of bellows: the ridges and the projecting parts of the coat collectively exhibiting a shade different from that of the hollows, which were lined with small ditch-like accumulations of stone and mortar-dust.[35]

To a late-nineteenth- and early-twentieth-century readership, these descriptions must have struck home as old-fashioned, maybe even a little bizarre, given that by this time the ready-made clothing industry was in full swing and there was a definite move towards the acquisition of new clothing by working-class people.

Thoreau likewise rails against the new trends when he admonishes: 'Do not trouble yourself much to get new things, whether clothes or friends. Turn the old; return to them. Things do not change; we change. Sell your clothes and keep your thoughts. God will see that you do not want society.'[36] The phrase, 'things do not change; we change' is a sure indication that the external world was, in fact, changing but that the human condition along with basic human needs remained the same. In other words, Thoreau describes the way that consumerism swept people along with it while he regretted the old ways that were left behind.

Thoreau came from a relatively wealthy background; perhaps it is 'easy' for the middle classes to rail against change when the struggle for material goods is absent. Not so with Hardy's background and upbringing, born as he was into a class of master masons in a quiet English hamlet. Although Hardy achieved prosperity as he became a successful writer, he always remembered his Dorset roots and wrote best about, and empathised with, the poor and the artisan classes, recognising, as he put it, the competing claims of 'progress' (change and urbanisation) and 'picturesqueness' (holding onto the old ways). As he wrote in his well-known essay, 'The Dorsetshire Labourer' (1883):

> It is only the old story that progress and picturesqueness do not harmonise. They [the Dorsetshire labourers] are losing their individuality, but they are widening the range of their ideas and gaining in freedom. It is too much to expect them to remain stagnant and old-fashioned for the pleasure of romantic spectators.[37]

Hardy was not alone in mourning the passing of the old agricultural and country ways. William Henry Hudson (1841–1922) was an almost exact contemporary: essayist, novelist, naturalist and ornithologist (and a founding member of the RSPB), he grew up on the pampas of Argentina before settling in England in 1869. An admirer of Henry David Thoreau[38] and a friend of Edward Thomas, Hudson's love of the countryside and hatred of the town is captured in his writing: many regard his masterpiece to be his 1910 publication, *A Shepherd's Life*. Hudson's work is sometimes compared to that of the naturalist Richard Jefferies (1848–87), but as Adam Thorpe observes:

> The chief difference between them is that Jefferies was a native Wiltshireman, and Hudson a foreigner, even to England: the former, especially in the brilliant *Hodge and His Masters* (1880), is the farmer's son telling us in knowing detail what late Victorian farm-life consisted of; Hudson is the inquisitive stranger in the rapt process of finding out.[39]

Unusually for his time, the focus of Hudson's observations is the poor whose lives have been forgotten:

> But of the humble cottagers, the true people of the vale who were rooted in the soil, and flourished and died like trees in the same place – of these no memory exists. We only know that they lived and laboured; that when they died, three or four a year, three or four hundred in a century, they were buried in the little shady churchyard, each with a green mound over him to mark the spot. But in time these 'mouldering heaps' subsided, the bodies turned to dust, and another and yet other generations were laid in the same place among the forgotten dead, to be themselves in turn forgotten. Yet I would rather know the histories of these humble, unremembered lives than of the great ones of the vale who have left us a memory.[40]

With the precarious economic situation of agricultural labourers whose wages in the southern English countryside were already shockingly low, one of the few abiding 'memories' that Hudson alludes to is that of the 'Swing Riots' of 1830 and the smashing by labourers of threshing machines that were depriving them of vital employment. This unrest is sometimes referred to as the 'Last Labourers' Revolt': the riots were so harshly suppressed that revolt on a similar scale did not reoccur. With regard to the law, 'the "enormity of the crime" was an expression as constantly used in the case of the theft of a loaf of bread, or of an old coat hanging on a hedge by some ill-clad, half-starved wretch, as in cases of burglary, arson, rape and murder'.[41] 'I find', says Hudson, 'another case of a sentence of transportation for life on a youth of 18, named Edward Baker, for stealing a pocket handkerchief'.[42] Elsewhere Hudson talks of a strong man's paltry wages of seven shillings a week, 'a sum barely sufficient to keep him and his family from starvation and rags'.[43] Hudson's references to the hard lives of the poor and the immediacy of daily existence are poignant; being able to plan would be preferable to the more usual hand-to-mouth existence but even so, small pleasures become greater ones:

> Before a stall in the marketplace [Salisbury] a child is standing with her mother – a little girl of about twelve, blue-eyed, light-haired, with thin arms and legs, dressed, poorly enough, for her holiday. The mother, stoutish, in her best but much-worn black gown and a brown straw, out-of-shape hat, decorated with bits of ribbon and a few soiled and frayed artificial flowers. Probably she is the wife of a labourer who works hard to keep himself and family on fourteen shillings a week; and she, too, shows, in her hard hands and sunburnt face, with little wrinkles appearing, that she is a hard worker; but she is very jolly, for she is in Salisbury on market day, in fine weather, with several shillings in her purse –

a shilling for the fares, and perhaps eightpence for refreshments, and the rest to be expended in necessaries for the house.[44]

In *A Shepherd's Life*, Hudson's focus is the shepherd Caleb Bawcombe whose flocks graze the Wiltshire, Hampshire and Dorset borders and whose recollections Hudson carefully records and which are finally shaped while he is staying in the Lamb Inn in the Wiltshire village of Hindon in the spring and summer of 1909. Shepherds are traditionally regarded as having a special kind of wisdom, the fruit of long and solitary hours quietly observing the natural world. The image of Christ as the 'Good Shepherd' tending his sheep has contributed significantly not only to Christian iconography but also to the enduring symbolism of the shepherd in literature over time: for example, Gabriel Oak in Hardy's *Far From the Madding Crowd* (1874) takes upon himself the role of Bathsheba Everdene's 'good shepherd' through all the vagaries of her life. There is no sentimentality in Hudson's descriptions either of Caleb or of other shepherds in his writing, however, whose clothing Hudson often depicts in some detail such as that of a young shepherd in Salisbury 'coming along towards me with that half-slouching, half-swinging gait peculiar to the men of the downs, especially when they are in the town on pleasure bent' and wearing 'a grey suit and thick, iron-shod boots and brown leggings, with a soft, felt hat thrust jauntily on the back of his head'.[45]

Caleb's father Isaac was born in 1800: as Caleb recalls, he wore the dress of an old order of pensioners to which he had been admitted – a soft, broad, white felt hat, thick boots and brown leather leggings, and a long grey cloth overcoat with red collar and brass buttons. Even after working as head shepherd for almost half a century, Isaac would not accept an increase of wages: 'Seven shillings a week he had always had; and that small sum, with something his wife earned by making highly finished smock-frocks, had been sufficient to keep them all in a decent way'.[46]

Hudson offers us some fascinating insights into the importance of clothing in very poor people's lives along with the creativity expended in maintaining a 'neat', even if not quite 'fashionable', appearance. He describes a boy whose father died when he was twelve years old: 'But the women had a tender feeling for him, because, although motherless and very poor, he yet contrived to be always clean and neat. He took the greatest care of his poor clothes, washing them and mending them himself'.[47] And then there is the old man in labourer's clothes who stumps into the church 'with his ponderous, iron-shod boots', and who, 'without taking off his old, rusty hat, began shouting at the church cleaner about a pair of trousers he had given her to mend, which he wanted badly'.[48] Elsewhere, 'iron-shod boots' (of which actual examples survive in museum collections such as that of the Museum of English Rural Life, University of Reading), are described by Hudson as good for tramping down roots, loose earth and dead leaves in order to break into a hedgehog's nest.[49]

Notwithstanding such colourful descriptions, stories of dire need are sadly repeated by Hudson: he recalls a farmer's wife, Mrs Ellerby, who takes pity on one 'Old Nance' who, having left Warminster workhouse, seeks employment with the daughter of her former mistress. All that Mr and Mrs Ellerby can do is to give her the job of crow scaring, one of the lowest-paid and most monotonous of agricultural jobs. The farmer, Mr Ellerby, gives her better clothes, 'an old felt hat, a big old frieze overcoat, and a pair of old leather leggings'. She ties on the hat with a strip of cloth and fastens the coat at the waist with a cord.[50] Such references to the makeshift nature of much working-class clothing remind us in our overstocked world that better access to clothing was once a necessity; yet the advent of fast fashion reveals democratisation gone to excess.

Nature fights back

Nature, whether in realistic/representational or stylised form, has long provided the inspiration for beautiful textiles used to adorn our bodies and our homes: exquisite, embroidered clothing can be seen, for example, in portraits by William Larkin (*c.* 1580–1619) at Rangers House in Blackheath, London; or embellished embroidered eighteenth-century silks for men's suits and waistcoats; or the magnificence of court dresses. Then there are the superlative woven silks designed by Anna Maria Garthwaite (1689/90–1763). Nathalie Rothstein observes that it was in the decade 1743–53 that a 'distinctly English version of Rococo' emerged and that whereas French silk designs continued to consist of stylised, albeit imaginative and decorative motifs, what was distinctive about the English interpretation of Rococo was 'an accurate rendering of botanical detail'.[51] Garthwaite introduced a plethora of ordinary plants into her designs of 1743 and 1744 but treated them botanically: daisies, lilies of the valley, pinks, holly leaves, heartsease (wild pansy) as well as rarer varieties such as Solomon's seal. She had certain favourites that appear frequently, for example, convolvulus, honeysuckle and auriculas as well as those that were still exotic at the time, such as several varieties of lily, begonias and an orchid. Her first aloe leaves were introduced in 1738 (still appearing in 1743). None of her designs show any indication of being a copy of a print from a flower book but suggest that she made botanical studies herself and then converted them into designs suitable for silks. She could well, says Rothstein, have been inspired by the superlative botanical artist Georg Dionysius Ehret (1708–70), who also drew auriculas and aloe (Figures 5.3 and 5.4).

In 1978 the Victoria and Albert Museum, London, acquired an album of 223 designs of some of the most spectacular and botanically correct textile designs by William Kilburn (1745–1818) executed between 1788 and 1792. We cannot be certain of the provenance of any existing textiles linked to Kilburn, but we know that after he completed an apprenticeship to Jonathan Sisson (owner of a cotton and linen printing factory at Lucan, eight miles outside Dublin) Kilburn moved to London and settled in Bermondsey where he earned a living selling his designs to calico printers, London being the centre of the industry at the time. Kilburn was also employed by the botanist William Curtis to produce some of the plates for his Flora Londinensis (1777–87). Either signed or initialled, Kilburn's work is finely executed and botanically exact. In search of more lucrative employment, Kilburn accepted a job as manager for a calico-printing factory at Wallington,

Figure 5.3 Waistcoat, British, of silk, wool and metal fibres. Fabric designed by Anna Maria Garthwaite (1689/90–1763) and woven by Peter Lekeux (1716–68), 1747. Courtesy of the Metropolitan Museum of Art, New York, USA (Purchase, Irene Lewisohn Bequest, 1966).

Figure 5.4 Skirt panel of silk, Spitalfields, London. Fabric designed by Anna Maria Garthwaite (1688–1763), 1749. Courtesy of the Metropolitan Museum of Art, New York, USA (Rogers Fund, 2004).

Surrey, purchasing the factory outright seven years later. His designs were plagiarised, leading a group of manufacturers to petition Parliament in 1787 to afford some legal protection against the 'base and mean Copies' of their 'new and elegant Patterns'. Called before the committee of enquiry to prove the allegations, Kilburn declared that popular patterns of his were 'immediately copied upon Coarser Cloth and in bad Colours' so that in three years he had lost a thousand pounds. In May 1787 a bill was passed, 'An Act for the Encouragement of the Arts of designing and printing Linens, Cottons, Calicoes and Muslins, by investing the Properties thereof in the Designers, Printers and Proprietors for a limited Time' (two months) and although the act worked well initially, the London trade declined and Kilburn was declared bankrupt in 1802 as competition from the Lancashire textile trade increased (Figure 5.5).

Kilburn's designs would have been block-printed; this was the technique used since the art of printing came to Europe from India in the late seventeenth century. Copper-plate printing superseded block-printing from around 1760, facilitating larger repeats and more finely detailed impressions; however, with rare exceptions plate-printed cottons were monochrome – purple, red or indigo-

Figure 5.5 William Kilburn (1745–1818), Viola Tricolor (Wild Pansy), *c.* 1770–90. Photo by National Museum & Galleries of Wales Enterprises Limited/Heritage Images/ Hulton Archive/via Getty Images. Source: Flora Londinensis.

blue on white. By the 1790s the standard of block-printed textiles had improved considerably and to achieve the fine lines and detail we see in Kilburn's designs, thin copper strips and pins would have been hammered into the block.

Kilburn's patterns were described in 1792 by a contemporary, Charles O'Brien, as 'perhaps the nearest approaches to nature in drawing'.[52] The designs used floral motifs, accessorised with leaves, shells, ribbons or architectural elements. The flowers and plants are mostly executed in a naturalistic fashion, identifiable species being mixed with imaginative and fantastic inventions, but evidencing a knowledge of plant form and structure, undoubtedly the result of Kilburn's training in botanical illustration. Trailing plants such as convolvulus or common vetch sometimes determine the meandering pattern, while other plants appear with roots to create a border or to add feather detail. Identifiable wild and garden plants can be seen, such as roses, daffodils, narcissi, jasmine, bluebells, iris, lily-of-the-valley, pelargonium and even a cactus. The largest group of designs are the floral arabesques and trails on a white ground, a style which derived from English silk designs of the 1740s and 1750s in which natural forms of leaves and flowers were sometimes intermixed with ornaments after the French Rococo taste. French silk designs often featured ribbons and Kilburn replaces these with striped ribbon-like leaves of an ornamental grass, sometimes tied in knots and bows with single sprigs or small bunches of flowers scattered over a white or pastel ground. Perhaps the most original element of Kilburn's designs is his use of seaweed motifs, Charles O'Brien stating that Kilburn's patterns for 1790 'run chiefly on an imitation of seaweed, and, in effect, at least excelled what any other printer exhibited'.[53] The fine tracery of the seaweed is used to create an 'all-over' pattern with or without scattered flowers, or else it is bunched with other plants, corals, mosses or skeleton leaves. 'Dark-ground' floral chintzes enjoyed a vogue in the last decade of the eighteenth century (independent evidence from another pattern book establishing the date for this style as *c.* 1790–94) both for dress and for furnishings, and some of Kilburn's seaweed patterns occur on such grounds, ranging from black to plum with highlights of white flowers such as jasmine. The interest in botany that manifested itself in these textiles illustrates the ways in which nature has inspired artists and fashion and textile designers and the deep connections that lie between them.

Nature and the Arts and Crafts Movement

The developments in textile design evidenced by the work of Garthwaite and Kilburn occurred just as the industrialisation of the cotton industry began to change relationships with the natural world, and this transition is reflected in the words of John Ruskin (1819–1900). In his autobiographical work, *Praeterita*, Kenneth Clark draws attention to the fact that Ruskin's literary work, in his own words, was done 'as quietly and methodically as a piece of tapestry'. Ruskin himself likens the art of writing to that of sewing and embroidery:

> I knew exactly what I had got to say, put the words firmly in their places like so many stitches, hemmed the edges of chapters round with what seemed to me graceful flourishes, touched them finally with my cunningest points of colour, and read the work to Papa and Mama at breakfast next morning, as a girl shows her sampler.[54]

It seems fitting that the great promoter of the Arts and Crafts Movement should pay attention thus to the (symbolic) importance of needlework. Ruskin writes using textiles as imagery and metaphor: for example, he speaks of a private tutor, Osborne Gordon, who arrived in 1839: 'Taking up the ravelled ends of yet workable and spinnable flax in me, he began to twist them, at first through much wholesome pain, into such tenor as they were really capable of.'[55] Ruskin was brought up in the sight and knowledge of his mother's needlework skills, who, at the age of seven or eight, went to a day school where she was taught evangelical principles and became the pattern girl and best needlewoman in the school.[56] He also recalls his nurse Anne as being an expert in packing clothing, 'unrivalled' in the 'flatness and precision of her in-laying of dresses'.[57] Who packs and folds with such precision now, except perhaps for Marie Kondo?!

Ruskin maintained an interest in textiles. Towards the end of his life, he identified the Langdale Linen Industry – set up in Westmorland (now Cumbria) by Alfred Fleming, with Ruskin's support and patronage and building on the work of Susanne Beever – as his most successful practical attempt to improve a local economy through the revival of rural arts. Ruskin preached truth to local materials and traditional craft skills, job satisfaction gained through handwork as opposed to factory work and making for need and joy rather than profit. The Langdale Linen Industry also promoted 'worthwhile' work for women.[58] The Ruskin Museum contains an extensive collection of hand-spun, hand-woven linen, including items embroidered incorporating themes from nature, and many fine examples of 'Ruskin Lace', a form of cut or reticella lace, and needle lace, inspired by the sumptuous ruffs and collars worn by sitters in portraits by Titian, Tintoretto and Veronese.

From the last quarter of the nineteenth century, the development of the ready-made clothing industry and the expansion of department stores and, later, chain stores retailing 'democratised' fashion, prompted some highly critical reactions by artistic groups and called into question the mass production of clothing, from a labour and environmental point of view and also from an aesthetic one: modern fashion, in fact, fashion by definition, was without soul and individuality and those who produced it were mostly exploited in the workplace and achieved little satisfaction from their work. Sweated labour (discussed in Chapter 4) was just one – albeit a significant – aspect of the consequences of increased accessibility to cheaper, ready-made clothing. Rejecting decorative elaboration and mechanised manufacture, the work of William Morris and his followers in the Arts and Crafts Movement aimed to revive the craft aspects of production in order to return to more beautiful, individual and less standardised products. Theirs was a quest for truth to material, structure and function: simple forms from nature, vernacular art and well-made items for use rather than display. Morris eschewed the new aniline dyes: the company produced fabrics using natural colours that contrasted with the new, commercially mass-manufactured dyes discussed in Chapter 2. (His daughter May Morris (1862–1938) was to share her father's enthusiasm for natural dyes although towards the end of her life she used brighter threads produced by synthetic dyeing.) Dress also featured in the form of simple clothing, sometimes made from hand-woven fabrics and worn with handcrafted jewellery. Morris's wife, Jane (née Burden, 1839–1914), was highly influential in her adoption of alternative dress styles as seen in the well-known images of Jane wearing voluminous folds of fabric deflecting attention away from the waistline, which at this time was 'fashionably' corseted to produce a tiny waist. In Rossetti's well-known portrait entitled 'The Day Dream' (1880), Jane wears an unconventional, beautiful silk green dress (see also Figure 5.6).

May Morris adopted her mother's 'Pre-Raphaelite' dress sense, wearing elements of exotic/foreign dress such as a North African-style cloak embroidered with coloured silks in chain, satin, and long and short stitch on fine wool and edged with silk braid. In photographs May can be seen in relatively loose (in comparison with the fashions of the time), sometimes slightly high-waisted (from about 1900) clothing, often with unrestricting sleeves (at least above the elbow) that references historic dress. In a Valentine's card made and sent by May

Figure 5.6 Dante Gabriel Rossetti (1828–82), Jane Morris: Study for 'Mariana', 1868. Drawing: red, brown, off-white and black chalk on tan paper; four sheets butt-joined (and slightly tented). Courtesy of the Metropolitan Museum of Art, New York, USA (Gift of Jessie Lemont Trausil, 1947).

to George Bernard Shaw in 1886 (now in the British Museum), she illustrates such dresses. As Jenny Lister points out, given May's unconventional upbringing, dressed in the simple, practical clothes chosen by her mother and surrounded by her father's experimental textiles, it comes as no surprise that May took the matter of dress seriously.[59] Unfortunately, few of May's clothes or dress designs survive to offer evidence of May's attitude to the meaning and value of clothing: 'While her appearance might have seemed unusual, striking, or even odd to some, from a modern perspective May was the consummate practitioner of the art of dress, applying the same thought and expertise to her clothes as she did to her embroidered textiles.'[60] Interestingly, May made a lecture tour in North America in the winter of 1909–10, which included lectures on 'Historic Dress' and 'Design in Dress', but frustratingly no details of these lectures survive, although one report states that she criticised tight lacing and cheap ready-made clothing, arguing instead for natural flowing dresses because they were 'more artistic and much more appealing' (Figure 5.7; for May's needlework, see Figure 5.8).[61]

In 1885, with her mother and aunt as role models, May Morris became the manager of the Morris and Co. embroidery department at the age of twenty-three. She held this position for eleven years, and her work in the 1880s included

Figure 5.7 May Morris (1862–1938), 1908. Photo by George C. Beresford/Hulton Archive/via Getty Images.

Figure 5.8 Bed of William Morris. Tapestries designed by May Morris. Kelmscott Manor, Oxfordshire, UK. Courtesy of Culture Club/Hulton Archive/via Getty Images.

designs for wallpapers as well as embroideries and stitched panels designed by her father. In 1896, her father died, after which she went on to pursue varied interests, including teaching, writing, editing and private embroidery projects and commissions. Jan Marsh observes that her work exemplifies the first principle of the Arts and Crafts Movement, 'that the designing and making of an object be by the same person, in a craft process both aesthetic and practical'.[62] May inherited from her father a devotion to meticulous craft practice that was in line with single pieces rather than machine-made batches.[63] She was herself committed to the integration of design and making, describing the 'modern' estrangement between designer and executant as 'a disastrous division of *labour*, with disastrous results'.[64] Whereas her father's textile designs incorporated motifs like pomegranates and acanthus, May favoured English hedgerow and meadow plants, often based upon her own botanical drawings. Her work also reflects her historical knowledge, style and stitching in references to earlier crewel work, fine eighteenth-century silk and beadwork or else folkloric patterning.[65] From 1897 she taught embroidery practice and design at the Central School of Arts and Crafts (under W. R. Lethaby), at Birmingham School of Art and at Hammersmith Art School, encouraging the teaching of complex historic techniques in order, observes Linda Parry, to revive manual dexterity, skills and knowledge that formed the basis for craft teaching in the first half of the twentieth century and creating 'a legacy that is still at the heart of art education today'.[66] In 1907 she founded the Women's Guild of Arts, for those working on an independent basis in arts and crafts of all kinds. (This was to compensate for the fact that the existing Art Workers' Guild did not at the time admit women into its professional and social networking circle, remaining closed to women until 1972.) May's book, *Decorative Needlework* (1893) has become a classic.

In *Decorative Needlework*, May expounds on her father's Arts and Crafts philosophy: 'The desire of and feeling for beauty, realized in a work of definite utility, are the vital and essential elements of this [embroidery] as of all other branches of art.'[67] Importantly, she adds that work 'done at the demand of fashion or caprice', and that done '*inevitably*, that is, for its own sake, are as widely dissimilar as can be: the first being discarded in a month or so as ridiculous and out of date, and the other remaining with us in all its dignity of beauty and fitness, to be guarded as long as may be against the unavoidable wear and tear of time'.[68] Noting the division 'in recent times' between plain sewing and embroidery (excepting the 'body-linen of a very fine lady . . . wrought by what under-paid work-girl she does not know or care'),[69] the book covers aspects of the history of embroidery, emphasising the beauty of medieval embroidery as the pinnacle of achievement reached in the twelfth to the fourteenth centuries after which, as she sees it, embroidery in the main degenerates.[70] Then, much of the first half of the book discusses embroidery stitches and various techniques including couching, appliqué, patchwork and quilting, as well as the practical aspects of 'setting to work'. In the latter May contrasts past and contemporary working practices:

> The old hand loom can be seen figured in many of the medieval manuscripts, where ladies are drawn carding, spinning, weaving, and embroidering, sitting in pretty gardens, the blue sky overhead, with garlands or jewels in their hair, and graceful gowns on their bodies – a different picture from that presented by our latter-day weaving-sheds, where every hour spent in the hot exhausted air among the clatter and crash of machinery is an undeserved penance to our work girls.[71]

In chapter 7 she discusses the significance of design, which she describes as 'the very soul and essence of beautiful embroidery, as it is of every other art, exalted or humble',[72] including the importance of symmetry, order and balance, especially in relation to the need to 'recall' rather than to copy nature.[73] Referencing John Ruskin's *Elements of Drawing*, she underscores the importance of using contrast in good design,[74] advising subsequently on the effective use of lines and curves in chapter 9 in which the careful copying of a single leaf from each of the different plants and leaves accessible to us constitutes an excellent study for simple and complex curves.[75] Finally, chapter 10 focuses on the importance of simple colour schemes; May shows a sophisticated understanding of the different effects of colour on different fabric grounds, for example, she recommends that yellow on a wool ground be used sparingly whereas on a silk ground it can be used on a larger area taking into account the way in which silk reflects and breaks up a larger area of one colour.[76]

As we have seen, both Jane and May Morris wore unconventional, loose styles when compared to the fashionable boned corsets of the latter decades of the nineteenth century, tight lacing thought to displace the internal organs and distort posture, while voluminous and heavy fabrics impeded movement for women who were beginning to enter the professions and embark on a more active life. The reform of fashionable dress was for both health and artistic reasons and was an important part of the Aesthetic Movement in which the shop Liberty & Co. (established by Arthur Lasenby Liberty) situated on Regent Street, London, participated. The Costume Department was opened in 1884 by the architect E. W. Godwin (1833–86) and the soft, draping Liberty silks, velvets and cashmeres (which became known as 'Art Fabrics') were made up into soft, flowing 'aesthetic' styles, often inspired by historic originals. Designs were often loosely based on historic costume and designated as 'Greek' or 'Medieval', while the typical 'aesthetic dress' had a square or a round neck and was softly gathered with a high waist held with a belt or sash.

Embroidery enjoyed a revival at this time and Liberty & Co. imported antique embroideries from Europe, Japan, China and the Near East. More usually associated with the traditional shaping and decoration applied to the smock-frock (the over garment worn widely by working-class men up until the 1860s and 1870s), smocking enjoyed a revival.[77] Applied to dresses, it gave a degree of 'elasticity' (and therefore comfort) to a garment and with that a more casual look than the typically fashionable small-waisted and corseted gowns of the period. *Weldon's Practical Smocking* referred to smocking being more than ever in vogue in 1887/8 both for children's 'artistic costumes' and for women's blouses and gowns, with smocking applied, for example, at the bust and waist (the intermediate space being left full and baggy) and on the sleeves at shoulder and wrist.[78] The sculptor Hamo Thornycroft designed for his wife a dress of Liberty striped Indian silk with puff sleeves in *c.* 1881, which had a square neck and a looped-up overskirt, now in the Victoria and Albert Museum. Significantly, the Thornycrofts were founder members of the Healthy and Artistic Dress Union in 1890, which launched a journal called *Aglaia* in 1893. It featured designs for reformed dress for men, women and children by the artists Henry Holiday and Walter Crane and some of the designs in the Liberty catalogue of the 1890s parallel the designs by Crane (Figure 5.9).[79]

As well as introducing English-made cashmere, Liberty also promoted British industry, and with Sir Frank Warner, set up the British Silk Association in 1887 in an attempt to revive both the hand-woven silks of Spitalfields and the machine-woven silks of Macclesfield, which were facing increasing foreign competition, especially from France. *The Queen* was particularly enthusiastic about Liberty velveteens 'in hues borrowed from nature' which suggested 'endless possibilities in the way of tea gowns, dinner dresses, opera cloaks . . . and picturesque frocks for children of all ages'.[80] In 1905, Liberty published a lavish costume catalogue, *Dress and Decoration*, a series of twelve coloured plates, reproduced from watercolours by H. E. Howarth, showing

Figure 5.9 Smocked silk dress, 1890s, by Liberty of London. Courtesy of the Metropolitan Museum of Art, New York, USA (Irene Lewisohn Trust Gift, 1986).

the costumes in typical Liberty room settings. Each plate was accompanied by a brief description, enclosed in a decorative border, with both border and typeface echoing William Morris's Kelmscott Press, adding to the artistic effect of the whole publication. Each of the costumes was given a woman's name, and most of the settings were in the typical Liberty Arts and Crafts style, with a strong Glasgow School influence in the motifs. High-waisted empire styles were included such as 'Amelia', 'Helen' and 'Josephine', the latter an evening dress in silk crepe with hand embroidery in blue and green.[81] Liberty 'shop walkers' wore medieval-style clothing (it is not clear when this practice was introduced but it was discontinued in 1932) – medieval-style dresses in purple or brown velvet, with embroidered motifs outlining the low square neck and simulating a medieval girdle.[82]

Liberty also played an important role in the revival of embroidery: the first embroideries sold by the store were Eastern imports, such as Japanese *fukusas* and fine woollen Indian embroidered shawls from Kashmir, Lahore, Amritsar and Delhi and Chinese silk shawls, embroidered in white and coloured silks with long silk fringes. Then came embroidered table covers and hangings from Algiers, Turkey and Persia and these were supplemented by a variety of European embroideries. In the 1880s and 1890s, Liberty sponsored embroidery exhibitions. Some of the most original of the Liberty embroideries were those commissioned by Ann Macbeth (1875–1948) in the Art Nouveau style, which included cushion covers and decorative panels and featured appliqué and embroidery typical of Glasgow School motifs while there were others with pictorial designs of ladies in artistic dress. Ann Macbeth studied at the Glasgow School of Art from 1897 to 1899 and was appointed as an assistant to Jessie Newbery, who had established embroidery classes at the school in 1894. She was an outstanding embroiderer and teacher, and her book *Educational Needlecraft* (1911) changed the status of the teaching of sewing in the twentieth century. Some of Newbery's designs for Liberty could be bought ready-worked, but many were adapted as transfers (to be ironed onto fabric) for embroidery to be used on both dress and furnishings. Liberty embroidery silks were excellent for their quality and colours and the range of designs included those for narrow borders. According to Clare Hunter (community textile artist and textile curator), the Glasgow embroiderers (Jessie Newbery, Ann Macbeth and the Macdonald sisters,) left 'the legacy of textile art, a term coined later, which others would embrace, experiment with and explore, investigating the limitless possibilities of needlework's materials and techniques to express their professional art'.[83] All this is a far cry from the disconnect that exists mostly between the making and wearing of clothes today. By paying attention, and by viewing our clothes as individual things of beauty and utility, we can connect to alternative values than those foisted upon us by manipulative marketing and become more fully aware of their true value far beyond that of disposable commodities.

Philosophies of dress

In the nineteenth and twentieth centuries, influential ideas about the role of textiles, dress and making were formulated by inspirational people, some of which were discussed in the previous chapter in relation to a 'return to nature'. Others have used fabric and clothing to explore radical politics and economics. Mahatma Gandhi (1869–1948), lawyer, politician, social activist and writer, who became the leader of the nationalist movement against the British rule of India, attached great significance to the source and ideal simplicity of cloth and clothing. After predicting (in December 1920) Indian independence, Gandhi travelled the length and breadth of India, preaching traditional cotton-weaving methods and organising bonfires to burn imported fabrics, calling on Indians to boycott British textiles, alcohol and manufactured goods.[1] On his long walks in which he peacefully proclaimed and enacted civil disobedience, he wore hand-woven cotton cloth and his daily routine was immutable: prayer in the morning, walking through the day, hand-spinning cotton in the evening, writing articles for his journal at night.[2] The slowness of his walking constituted a rejection of speed – 'the Mahatma's mistrust of the machine, accelerated consumption, mindless productivism':

> For Gandhi, the real opposition wasn't between East and West, but rather between a civilization of speed, machinery and the accumulation of forces and one of transmission, prayer and manual labour. Which doesn't imply, however, that the choice is between the inertia of tradition and the conqueror's dynamism, but rather between two energies: the energy of the immemorial and the energy of change.[3]

The 'two energies' described here are not unlike, albeit in a different context, the poet Edward Thomas's distinction between the 'two incompatible desires, the one for going on and on over the earth, the other that would settle for ever, in one place as in a grave and have nothing to do with change'.[4] For Gandhi it was important to strip back every aspect of his life: from his early days in

London wearing a greatcoat, double-breasted waistcoat and striped trousers, carrying a silver-knobbed walking stick, he gradually simplified his attire until in his last years he was dressed only in a loincloth of hand-woven white cotton.[5] He set great value on indigenous crafts, produced locally. He gave the spinning wheel – which had been known in the Middle East from *c.* 1260 and appeared in northern India in the mid-thirteenth/early fourteenth centuries, having in all probability come from Western Asia[6] – a new lease of life, and considered it a duty to weave by hand every day. 'To work with your hands', writes Gros pertinently, 'is to reject exploitation of others'.[7] It is also an implicit critique of the status quo. This chapter explores the way in which, in the wake of the Arts and Crafts Movement, alternatives were put forward to counter the dearth of creativity in fashion that resulted from the destructive aspects of industrialisation.

Oscar Wilde: 'The Philosophy of Dress'

In Chapter 5 the role of Liberty was considered in its popularisation of the values of artistic dress. Two Liberty tea gowns were featured in the July 1887 issue of *The Lady's World*[8] which was edited by Constance Lloyd, the wife of Oscar Wilde (1854–1900). Of particular interest in the context of a reappraisal of the aesthetics and values represented by fashion in the final decades of the nineteenth century are Oscar Wilde's (rather overlooked) discourses on dress. Originally published as an article in the *New York Tribune* (19 April 1885), Wilde's 'The Philosophy of Dress' not only questions the very basis of contemporary fashion but also provides a fascinating window onto Wilde's time and an insight into aestheticism and that movement's relationship to dress.[9] Wilde acknowledges the work of fashion couturiers, in particular that of the much-lauded Englishman working in Paris, Charles Frederick Worth (1825–95), referring to 'the gorgeous costumes of M. Worth's *atelier*' as 'curious things to look at, but entirely unfit for use'. His reasoning is that beauty is in the human form first and foremost, that it 'comes from within, and not from without', and 'not from any added prettiness', and that therefore 'the beauty of a dress depends entirely and absolutely on the loveliness it shields, and on the freedom and motion that it does not impede'. According to Wilde, knowledge of the human form through drawing should be acquired young, as early as children learn to write. Wilde's views on size (which, he says, has nothing to do with beauty) are interesting and offer a critique of fashions that, for example, widen the hips or make small the waist through 'the tyranny of tight lacing'. Consequently, he is highly critical of false padding and structures that exemplify unnaturally the contours of the female figure: the farthingale, hoop, crinoline and, most recently, the Dress-improver or crinolette (bustle). The laws of architecture in which proportion rules are, in fact, the same as the laws of dress – or should be. Probably referring to the bustle – and the line it drew from the waist horizontally outwards at the rear – Wilde observes that in 'modern costume' this horizontal line is used too often, while the vertical one is not used enough and the oblique very rarely, while in a gown a high waist is desirable because it gives the opportunity for long folds of fabric to fall to the ground (ideally from the shoulders and not the waist), giving an impression of tallness and grace.

As for colour, Wilde rails against the 'anarchy of aniline dyes'. He advises on the use of, at most, three colours in an ensemble and fewer in a small person. He describes 'bad colours' as Albert blue, magenta and arsenic green along with 'the colors [*sic*] of aniline dyes generally'. By contrast, a 'good color always gives one pleasure' and the 'tertiary and secondary colors are for general use the safest, as they do not show wear easily, and besides give one a sense of repose and quiet'. Contrary, he says, to what M. Worth may say, 'a dress should not be a steam whistle': in other words, it should not draw attention in a loud manner to the approach of the woman wearing it. Meanwhile, patterns should not be too definite or too big, he says. The amount of money spent on dress in America is 'something almost fabulous' and is due, says Wilde, not to the 'magnificence of the apparel' but, rather, to 'that unhealthy necessity for change which Fashion imposes on its beautiful and misguided votaries' (followers). He sets up fashion as the great enemy of art: 'Fashion rests upon folly. Art rests upon law. Fashion is ephemeral. Art is eternal. Indeed what is fashion really? A fashion is merely a form of ugliness so absolutely intolerable that we have to alter it every six months.' So, fashion ('the constant evolution of horror from horror') for Wilde is the antithesis of what is eternally beautiful, because 'what is beautiful looks always new and always delightful, and can no more become old-fashioned than a flower can'. Fashion, on the other hand, takes no heed of individuality, of whether a woman is tall or short, fair or dark, stately or slight, 'but bids them [women] all be attired exactly in the same way, until she [fashion] can invent some new wickedness'.

Wilde objects to ready-made frills and flounces, applied in abundance to clothing especially after mid-century when the use of the sewing machine enabled more decoration to be added easily. Thus, he says, 'a well-made dress should last almost as long as a shawl':

And what I mean by a well-made dress is a simple dress that hangs from the shoulders, that takes its shape from the figure and its folds from the movements of the girl who wears it, and what I mean by a badly-made dress is an elaborate structure of heterogenous materials, which, having been first cut to pieces with the shears, and then sewn together by the machine, are ultimately so covered with frills and bows and flounces as to become execrable to look at, expensive to pay for, and absolutely useless to wear.

Finally, Wilde discusses fabric. Once again, his comments provide an interesting window onto his time but they are also relevant to ours. He refers to Dr Gustav Jaeger, professor of zoology and physiology at the University of Stuttgart, whose well-known views on the importance of wearing wool were published in 'Essays on Health Culture' (1887), in which he advocated his 'sanitary woollen system' advising the wearing of wool rather than many layers of linen for warmth. Wool absorbs and distributes moisture and was, according to Jaeger, the fabric of the future. In addition, wool gives soft lines to clothing (whereas satin, for example, crumples and, as a hard fabric, gives hard lines).

Mary Eliza Haweis: *The Art of Dress*

Six years prior to the publication of Oscar Wilde's essay, *The Art of Dress* (1879) by Mary Eliza Haweis (she usually gave her name as Mrs H. R. Haweis) voices anti-fashion sentiments that constitute a salient feature of the last three decades of the nineteenth century. Using the term 'dress' (as distinct from 'fashion'), she argues that the three great requirements of dress are to protect, to conceal, to display.[10] Dress, she believes, is distinct from 'clothing' because it has been elevated into a fine art. Her book exemplifies in some detail three rules to be observed: that it shall not contradict the natural lines of the body, that the proportions of dress shall obey the proportions of the body, that the dress shall reasonably express the character of the wearer.[11] With regard to dress expressing individuality, the problem with fashion is that it leads people to follow styles blindly whether or not they suit them: 'Englishwomen will never efface their sad reputation for ill-dressing and general want of taste until they do think more for themselves, and individualise their daily garb as a part of their individual character.'[12]

Acknowledging the importance of apparel in influencing the mind, she says, 'a new colour seems to bring a new atmosphere with it, and changes, oddly enough, the level of thought'.[13] By contrast, fashion 'turns a ceaseless wheel for the benefit of some millinery-master'; yet she goes on to say that fashion is a tendency worthy of study.[14] Any part of dress, like any part of architecture, she believes, which has no *raison d'être*, and does not belong to the rest, and form part of a harmonious whole, is ungraceful and uncomfortable-looking – and is, in fact, bad in art.[15]

Haweis has much good advice that stands up to scrutiny in the context of twenty-first-century challenges. She rails against wastefulness in dress, advising economy, arguing that 'in thoroughly good patterns every fragment of stuff cut away has its use and place in some other position, and every line and corner is filled up and accounted for'. As an example of this she describes the 'old pattern of a man's shirt' whereby 'each morsel taken off is needed elsewhere, in gusset or welt, and none of the linen is thrown away'.[16] She also underlines the importance of quality fabric and having fewer pieces of well-made clothing that do not follow the vagaries of fashion.[17] Furthermore, the details of dress should have a function and not exist purely for the sake of decoration, a comment on the 'frivolities' of contemporary fashion:

> A hood that is seen to be incapable of going over the head; bows (which are nothing but strings tied together) stuck about the dress in an aimless manner, whereby no possible means could two portions be fastened to each other; clasps and buckles sewn to parts which they neither unite nor support; buttons which do not button; lacings that cannot lace, and begin and end for no reason; all lines ending no-where and nohow . . . are intolerable to taste.[18]

Perhaps her best-known tirade is that against the wearing of extreme corsets although she qualifies this: 'People who refuse to wear any corset at all look very slovenly; but we must protest against a machine that, pretending to be a servant, is, in fact, a tyrant – that, aspiring to embrace, hugs like a bear – crushing in the ribs, injuring the lungs and heart, the stomach, and many other internal organs.'[19] In chapter 10 she refers to 'Pre-Raphaelite' dress, which she says would be better termed 'Art-Protestant', referring to the reign of Edward III, from 1327 to 1357.[20] She extols a natural waist rather than tight lacing.[21] Haweis laments fashions such as the crinoline worn by children some twenty years previously[22] as well as the use of harsh aniline dyes.[23] She advocates the use of soft cream colours instead of harsh white produced by washing powder and chloride of lime.[24] A recurring theme through the book is the need to dress according to 'nature', which definition is, of course, open to interpretation: 'When the common style of dress is very ugly it will often be found to be based on a direct contradiction of nature, and this is the undeniable abuse of dress.'[25] Chapter 8 focuses on jewellery and Haweis describes uncut stones as often 'extremely beautiful'[26] while she particularly admires the simplicity of Greek and Etruscan pieces.

Eric Gill: *Clothes*

The controversial sculptor, typeface designer and printmaker Eric Gill is often associated with William Morris and the Arts and Crafts Movement, inheriting – some thirty years after the death of Morris – similar views on the (mostly) disastrous impact of industrialisation on art, design and culture. Gill offers a particularly damning assessment of modern fashion and marketing practices in the early 1930s. His book *Clothes* (1931) provides fascinating insights into some alternatives to fashion, the function and meanings of clothes and their relationship with art, and the importance of reform of the 'principles' that underlie how we dress in order that we might dress better. Gill's adherence to William Morris's tenets of beauty and good design – along with the conditions in which art should be made – is striking throughout as when he exhorts the reader: 'Let us put everything out on to the lawn and not bring anything in again which is not strictly useful, or even more strictly useless – either absolutely necessary for comfort or convenience or absolutely delightful in itself. Away with the knick-knacks and frills.'[27] Gill believed that the lack of beauty in society was due less to people not knowing what beauty is and more to the fact that contemporary design was the result of 'an industrial system which, having driven all ordinary workmen into factories and deprived them of any artistic responsibility for what they do or make', effectively makes 'art a mystery and places the artist on a pedestal'.[28] In other words, art in contemporary society is only to be found in luxury goods which are too expensive for most people to acquire.[29] Gill argues that 'the whole affair of the modern State and its commercialism and industrialism is built upon Puritanism';[30] he sees this as a structural problem embedded in the 'economic' (Gill does not use this term as such) mechanisms that underpin industrialism and capitalism. (There are parallels here with critiques of the economic systems of our own time discussed in Chapter 4.) Indeed, according to Gill:

> Industrialism means servile labour; it means standardized labour and it means the standardized product. It means that the things which everybody needs or thinks necessary will be made to standard patterns and only what are conceived to be luxuries will be made according to the individual's desire.[31]

'[I]ndustrialism', opines Gill, 'is based upon an ultimate *disrespect for the human being as artist* – it is a denial of the ultimate significance of human acts, the collaborating of man with God in creating'.[32] In summary, says Gill, 'Puritanism and Industrialism are the twin powers, the wedded powers that rule our world' and 'what', he asks, 'could be more unchristian than either?'[33] Gill's definition of an artist is someone who 'seeks beauty and the making of beautiful things', whereas for him 'the architect, the builder, the designer of furniture and clothes are no longer professionally concerned with beauty and are therefore, in the Victorian sense of the word, no longer artists, but engineers'.[34] Meanwhile, for the artist there is now no work except the making of luxuries or 'museum pieces'.[35] Thus, artistic endeavour is not grounded within daily work but has become something beyond the reach of most people.

Gill begins from the premise that fashions for men are a 'present tyranny' in which the 'universal' adoption of the 'counting-house clerk's coats and trouserings' are imposed.[36] It is likely that Gill is referring to the jobs which serve business and financial success: 'The counting-house has swallowed everything. All men wear the clothes of clerks. All men wear the clothes of the puritan man of business who sees no justification for any human activity but financial success'.[37] The clothing referred to is presumably the male suit, which, as we have seen was, by the 1930s, mostly mass-produced and standardised in terms of its design. Whereas in the past there was a diversity in clothing, Gill sees only uniformity around him, in which 'the counting-house sets the fashion' and has 'swallowed everything else'.[38] Gill is essentially anti-fashion in his views, seeing fashion as no more than a means by which profits are made and change is encouraged and adopted for its own sake. Of contemporary women's fashions he says:

> Few women yet realize that ornament cannot be done by machinery, and many still cover themselves with the patterns which we associate with nineteenth-century wallpapers. They are terribly at the mercy of shopkeepers who vie with one another in bringing out what they call new 'fashions'. They are addicted to all sorts of illogical cuttings and shapings for which there is neither rhyme nor reason, and not even the excuse that it expresses the fancifulness of the manufacturer; for it does no such thing: it expresses nothing but the manufacturers' haste to bring out something 'new'.[39]

Gill believes that women's clothes are generally better than men's although he takes exception to a surfeit of 'ornament' (by which he may mean both surface pattern as well as machine-made trimmings). He also takes a dim view of the democratisation of clothing brought about by the advent of mass production, displaying a transparently class-biased view of the existing social hierarchies: 'The dresses of the majority of women are horribly cheap, and even great ladies, and especially queens, are dressed no better than factory-girls.'[40]

Writing in detail about the function of clothes, he thinks neither that clothes are 'unnatural' nor the converse – that nakedness is inherently natural: 'Clothes belong to man; man is a clothed animal; clothes are natural to him.'[41] Gill's logic is that, just as the skin is part of a human being – '[T]he skin itself is a suit of clothes, a body-fitting underwear, an intimate garment'[42] – so are our clothes. The fact that we prefix the word 'naked' to a man without clothes indicates that clothes are part of man: 'Clothes, in fact, are as much a part of man as his skin, and to say that the primary significance of clothes is warmth, shelter and decency is the same as saying that warmth, shelter and decency are the primary significance of his skin.'[43] For Gill, the logic goes that 'those who in theory most despise clothes most hate the body, and those who most love the body most honour clothes'[44] and he reconciles 'the love of clothes and the worship of the nude' because 'clothes made of cloth or wool and clothes made of skin and hair are simply different kinds of clothes appropriate to different occasions'.[45]

Turning the proverb 'cutting one's coat according to one's cloth' on its head and, perhaps most interestingly, showing how 'all other matters have relevance in a book on clothes' and that clothing is linked to 'politics and industrialism, religion and piety, war, pestilence and famine [which] are all matters which have their bearing on everything else', he adds, 'if a peg be a thing to hang a coat on, a coat may be a peg on which to hang the remainder of creation'.[46] Gill's observation that clothes have significance beyond what is often taken as their primary function (i.e. 'clothes as houses', in which clothes may 'be regarded as part of the housing problem', that is, they provide warmth) is enlightening and segues into discussion of the fact that 'they are not merely housing in the sense of warmth and shelter'.[47] Indeed, the primary significance of clothes has never been warmth, shelter and privacy[48] even though many people assume that usefulness is their primary function.[49] 'To be without one's boots', says Gill, 'is not merely to be without protection from the stones; it is as ignominious as to be without one's hat'.[50] Further, 'to be without gloves is not merely to have dirty hands; it is to be lacking in human dignity, to be without a proper sense of the enormous significance of contact. The glove is a veil as much as a shield, it hides the hand as much as it protects it'.[51] And 'the central truth of the matter', is that 'Clothes are for dignity and adornment'.[52] Unfortunately, he says, 'dress as befits human dignity' is found today only among people 'who have so far escaped our Puritanism and Industrialism – our scientific materialism'. For Gill those free from the influence of the latter include 'ecclesiastics in their churches, judges and lawyers in their courts, monks and nuns in their convents and, generally speaking, women'.[53]

Although rationality may be what distinguishes man from other animals, it is not easily apparent in the matter of clothes:[54] in an enlighteningly contemporary manner, he questions the basis on which men and women's clothes are different, asking, for example, that if a girl plays tennis in a thin short dress, 'why should a man think it necessary to wear long trousers and a shirt with sleeves to the wrist?'[55] According to Gill, the 'violent contrast between the clothes of modern 'western' men and women has clearly little or nothing to do with any difference of physique' and it is a 'nonsense' that associates men with trousers and women with skirts.[56] Equality is needed: there is too much difference between boys' and girls' clothing.[57] The distinctions between men's and women's clothes are to be accounted for by the fact that their respective 'architecture' has developed upon two distinct and divergent lines. He likens the makers of clothes to different types of architects: for men it is the tailor, a person who cuts out (from the French *tailleur*, to cut) and for women, the dressmaker, 'that is to say simply a person who makes dresses'.[58] Gill makes the distinction between the seams used by tailors (not good!) and the creases and folds used by dressmakers (good!).[59] In theory, men's clothes, because they are cut (as opposed to relying on folding and creasing), should fit a man well.

Gill voices the concerns of others (in respect of fit and fabric quality) who opposed the ready-made clothing manufacturing system as it had evolved by this time: 'As most men cannot afford to have clothes made specially for them and have to wear ready-made suits, it follows that most men wear clothes that do not properly fit them' because a tailor 'imagines a ready-made man and cuts the clothes to fit him'. 'Yet fitting', says Gill, 'is the one thing we have not got in modern ready-made tailoring' and a further problem is that 'tailoring as a universal method of making clothes is dependent upon cheap materials'.[60]

In the third chapter, entitled 'Clothes as Workshops', Gill considers the processes of the making and wearing of clothes and takes an original stance as to their aesthetic and artistic value. Given, he says, that 'it is not as the result of logical processes of thought that people wear the clothes they do', it is therefore 'as works of art that we must primarily judge the clothes and as artists that we must look on man and woman'. Indeed, he asserts that 'every man is an artist in the matter of clothes'.[61] Interestingly, Gill does not see the factory system as intrinsically deleterious to good design and high-quality execution, but he addresses the topic of labour, pointing to the fact that 'the making in factories of articles of clothing and household use more cheaply than they were formerly made by the housewife and the supply of every sort of tinned food and food in packets has deprived the suburban housewife of nine-tenths of her occupation.[62] While his views on the need for equality in men and women's clothing are refreshingly modern, his approach to the roles of women is cringingly traditional and patriarchal. The industrial system in theory means that people have more leisure to do the things they want to do, but Gill asserts that we should have joy not only in leisure but also in our work,[63] and that there is too gaping a divide between work and leisure, with work becoming unfulfilling. A craft process such as weaving – commonplace before the advent of mass production – has now become a fine art and 'the hand-loom weaver is as much a self-conscious artist as the musician or the poet; now, however, only a few highly cultured people may, if they are rich enough, indulge in hand-woven cloth.[64] Gill does not eschew industrial methods per se, but advocates that it is better that they are used to make simple things really well so that we should 'have done with this half-hearted muddle wherein machine-made things are slobbered over with the dregs of pre-industrial ornament.[65] In other words, clothing made by mass-production methods should be simple rather than display 'machine-made ornament', the stupidity of which artists in the 1890s were alone in seeing.[66] Gill implies a comparison between the simplicity of clothing and that of church ornament, pointing out that 'the grandest buildings in the world are not always those which are covered with sculpture or paintings.[67] Thus, in a world of mass production, 'good things are plain things, and here the factory-hand, though still foolishly hankering after the ornamental exuberance of a past age, is as good a critic as his masters' while well-made factory clothing constitutes 'rational garments as befits rational souls.[68]

So what is Gill's solution to the problem of the mundane nature of labour, the lack both of artistic enterprise and of dignity in contemporary clothing? Central to Gill's vision is that our material things should be 'good', and 'they can only be good when they are the fruit of love, when there has been great joy at their making.[69] '[T]he making of clothes is an art and so also is the wearing of them, and . . . man . . . naturally delights in dressing up.[70] Gill's underlying *philosophy* about the need for dignity and beauty in clothing is perhaps more interesting and convincing than the way he suggests it should be put into practice. Gill shows admiration for the clothes of the clergyman (the cassock and the surplice, the alb and the chasuble, the stole and the cope), who, he says, is the only person who seems not to hide his profession.[71] More interesting is that he advises a non-gendered style of dress, saying that English and European men need 'to rid themselves of the preposterous notions that trousers are specially a male garment, and that skirts are specially for women,[72] exhorting men and women's wardrobes alike to consist of 'shirts' and 'shorts' and 'tunics', with emphasis on tunics.[73] Gill gives specific details for the kind of tunic to be worn: 'with a belt (girdle) to bind it at the waist' and as for length, it should be 'a few inches below the belly' for boys and girls, while for men and women 'as befits their greater age and self-consciousness and the more obvious development of their organs', it should reach to the knee or below.[74] With the tunic Gill recommends 'full cloaks and mantles embroidered according to fancy and lined with fur or wool according to season' and that 'in very cold climates full-length hose will be worn, and the tunic, otherwise short in the arm or with no arms at all, will be worn with long sleeves'.[75] He also advocates 'plain strong boots for the feet and plain strong caps for the head'.[76] Reform should thus take the direction of man's adoption of the dress of women rather than the adoption of the dress of men by women.[77]

In conclusion, Gill summarises the central thesis of his book, which is that clothes should be worn to honour the human body (not cover it) and to 'honour them as temples of the Holy Ghost'.[78] 'And clothes', he says finally, 'are not the rags with which man covers his filthiness, but the habit in which he walks with his Master'.[79] Whatever our views about the man himself and the way he conducted his (highly controversial) personal life, both in the context of his time and out of it, Gill's narrative on clothing and on how we might dress 'better' are enlightening and thought-provoking in a consideration of alternatives to fashion. Perhaps most striking in terms of its relevance for contemporary capitalist societies bent on destruction through limitless growth and consumption is his observation that 'we are still obsessed by the notion that only by mass production can we feed and clothe our vast populations'.[80]

Conclusion

The critiques of fashion considered in the previous chapter reflect a particular response to the rapid industrial/technological and retail developments that had taken place in Britain since the late eighteenth century. In the twentieth century in the United States, the visionary Liberty Hyde Bailey sought answers to practical and philosophical questions about the nature of human consumption and its impact on both the natural world and on less industrialised, vulnerable and poor societies. In his extraordinary book, *The Holy Earth*, much of which resonates with our contemporary concerns, he wrote in 1915:

> We have been greatly engaged in digging up the stored resources, and in destroying vast products of the earth for some small kernel that we can apply to our necessities or add to our enjoyments. We excavate the best of the coal and cast away the remainder; blast the minerals and metals from underneath the crust, and leave the earth raw and sore; we box the pines for turpentine and abandon the growths of limitless years to fire and devastation; sweep the forests with the besom of destruction; pull the fish from the rivers and ponds without making any adequate provision for renewal; exterminate whole races of animals; choke the streams with refuse and dross; rob the land of its available stores, denuding the surface, exposing great areas to erosion.[1]

He goes on to suggest: 'There are more fundamental satisfactions than "thrills". There is more heart-ease in frugality than in surfeit. There is no real relish except when the appetite is keen. We are now provided with all sorts of things that nobody ever should want.'[2] The environmental movement took a huge leap forward with the publication of Rachel Carson's seminal *Silent Spring* in 1962. But it was only with the advent of fast fashion and the drive for retail giants to outsource described in the earlier part of this book that the consumption of clothing became closely linked to climate crisis.

In this book I have returned frequently to the seeming contradictions between clothing and fashion: the way in which both have the power to transform our lives and ourselves. However, at the same time the realities of the fashion industry as it operates today are at odds with so much that we seek:

a panacea for climate crisis, the righting of injustices in employment in terms of pay and conditions, and destruction of the prejudices perpetuated by simplistic binary clothing systems. The University of Antwerp's October 2021 conference organised as part of the 'Responsible Fashion Series' asked, 'Can Fashion Save the World?' The inference that fashion has such a degree of transformative potential might be described as mere provocation, especially in the wake of the Covid-19 pandemic when fashion journalists asked whether fashion would survive a world in lockdown along with their lockdown, 'casual' wardrobes! And as Jess Cartner-Morley writes: fashion has 'come to symbolise everything that is wrong with the modern world – from carbon emissions to global inequality and from crass materialism to unrealistic beauty standards'.[3] But if fashion has the potential to destroy so much, maybe it also has the potential to rebuild it? And what is the industry itself doing to make things more sustainable?

Unfortunately, the word 'sustainable' has, even over the course of the last two years while I have been writing this book, become in a very real sense synonymous with greenwashing. For now we have to go far beyond just 'raising awareness' around sustainability, even if that is the first step. Greta Thunberg's indictment of world leaders engaging in political 'blah blah blah' when meeting in Glasgow for COP 26 in November 2021 could appositely be applied to the mass fashion retailing industry's labelling of their products as 'responsibly sourced': what does that even mean? Other retailers proclaim that their products 'contain recycled polyester', or that they are recycled from plastic bottles. Perhaps these initiatives seem 'better than nothing', but are they really anything more than greenwashing? And in any case the plethora of polyester and plastic bottles used to make recycled polyester should not have been around in the first place while such recycling initiatives lull the customers into a false sense of doing their bit to 'save the environment', when the real issues are about controlling/eliminating waste and overconsumption. One of the greatest challenges is to change our impatient, fast-fashion mindset to embrace individualism and longevity (e.g. allowing our jeans to wear gradually and develop their own rips and faded areas rather than buying ones that already look worn but that are, in fact, new).[4]

Greenwashing doesn't stop repeat buying; if we think we are buying from a 'green' retailer, then we can more easily justify that purchase because we are told that we are buying 'responsibly'. Indeed, a report on greenwashing, published in September 2021 by Eco-Age and the Geneva Centre for Business and Human Rights identifies 'greenwishing' – fancying oneself less environmentally harmful than one is in reality – to be a real problem in fashion. The same report states that while 'all major fashion brands claim to be engaged in sustainability efforts

. . . many are struggling and indeed failing, because they are using a flawed definition of sustainability, unscientific methods and selective implementation'.[5] In June 2022, Laurie Havelock reported in the *Independent* that 'the world's largest fashion firms are not doing enough to hit vital sustainability goals' with the thirty biggest clothing makers in the world having either 'stalled or lapsed across a number of key sustainability issues', according to the Business of Fashion Sustainability Index which measures performance across emissions, transparency, water and chemicals, waste, materials and workers' rights.[6] On the other hand, in 2019 it was mooted that 'secret sustainability' is on the rise, with companies loath to talk about their 'ecological credentials' fearing that customers believe that sustainable clothing and food will be more expensive and that quality will suffer and so they will stop buying from them.[7]

But it is not all doom and gloom: we can be heartened by the fact that sales of second-hand clothing are on the rise and that even London Fashion Week in February 2020 promoted clothes swapping for the first time, in which the currency was clothing rather than cash.[8] And scepticism about the large profit-hungry retailers is not to gainsay the astonishing creativity to be found in initiatives by some companies and by individuals with vision who need to make a profit from their businesses but not at the expense of ignoring ethical working practices or environmental degradation. Gordon and Hill point out: 'Combining philosophy and action, the present and future generations of designers and manufacturers have the potential to enact real and positive change for the environment'.[9] Sarah Bellos, CEO of Stony Creek Colors – a company founded in 2012 that makes natural indigo dyes for independent designers – says: 'I believe it takes smaller companies to prove it's possible before bigger companies will take the leap'.[10] In relation to dyeing there are also technological leaps such as 'air-dyeing', which allows fabrics to be dyed in a way so as to cut down the vast amounts of water required in traditional vat-dyeing processes.[11] With the production of denim being one of the most heavily intensive and polluting industries, a number of companies focus on ameliorating its effect on the environment in various ways. In fact, the denim industry has been quick to respond to the need for responsible solutions, 'placing itself at the very forefront of the conversation about innovation and sustainability'.[12] For example, Jeanologia (founded in 1994 in Valencia, Spain) aims to lead the transformation of the textile industry by using disruptive technologies such as lasers to replace sandblasting and chemical bleaching of denim; ozone to fade fabric without using chemicals; and e-Flow, a washing system that uses microscopic 'nanobubbles' and cuts water usage by 90 per cent.[13] Meanwhile, the American company Blue Delta Jeans in Oxford,

Mississippi, offers a bespoke service that sizes and individually hand-makes jeans based on customer measurements given online.[14] Hiut Denim in Wales, UK, makes small runs of artisanal jeans, revitalising local manufacture in the town of Cardigan using organically grown denim and offering a lifetime repairs service.[15]

Some designers have been courageous in offering radical approaches to fashion. For example, Stella McCartney, who is vegetarian and an ardent supporter of People for the Ethical Treatment of Animals (PETA), introduced 'vegan' leather into her collections and others have followed suit. (New Jersey-based company Modern Meadow is one example of an enterprise that develops the technology for producing materials without the use of either animals or products from the petrochemical industry.)[16] In 2010 McCartney banned the use of PVC in her company. Furthermore, hers was one of the first high-profile fashion companies to make the switch completely from virgin or new cashmere to 'regenerated' or reclaimed cashmere made from post-manufacturing waste such as cuttings gathered from the factory floor.[17] Those closely related to music celebrities such as Stella McCartney or music celebrities in their own right such as Bono and his wife Ali Newson – who formed the eco-label Edun in 2002 – hold much influence over their customer base (Figure C.1).

Figure C.1 Model dressed as a cow for Stella McCartney runway at Paris Fashion Week (Womenswear, Fall/Winter 2020/21), March 2020. Photo by Peter White/via Getty Images.

Rather than focusing on just one element – such as the elimination of waste or the use of water, for example – Stella McCartney takes an all-embracing approach to issues around sustainability: since 2013, she has produced an Environmental Profit and Loss report (EP&L) which measures her supply chain's impact from farms to finished products.[18] The EP&L system was developed by Kering with PricewaterhouseCoopers. It analyses six major categories (greenhouse-gas emissions, air pollution, water pollution, water conservation, waste and land-use) and places a monetary value on environmental changes in each caused by the company's practices.[19]

Meanwhile, American company Patagonia not only advertises its eco-credentials but also offers a repair service called 'Worn Wear', selling used Patagonia products through their website. Patagonia states: 'If you own a Patagonia product that's well beyond repair, please return it to us so that we can recycle it into something new or repurpose what can't yet be recycled.'[20] The company gives advice in an accessible and cartoon format on the do's and don'ts of recycling/donating clothes (ideally, this should be locally), emphasising the importance of giving responsibly: donating appropriate, clean clothing and not simply offloading one's waste onto others who then have to take time sorting through it and disposing of it as necessary. It gives detailed information about the fabric used for each product line as well as a glossary of all the fabrics used by the company (including recycled polyester, recycled cashmere, recycled wool and recycled cotton). It also supports Fair Trade and in 2021, the company made the claim that it offers 'more Fair Trade Certified sewn styles than any other apparel brand'. To date, Patagonia's Fair Trade programme has impacted more than 64,000 workers in ten countries around the globe while continuing 'to work to find a permanent solution to ensure all workers who make our clothing earn a living wage'.[21] Patagonia does not have a specific time limit for returns and offers an 'ironclad guarantee':

> We guarantee everything we make. If you are not satisfied with one of our products at the time you receive it, or if one of our products does not perform to your satisfaction, return it to the store you bought it from or to Patagonia for a repair, replacement or refund. Damage due to wear and tear will be repaired at a reasonable charge.[22]

The Sustainable Apparel Coalition (SAC) – a San Francisco-based global, multi-stakeholder non-profit alliance for the fashion industry – was founded by Patagonia. It is made up of over 250 leading apparel, footwear and textile brands, retailers, suppliers, service providers, trade associations, non-profits,

NGOs and academic institutions working to reduce environmental impact and promote social justice throughout the global value chain. As explained on the SAC's website:

> The Coalition develops the Higg Index, a suite of tools that standardizes value chain sustainability measurements for all industry participants. These tools measure environmental and social labor impacts across the value chain. With this data, the industry can identify hotspots, continuously improve sustainability performance, and achieve the environmental and social transparency consumers are demanding. By joining forces in a Coalition, we can address the urgent, systemic challenges that are impossible to change alone.[23]

Notwithstanding these initiatives, Patagonia remains a large company with global reach and customers worldwide while spearheading 'slow fashion', which, says Dana Thomas, champions localisation and regionalism rather than massification: 'It honors craftsmanship and respects tradition while embracing modern technology to make production cleaner and more efficient.'[24] But as a large-scale industry, Patagonia can be considered to be an example of 'massification'. Many see the solutions to the problems of the fast-fashion industry to lie in smaller-scale circular or closed loop systems where nothing goes to waste. For example, the American company Evrnu (based in Seattle) uses molecularly regenerated fibre made of 100 per cent post-consumer waste: it describes itself as 'a textile innovations company creating a circular ecosystem' using 'multiple lifecycle fiber technologies' for the creation of 'engineered fibers with extraordinary performance and environmental advantages, made from discarded clothing.'[25] Not dissimilarly, the vision of Nottingham-based Worn Again Technologies is 'to eradicate textile waste' and to create 'a world where resources are kept in constant circulation': 'Our advanced recycling technology that recaptures raw materials from non-reusable products (textiles, PET bottles and packaging) is being brought to life by an expert team and strategic partners who have a shared ambition of creating a circular world.'[26] Meanwhile Econyl uses regenerated nylon composed of used carpets, old fishing nets and fabric scraps to make 'virgin' nylon that can be recycled repeatedly.[27] While wearing vintage, buying second-hand, swapping, renting and upcycling are positive steps, as Orsola de Castro observes, we also need *circular* models – which means from fibre back to fibre.[28]

The American company Eileen Fisher proclaims on its website its commitment to circular design: through its Renew take-back programme, for example, Eileen Fisher garments returned to the company are resold as they are or recycled/

upcycled into something entirely new. The text of the website video is a simple but accessible summary of the company's mission for circularity:

> The clothing you wear matters:
> It's about more than style.
> These choices have an impact beyond your closet.
> Every year the average American throws out 81 pounds of textiles:
> Most of these fabrics can't biodegrade.
> That has a very real impact on the environment.
> So how do you solve clothing waste?
> It starts by thinking differently.
> By wearing our clothes
> You're participating in a circular system,
> One that cares about how clothes are made
> And where they end up.
> From the beginning ours are designed to last:
> Timeless styles;
> Quality fabrics;
> Responsibly sourced.
> Instead of discarding them we ask that you bring them back when you're done.
> We'll make sure they have a new life,
> Either by reselling the pieces that can be re-worn
> Or turning the others into something entirely new.
> At Elieen Fisher we imagine a future where waste is a thing of the past
> One where we leave the places we touch
> Better than we found them.[29]

Other companies focus on eliminating the problem of overproduction at the start of the manufacturing process. For example, Unmade – founded in 2013 in London by two innovative engineers and a knitwear designer – is an on-demand knitwear and print platform that facilitates the production of one-off or short-run garments and sweaters at a mass level. Describing itself as 'a global fashion SaaS (Software as a Service) company working with some of the most recognisable fashion, lifestyle, and sportswear brands', with a mission 'to bring the fashion supply-chain into the 21st century by shifting the industry towards consumer-driven, on-demand production, and away from mass consumption', Unmade developed a computer programme that can be grafted onto a factory's existing knitting machine and instructs the machine to knit a purple crewneck, then a red v-neck and so on.[30]

A different approach is to avoid large production runs and maintain transparency by keeping production either relatively local or on a sufficiently small scale in order to avoid the problems that subcontracting of supply brings with it while also maintaining control of design, sourcing of fabrics, production and retail under the banner of one company such as that of the British company Cabbages & Roses, founded in 2000. I talked to founder and creative director Christina Strutt in January 2022 in her beautiful shop in Bruton, Somerset (warehouse and offices are located here too), and she explained the ethos of the company: to make and sell clothes that will last, that are multi-generational (the age-range of customers is approximately thirty to eighty) and that are far from the relentlessness of fast-changing fashion trends and much more about aesthetics, functionality and timeless design. A large proportion of the clothes are manufactured in the UK, with lambswool jumpers knitted in Scotland and many of the coats, dresses, shirts and so on made in small quantities in a factory in north London. Clothing is designed to remain relevant for many years, often going perfectly with something designed five years earlier. There are two collections per year and production runs are small (usually fifteen to thirty pieces across five sizes), and instead of constantly working *ahead* of the seasons, 'you will always find a warm coat when it is cold and a beautiful summer frock when the sunshine finally appears':

> Some people like to call this slow fashion, but we just think it is good to be able to buy something that will be immediately useful to you. We also make things to last, that are to be cherished and handed down from one person to the next year after year.[31]

In seeking solutions for the future, there are tensions between large and small retail operations, with 'small' being much easier to control. 'Small' also runs counter to the growth paradigm which is mostly about making increasing profits for the few.

On the other hand, when it comes to coordinating efforts towards sustainability, large-scale initiatives such as the 'Global Fashion Agenda' (GFA) have the potential to make a greater impact. The latter brings together members of the fashion industry, multilateral organisations, industry associations and policymakers to find common solutions to accelerate social and environmental sustainability. The GFA organises the well-known business event on sustainability in fashion, the Copenhagen Fashion Summit, which, according to GFA, 'has been leading the movement for over a decade' with an online event launched in 2020 described as 'a hybrid of pre-produced premium digital content, live sessions, and an online Innovation Forum that connects the fashion industry with the world's leading innovators to keep the sustainability agenda alive'.[32] In 2021, the

Copenhagen Fashion Summit's theme was 'Prosperity Vs Growth', a contention already discussed in Chapter 4. The trade show Première Vision, meanwhile, has developed 'Smart Creation' which showcases new sustainable materials in one area of the exhibition and has an online video explaining its approach.[33]

Sustainable initiatives are not always the most visible ones: in fact, the converse is more likely to be true. In their study *Sustainability and the Social Fabric: Europe's New Textile Industries*,[34] Clio Padovani and Paul Whittaker shift the emphasis away from the materiality of textile production to 'social sustainability' and the industry's relationships with the communities from which the products originate, case-studying design entrepreneurs, artisans and textile businesses, from Harris Tweed in Scotland to luxury woollen mills in Italy. The authors explore new centres of textile manufacturing that have emerged from economic decline, responding creatively and producing socially inclusive approaches to textile production. Demonstrating how some companies are rebuilding the local social fabric to encourage consumer participation through education, enterprise, health and well-being, innovative business models that are economically successful and that, at the same time, support wider societal issues, are a force for change.

It is evident from this brief account that much is being done in a variety of ways to address our addiction to the wastefulness of fast fashion, the constant drive for change and the social and environmental degradation with which it goes hand in hand. Although it is not our focus here, we must look to how the issues discussed in this book should inform the educational curriculum, both at primary and secondary level in general, but also specifically in terms of how we structure (fashion) design education. Some valuable suggestions are offered by Alice Payne in her book, *Designing Fashion's Future: Present Practice and Tactics for Sustainable Change*[35] which addresses such issues as how fashion designers design; how design functions within the industry; and how design practices can create sustainable pathways for fashion's future.

In concluding, we return to where we began to ask: how can an awareness of the past encourage us to pay attention, create fresh ideas and forge new directions? By elucidating the context in which textiles and clothing have been made, the roles they play in our daily lives and the extraordinary ways in which they have become part of our language and our culture often far beyond their material value, history encourages reflection and an understanding of the path already trodden along the way to this point; the way-markers facing us and the possible routes ahead. Knowledge of past practices should act as a warning that too much is at stake for us to repeat mistakes and reminds us in stark terms that our current and future footfall have to be radically different. We should value and celebrate the beauty of textiles and clothing both in the past and in the present and the extraordinary work of people who eked out the lives of clothing for their families in the humble cottage or makeshift shelter or of those who made sumptuous garments for the wealthy. And today, we should interrogate manufacturers and retailers, asking, 'who made my clothes?', acknowledging the 'sweated' labour of the past and directly addressing the denial of living wages and decent working conditions that persist in the textile and clothing factories throughout the world today.

As Clare Hunter points out, in the past the work of embroiderers, for example, remained mostly uncelebrated and anonymous, and while needlework (such as the Bayeux Tapestry) might be of historical value, donated to and collected by museums, without the necessary provenance, the creators cannot secure a part in its story.[36] Hunter includes in her eulogy the extraordinary body of work known as 'Opus Anglicanum', explaining how the English Reformation stripped churches of their textile wealth, with many ecclesiastical embroideries burned to extract their costly gold thread and jewels, their silk thread unpicked. The choicest were recycled for secular use but most were destroyed.[37] We should also acknowledge 'the unspoken power of needlework': Hunter suggests that Mary Queen of Scots (1542–87) embroidered in captivity to 'assert her sovereign power' and campaign for her reinstatement, but perhaps also to 'maintain self-control, create order and exercise choice among the tumult and humiliation of her life'.[38] These are benefits that even the simplest sewing and mending can confer. Even if we cannot go so far as to revive an era in which, as modernist painter Paul Nash described it, artist and craft practitioner did not divide their labours, we can perhaps hold as an ideal 'the designer craftsman or craftswoman who solves the problem of textile production by designing and cutting her own wood blocks, making her dyes and printing direct upon stuffs'.[39]

And while one solution is to create local supply chains that enable on-demand made-to-measure clothes, we know that the nature of the global marketplace, along with the creator economy that relies on brands and the influencers that advertise and sell those brands,[40] together work against this as an exclusive way of obtaining our clothes in the twenty-first century. Olivia Yallop observes that between 2015 and 2016 the influencer industry passed its tipping point as Google searches for the term 'influencer' soared fivefold[41] and that the industry is 'propelled by an exhaustive cycle of excess, impermanence and disposability' with junklords such as MrBeast taking this to extremes: his videos are either about 'attaining things on an exaggerated scale or getting rid of them just as quickly'. Yallop describes junklord videos as 'pure consumerist pornography: a fantasy of endless "stuff" in a world that's rapidly running out of resources'.[42] It is estimated that in 2018, 3.7 million brand-sponsored influencer posts were uploaded to Instagram; by 2020, this had almost doubled.[43] Meanwhile TikTok (released in 2016) became THE influential video-focused social media platform during the Covid-19 pandemic. Covid has increased exponentially online clothing acquisition, benefiting the huge companies that promote fast fashion: Boohoo's sales surged by 45 per cent in the quarter to the end of May 2020; Asos added 3 million new customers and reported pandemic sales increases of 19 per cent; Amazon reported it had doubled its year-on-year net profit to $5.2 billion, and the value of its stock had increased by 97 per cent.[44] Notwithstanding the fact that in late 2019, a joint investigation by Grey and YouGov reported that 96 per cent of people in the UK do not trust what influencers say, for now, at least, the creator economy's growth trajectory looks set to continue with Business Insider reporting its value growing 50 per cent between 2020 and 2022, and forecast to reach $23.52 billion by the end of 2025.[45] Some have pointed to the lack of credible involvement from teenagers' 'heroes' such as Instagrammers, celebrities and pop-stars as one reason for the dearth of peer-to-peer pressure when it comes to seeing clothes as a vehicle for catalysing change.[46]

Surely the key is to be found in circular economic models based on using the fabrics and clothing we already have and one where we stop producing more from 'virgin' materials. For example, designer Soraya Wancour runs her business Studio Ama in Belgium. Here, garments and accessories are made from leftover materials from the local textile industry such as towels and sheets. They are produced by a social enterprise in the neighbourhood.[47] Such a model could replace the outsourcing of new, unsustainable clothing overseas: meanwhile, those to whom the rich West has already irresponsibly outsourced the manufacture of raw materials and finished clothing (and here there are thousands of jobs at stake) could be 're-employed' in making clothing and accessories from those that already exist. It may be unrealistic to think that we can stop the compulsion by brands and individuals to keep producing new clothing. However, the fact is that we have so much already and if we do not make use of it, it will be needlessly 'disposed of' (as when Burberry was reported to have destroyed £28.6 million of unsold clothing accessories and perfumes in 2017 in order to 'protect' the brand),[48] incinerated or thrown into landfill where it will produce greenhouse gases as it slowly decomposes. Alternatively, our clothing 'waste' is exported, filling landfill and destroying cultures and economies abroad (Figure C.2).

Figure C.2 Garment waste dumping site in Dhaka, Bangladesh. Courtesy of STORYPLUS/Moment via Getty Images.

As Orsola de Castro laments:

> That our cheap, unwanted, readily discarded fashion is making redundant the use of beautiful local cloth and costume is, to my mind, one of the greatest cultural disasters we have ever witnessed, on a par with burning books, or the destruction of ancient pottery during the Cultural Revolution in China. Western clothes may be cheaper to buy and seen as trendier than local craft offerings, but their cultural and environmental cost far outweighs any real benefit for local consumers.[49]

She concludes:

> We need to mend, repair and rewear, not just as individuals, but systematically as a society. Clothing end-of-life should be a shared responsibility, with brands being responsible for producing clothes that are durable and recyclable; local governments being responsible for providing adequate and readily available recycling facilities, supporting local infrastructures to include repairing as a high-street standard; and citizens being responsible for buying sensibly and looking after clothes, as well as engaging in activities such as swapping and renting, to actively prevent accelerated disposal.[50]

Idealistic? – Yes. Radical, because it turns on its head the current economic 'gospel' of growth and influencer culture that is fed by branding and waste? – Unashamedly so (Figure C.3).

Figure C.3 Stitching a bag made of wool woven in a checked pattern at the National Wool Museum, Wales, UK. Made by Rachel Worth, January, 2018. Photo by Rachel Worth.

As Sally Rooney's character Eileen in the novel *Beautiful World, Where Are You* says:

> I don't need all these cheap clothes and imported foods and plastic containers, I don't even think they improve my life. They just create waste and make me unhappy anyway. (Not that I'm comparing my dissatisfaction to the misery of actually oppressed peoples, I just mean that the lifestyle they sustain for us is not even satisfying, in my opinion.)[51]

The 'revolution' that needs to take place is not going to be born from the makers, but from us, the wearers: we are the customers and we have incredible power both individually and collectively because if we don't buy, the fast-fashion system dies. In a fascinating article, Russell Belk asserts: 'The idea that we make things a part of self by creating or altering them appears to be a universal human belief.'[52] Just as Thomas Hardy drew attention to the relationship between personality and clothing made by the wearer, so Belk says that a relationship should exist between incorporation of an object into one's extended self and the care and maintenance of that object. He cites one study in which the more strongly homeowners valued their dwellings, the more frequently or recently they reported mowing the grass, remodelling the house, painting the interior and dusting.[53] Jean-Paul Sartre in *Being and Nothingness* (1943) took the view that having and being are the central modes of existence, contrasting starkly with that of Karl Marx, who thought that doing, and particularly working, is central to existence and self-worth. In Marx's view, the problem with having is that it produces a false path to happiness through 'commodity fetishism'. In commodity fetishism, consumers worship goods and believe that goods have magical powers to bring happiness, provoking a pervasive and ongoing expectation that happiness lies in the next purchase.[54] More recently, Eva Wiseman suggests that what is missing from the stories about people struggling not to buy new clothes is 'an interrogation into why so many feel that need, into how capitalism turns people into addicts'.[55]

And when it comes to mass-produced items versus the handcrafted we may prefer the latter because it took longer to create, that is, more of others' selves were invested in it.[56] But whether we want to wear or appreciate clothing that has been worn by others is another matter: for example, Belk refers to the way in which second-hand clothing (e.g. underwear) worn close to its former owner does not sell and the fact that there is a taboo against reuse in this case because of the possibility of 'contamination'. On the other hand, when adolescent girls exchange clothing, they share not only friendship but also identities and in this way become 'soulmates'. This is an instance of positive contamination rather than the more commonly recognised negative contaminations.[57] Given that we do form attachments to our clothes (and that we can find it hard to part with them), it seems odd to think that renting clothing will become the way forward: is it 'sustainable' to be constantly washing or dry-cleaning clothes after they are returned from one person who rents them and before they are rented to someone else? Eva Wiseman says that a recent study revealed that renting clothes (which involves a large amount of transportation and dry-cleaning) is worse for the planet than throwing them away. She adds: 'Clothes rental businesses are as much of a solution to the problem of fast-fashion consumption as a tea towel is when faced with a flood – if we're serious about real change, somebody needs to try to turn off the tap.'[58] And, finally, we need to 'see our clothes not just as something we throw on, but as the entire ecosystem that they are':

> We all have to step up. Buy less. Wash our clothes differently. Repair or upcycle them more. Consider the impact of the material they are made of. Consider the supply chain that produces them. Consider the tenets of the company that created and distributed them. We need to fashion a personal style that does more good for the world than ill.[59]

We cannot reverse or rewrite history but we *can* question the relevance in the twenty-first century of a culture and a system that, in the past, produced poverty in the midst of apparent plenty while at the same time wreaking havoc with the environment of the towns and cities where that plenty was produced, and one that continues to produce global inequalities via the fast-fashion system, perpetuating values that are, frankly, unsustainable. 'In order to change the system', says Orsola de Castro, 'we must change the culture it thrives on, and rethinking the role of our existing clothes and objects could be the way to move from a culture of excess to one of abundance instead. In an age of dwindling resources, every way of reusing pre-existing materials makes economic as well as environmental sense'.[60] The system has to change: as pioneering Kate Fletcher explained when talking about her 'Earth Logic' Fashion Action Research Plan at the 'Responsible Fashion Series' Conference in October 2021, there is no 'business as usual' on a dead planet.[61]

Notes

Introduction

1 Quentin Bell, *On Human Finery* (1947, this edn London: Alison and Busby, 1992), 19.

2 Stewart Brand, *How Buildings Learn: What Happens After They're Built* (London: Penguin, 1995), 71.

3 Orsola de Castro, *Loved Clothes Last: How the Joy of Rewearing and Repairing Your Clothes Can Be a Revolutionary Act* (London: Penguin Life, 2021), 1.

4 Ibid., 14.

5 Kate Raworth, *Doughnut Economics: Seven Ways to Think Like a 21st Century Economist* (London: Penguin Random House, 2018), 102.

6 de Castro, *Loved Clothes Last*, XIV.

7 Cited in Edwina Ehrman, ed., *Fashioned from Nature* (London: V&A Publishing, 2018), 155.

8 de Castro, *Loved Clothes Last*, XIII.

9 Vanessa Friedman, 'The Biggest Fake News in Fashion', *New York Times*, 18 December 2018, https://www.nytimes.com/2018/12/18/fashion/fashion-second-biggest-polluter-fake-news.html (accessed 15 January 2020).

10 J. M. Keynes, 'Alfred Marshall, 1842-1924', *The Economic Journal*, 34, no. 135 (1924): 322.

11 Giorgio Riello, *Cotton: The Fabric That Made the Modern World* (Cambridge: Cambridge University Press, 2013), 29.

12 Dana Thomas, *Fashionopolis: The Price of Fast Fashion and the Future of Clothes* (London: Head of Zeus, 2019), 254–5.

13 Theodore Veblen, *The Theory of the Leisure Class: An Economic Study of Institutions* (New York: The Macmillan Company, 1899), 168.

14 Tim Jackson, *Prosperity Without Growth: Foundations for the Economy of Tomorrow* (London: Routledge, 2017), 114.

15 Malcolm McLaren, 'Hype-Allergic', *Details*, July 1992.

16 Virginia Woolf, *A Room of One's Own* (1929; this edn London: Penguin, 2004), ch. 4, 85–6.

17 Anne Laurence, *Women in England 1500-1760: A Social* History (1994; this edn London: Orion Books, 1996), 113.

18 Owen Owen opened as a drapery store in Liverpool in 1868, later becoming a chain of department stores in the UK and Canada. It ceased operations in 2007.

19 The origins of Dolcis go back to 1863 when John Upson began selling shoes from a street barrow on Woolwich market; the first store (in Woolwich) was called the Great Boot Provider. In 1920 the company went public and the name Dolcis appeared above shops. In 1998 it was bought by the Alexon group but was sold in a deal involving the Scottish entrepreneur John Kinnaird in 2006. It began trading online the next year but went into administration in 2008. Dolcis shops were rebranded as Barratt shoes.

20 Freeman Hardy Willis was named after three employees of the company (established in 1875), one of whom was Alfred Freeman, a Russian shoemaker who lived in St Pancras, London. For many years there was a branch in nearly every town in the UK. Acquired by Sears plc in 1929, it was later purchased by the British Shoe Corporation, which, in the early 1990s, converted nearly half of the 540 Freeman Hardy Willis branches into Hush Puppies stores, with the remainder sold to the entrepreneur Stephen Hinchcliffe. However, by 1996 the business had collapsed. After closure some forty former FHW stores were sold to Stead and Simpson.

21 Littlewoods was founded in Liverpool in 1923 as a football (soccer) pool business by John Moores (1896–1993) and two partners. Moores entered retailing in 1932 with a mail-order business and in 1937 opened the first Littlewoods store. By 2001, the company operated 118 Littlewoods stores offering a wide variety of clothing and household products; 181 Littlewoods Index catalogue shops, 99 of which were located within Littlewoods stores; and 24 Littlewoods Discount stores featuring a wide range of quality merchandise at discount prices. In addition to being the fourth largest clothing retailer in the UK and the fifth largest non-food retailer, Littlewoods was also the second largest home shopping company in the UK through its operation of such catalogues as Littlewoods, Janet Fraser, Burlington, Peter Craig, John Moores and Littlewoods Extra. The company was also involved in internet retailing through e-commerce sites. (Source https://www.referencefor business.com/history2/3/Littlewoods-plc.html#ixzz6IXlsBIQD (accessed 3 April 2020)).

22 George Orwell, *The Road to Wigan Pier* (1937; this edn London: Penguin Group, 1989), ch. 5.

23 Walker and Ling was established in Bath in 1892 by William Ling and Samuel Walker, who then opened a branch in Weston-Super-Mare in 1904. At the time of writing Walker and Ling is a successful drapery business. (See https://www .walkerandling.co.uk (accessed 3 April 2020).)

24 https://www.vvrouleaux.com (accessed 27 March 2020).

25 Lynn Knight, *The Button Box: Lifting the Lid on Women's Lives* (London: Chatto and Windus, 2016), 117.

26 Thomas Hardy, *The Woodlanders* (1887; this edn Harmondsworth: Penguin, 1981), ch. 5.

27 Claire Hunter, *Threads of Life: A History of the World Through the Eye of a Needle* (London: Hodder & Stoughton/Sceptre, 2019), 294.

28 Marie Kondo, *Spark Joy: An Illustrated Guide to the Japanese Art of Tidying* (London: Vermilion, 2016).

29 Philip B. Smith and Manfred Max-Neef, *Economics Unmasked: From Power and Greed to Compassion and the Common Good* (Cambridge: Green Books, 2013), 20.

Chapter 1

1 Kassia St Clair, *The Golden Thread: How Fabric Changed History* (London: John Murray, 2019), 37.

2 Ibid., 63; 97.

3 Riello, *Cotton*, 39–40.

4 St Clair, *The Golden Thread*, 2.

5 Ibid., 18.

6 de Castro, *Loved Clothes Last*, 21.

7 St Clair, *The Golden Thread*, 18.

8 George Lakoff and Mark Johnson, *Metaphors We Live By* (Chicago: University of Chicago Press), 2003.

9 Clemency Burton-Hill, 'The Dark Side of Nursery Rhymes', 11 June 2015, http://www.bbc.com/culture/story/20150610-the-dark-side-of-nursery-rhymes (accessed 19 April 2020).

10 *The Oxford Nursery Rhyme Book*, assembled by Iona and Peter Opie (Oxford: Oxford University Press, 1955; this edn 1979), 211.

11 See Edward Francis Rimbault (1816–76), *Nursery Rhymes, With the Tunes to Which They Are Still Sung in the Nurseries of England, Obtained Principally from Oral Tradition* (London: Cramer, Beale & Co., 1846). With lithographed plates by J. Brandard. https://www.momh.org.uk/exhibitions-detail-all.php?cat_id=2&prod_id=135&start_row=1

12 Burton-Hill, 'The Dark Side of Nursery Rhymes'.

13 *Ring a Ring O' Roses,*
    A pocketful of posies,
    Atishoo! Atishoo!
    We all fall down!

'Ring a Ring O' Roses' is thought to be a macabre parody on the horrors of the Great Plague of 1665. One of the first signs of the plague was a ring of rose-coloured spots, and, in an age when little was known about the spread of disease, a posy of herbs was considered protection against the plague. Sneezing was taken as a sure sign that you were about to die of it, and the last line 'We all fall down' omits the word 'dead'!

14 *The Oxford Nursery Rhyme Book*, 44.

15 Albert Jack, *Pop Goes the Weasel: The Secret Meanings of Nursery Rhymes* (London: Penguin, 2010), 8.

16 https://www.historic-uk.com/CultureUK/More-Nursery-Rhymes/ (accessed 20 April 2020).

17 *The Oxford Nursery Rhyme Book*, 71.

18 Melanie Tebbutt, *Making Ends Meet: Pawnbroking and Working-Class Credit* (London: Methuen, 1984).

19 Although the usage of the building has changed over the years, the current Eagle pub dating from the early twentieth century proudly sports a plaque outlining its association with the nursery rhyme.

20 *The Oxford Nursery Rhyme Book*, 26.

21 Jack, *Pop Goes the Weasel*, 55–7. The term 'Beghards' refers to impoverished members of a Christian brotherhood/group founded in Flanders in the thirteenth century who had fallen on hard times and from which the word 'beggar' derives; it is used here to refer to the Dutch in a derogatory way.

22 Aileen Ribeiro, 'Meet the Macaronis', *History Today*, 31 July 2019, https://www.historytoday.com/miscellanies/meet-macaronis (accessed 18 January 2022).

23 Jack, *Pop Goes the Weasel*, 270–1.

24 *The Oxford Nursery Rhyme Book*, 58.

25 Jack, *Pop Goes the Weasel*, 65.

26 *The Oxford Nursery Rhyme Book*, 32.

27 Ibid., 81.

28 Ibid., 60.

29 Ibid., 19.

30 George Eliot, *Adam Bede* (first published in serial form in Blackwood's Magazine, the first part appearing in the February edition of 1859; this edn, Harmondsworth: Penguin Popular Classics, 1994), ch. XII, 133.

31 *The Oxford Nursery Rhyme Book*, 124.

32 Ibid., 196.

33 Ibid., 194.

34 Ibid., 16.

35 Ibid., 36.

36 Ibid., 114.

37 Ibid., 115.

38 Ibid., 73.

39 Ibid., 122.

40 Ibid., 28–30.

41 Ibid., 37; Jack, *Pop Goes the Weasel*, 113–14.

42 *The Oxford Nursery Rhyme Book*, 53.

43 Ibid., 65.

44 Beatrix Potter, *The Tale of Peter Rabbit*, first published by Frederick Warne in 1902.

45 Jack, *Pop Goes the Weasel*, 139–40.

46 See https://www.collections.vam.ac.uk/item/O11107/pin-unknown/ (accessed 18 January 2022).

47 *The Oxford Nursery Rhyme Book*, 70.

48 This information is taken from Karen Baclawski, *The Guide to Historic Costume* (London: Batsford, 1995), 163–4. Baclawski writes: 'Pockets were displaced temporarily by reticules at the end of the eighteenth century when neo-classically inspired fashions could not easily accommodate the wearing of pockets. They re-appeared after about 1825 as skirts grew fuller, and then fell from favour again after dresses with integral pockets caught on in the 1840s. Pockets were usually triangular or pear-shaped with ribbon- or tape-bound slits. Eighteenth-century pockets were often embroidered, quilted or decorated at home, but were also available ready-made. Nineteenth century examples tended to be plainer.'

49 Jack, *Pop Goes the Weasel*, see 123–4.

50 Marcia Pointon, 'The Lives of Kitty Fisher', *Journal for Eighteenth Century Studies*, 27, no. 1 (October 2008): 77–97 (78–9).

51 *The Oxford Nursery Rhyme Book*, 63.

52 Ibid., 73.

53 Ibid., 100.

54 Ibid., 187.

55 Ibid., 69.

56 Ibid., 127.

57 Ibid., 148.

58 Ibid., 147.

59 Ibid., 149.

60 See, for example, 'The Surprising History of Aiken Drum': His hat was made of 'good cream cheese'; his coat of 'good roast beef'; his buttons of 'penny loaves'; his waistcoat of 'crust of pies'; his breeches of 'haggis bags', *The Oxford Nursery Rhyme Book*, 162.

61 *The Oxford Nursery Rhyme Book*, 156.

62 William Fiennes, *The Snow Geese* (Basingstoke: Picador, 2010), 76–7.

63 *The Oxford Nursery Rhyme Book*, 189.

Chapter 2

1 Geoffrey M. Hodgson, 'After 1929 Economics Changed: Will Economists Wake Up in 2009?' in 'How Should the Collapse of the World Financial System Affect Economics?', *Real-World Economics Review*, 48 (2008): 273–8.

2 Neil McKendrick, John Brewer and J. H. Plumb, *The Birth of a Consumer Society: The Commercialisation of Eighteenth-Century England* (London: Europa Publications, 1982), 97.

3 Ibid., 40.

4 R. S. Thomas, 'Hafod Lom', published in *Pietà* (London: Rupert Hart Davis, 1966).

5 Samuel Scriven, *Report on the Staffordshire Potteries* (London, 1843), vol. 14, C 2–5 cited in Margaret Drabble, *Arnold Bennett: A Biography* (London: Weidenfeld and Nicolson, 1974; this edn Futura Publications Ltd., 1975), 7.

6 Diana Crane, *Fashion and Its Social Agendas: Class, Gender, and Identity in Clothing* (Chicago: University of Chicago Press, 2000), 62.

7 Rachel Worth, *Fashion for the People: A History of Clothing at Marks & Spencer* (Oxford: Berg, 2007), 5.

8 Beverly Lemire, *Fashion's Favourite: The Cotton Trade and the Consumer in Britain, 1660-1800* (Oxford: Pasold Research Fund/Oxford University Press, 1991), 199 and 200.

9 Ibid., 145.

10 Ibid., 2.

11 Ibid., 168; 170; 172.

12 Ellen Leopold, 'The Manufacture of the Fashion System', in *Chic Thrills: A Fashion Reader*, edited by J. Ash and E. Wilson (London: Pandora, 1992), 113.

13 Ibid., 104.

14 Andrew Brooks, *Clothing Poverty: The Hidden World of Fast Fashion and Second-Hand Clothes* (London: Zed Books, 2015), 55 and 62.

15 Riello, *Cotton*, 2.

16 Lemire, *Fashion's Favourite*, 2.

17 Riello, *Cotton*, 238.

18 Ibid., 242.

19 Ibid., xxiv.

20 Jennifer Farley Gordon and Colleen Hill, *Sustainable Fashion: Past, Present and Future* (London: Bloomsbury, 2015), 61.

21 Riello, *Cotton*, 149.

22 Ibid., 18; 19.

23 Ibid., 212.

24 Ibid., 214.

25 Ibid., 254.

26 Ibid., 12.

27 See Lemire, *Fashion's Favourite*.

28 Riello, *Cotton*, 74–5.

29 Daniel Roche, *The Culture of Clothing: Dress and the Ancien Régime* (first published in 1989 and translated into English in 1994; this edn. Cambridge: Cambridge University Press, 1996), 138.

30 Riello, *Cotton*, 115–16.

31 Ibid., 86.

32 Ibid., 148.

33 Ibid., 119.

34 Ibid., 123.

35 Kimberley Chrisman-Campbell, 'From Baroque Elegance to the French Revolution 1700-1790', in *The Fashion Reader*, edited by Linda Welters and Abby Lillethun (Oxford: Berg, 2007), 18.

36 See C. Kidwell and M. Christman, *Suiting Everyone: The Democratization of Clothing in America* (Washington DC: Smithsonian Institute Press, published for the National Museum of History and Technology, 1974), 27. Also Elizabeth Wilson and Lou Taylor, *Through the Looking Glass: A History of Dress from 1860 to the Present Day* (London: BBC Books, 1989), 33.

37 See Pamela Sharpe, '"Cheapness and Economy": Manufacturing and Retailing Ready-Made Clothing in London and Essex 1830-50', *Textile History*, 26, no. 2 (1995): 203–13.

38 This section on Elias Moses & Son is taken from information found at https://www.tonyseymour.com/people/elias-moses/ (accessed 19 May 2021).

39 Ibid.

40 Christopher Breward, Edwina Ehrman and Caroline Evans, *The London Look: Fashion from Street to Catwalk* (New Haven: Yale University Press and the Museum of London, 2004), 32–3.

41 Katrina Honeyman, *Well-Suited: A History of the Leeds Clothing Industry, 1850-1990* (Oxford: Oxford University Press, 2000), 22.

42 Ibid., 2.

43 Eric Sigsworth, *Montague Burton: The Tailor of Taste* (Manchester: Manchester University Press, 1990), 14.

44 Honeyman, *Well-Suited*, 53.

45 Alison Adburgham, *Shops and Shopping, 1800-1914* (London: Barrie and Jenkins, 1981), 123.

46 Wilson and Taylor, *Through the Looking Glass*, 36.

47 Breward, Ehrman and Evans, *The London Look*, 37.

48 Lou Taylor, *Mourning Dress: A Costume and Social History* (London: George Allen and Unwin, 1983), 192–3.

49 Alison Beazley, 'The Heavy and Light Clothing Industries 1850-1920', *Costume*, 7 (1973): 55.

50 Kidwell and Christman, *Suiting Everyone*, 75.

51 Adburgham, *Shops and Shopping, 1800-1914*, 128.

52 Hamish Fraser, *The Coming of the Mass Market 1850-1914* (London: Macmillan, 1981), 177.

53 Leopold, 'The Manufacture of the Fashion System', 104–5.

54 Ibid., 108.

55 Jane Rendall, *Women in an Industrialising Society: England, 1750-1880* (Oxford: Basil Blackwell, 1990), 29.

56 Angela John, ed., *Unequal Opportunities: Women's Employment in England, 1800-1918* (Oxford: Basil Blackwell, 1985), 37.

57 Gordon and Hill, *Sustainable Fashion*, 110.

58 Leopold, 'The Manufacture of the Fashion System', 172–3.

59 Thomas, *Fashionopolis*, 273.

60 For more detail than space allows here, see Worth, *Fashion for the People.*

61 J. B. Jeffreys, *Retail Trading in Britain 1850-1950* (Cambridge: Cambridge University Press, 1954), 69–70.

62 George Barry Sutton, *C. and J. Clark 1833-1903: A History of Shoemaking in Street, Somerset* (York: William Sessions Ltd., 1979), 61.

63 Ibid., 12.

64 Ibid., 20; 21.

65 Ibid., 21; 187.

66 Ibid., 23.

67 Ibid., 32.

68 Ibid., 39.

69 Ibid., 34.

70 Ibid., 143.

71 Susannah Frankel, 'High Hopes', *The Guardian*, 7 February 1998: 38.

72 Thomas, *Fashionopolis*, 262.

73 https://www.aspiga.com (accessed 18 May 2021).

74 de Castro, *Loved Clothes Last*, 189.

75 Thomas, *Fashionopolis*, 283.

76 Simon Garfield, *Mauve: How One Man Invented a Colour That Changed the* World (Edinburgh: Canongate Books Ltd., 2018), 40–1.

77 Ibid., 41.

78 Ibid.

79 Ibid., 42.

80 Ibid., 44.

81 Ibid., 43.

82 Ibid., 44.

83 Ibid., 67.

84 Ibid., 45–6.

85 Ibid., 24–5.

86 Ibid., 37.

87 Ibid., 57.

88 Ibid., 62.

89 Ibid., 46.

90 Ibid., 63.

91 Ibid., 65.

92 Ibid., 66.

93 Ibid., 83.

94 Ibid., 84.

95 Ibid., 96–104.

96 Ibid., 9.

97 See for example, Ardalanish Weavers based on the island of Mull, https://www. ardalanish.com/weaving/natural-wool-colours-dyes/ (accessed 21 January 2022). The company uses natural, undyed wools in their products, namely Hebridean, Shetland and Manx Loaghtan fleeces (for dark, cream and brown colours, respectively) and then natural dyes to produce accents in their ranges such as woad for blues, madder root for red/pinks and onion for yellowish hues.

98 Garfield, *Mauve*, 170.

Chapter 3

1 Aldous Huxley, *Brave New World* (originally published in 1932, this edn London: Flamingo 1994), 49.

2 https://www.un.org/development/desa/en/news/population/world-population -prospects-2017.html (accessed 9 June 2020).

3 Brooks, *Clothing Poverty*, 68.

4 Ibid., 81.

5 Ibid., 229.

6 James Laver, *A Concise History of Costume* (London: Thames and Hudson), 62.

7 See Chapter 2 and my discussion of McKendrick, Brewer and Plumb, *The Birth of a Consumer Society*.

8 Adam Smith, *An Inquiry into the Nature and Causes of the Wealth of Nations* (1776; this edn New York: Modern Library, 1937), 821.

9 Georg Simmel, 'Fashion', *International Quarterly*, 10, no. 1 (October 1904): 138–9.

10 Raworth, *Doughnut Economics*, 110.

11 Smith and Max-Neef, *Economics Unmasked*, 86.

12 Brooks, *Clothing Poverty*, 35.

13 Jackson, *Prosperity Without Growth*, 115.

14 Russell Belk, 'Possessions and the Extended Self', *Journal of Consumer Research*, 15 (1988): 139–68.

15 Brooks, *Clothing Poverty*, 27.

16 Thomas, *Fashionopolis*, 35–6. Andrew Brooks observes that the quotas under the Multi-Fiber Arrangement (MFA), which restricted the imports of Chinese textiles and clothing to Europe, were removed in January 2005. *Clothing Poverty*, 40.

17 See the brilliant indictment of neoliberal economics, and of the misguided addiction to the promotion of GDP and globalisation by mainstream economists in Smith and Max-Neef, *Economics Unmasked*.

18 Ben Leapman, 'How an Industry in Tatters Cut Its Cloth for a Bright Future', *Evening Standard*, 21 November 1996: 36–7.

19 Cited by Dilys Williams in *Fashioned from Nature*, edited by Ehrman, 157.

20 Jackson, *Prosperity Without Growth*, 226.

21 Carlo Rivelli, *The Order of Time* (London: Penguin, 2019).

22 Raworth, *Doughnut Economics*, 280–1.

23 Gordon and Hill, *Sustainable Fashion*, 42.

24 Quoted in Thomas, *Fashionopolis*, 40.

25 Christian Dior, *Dior by Dior: The Autobiography of Christian Dior* (Harmondsworth: Penguin Books, 1958), 189.

26 Gordon and Hill, *Sustainable Fashion*, 48.

27 Ibid., 59.

28 Jackson, *Prosperity Without Growth*, 116.

29 https://www.un.org/sustainabledevelopment/sustainable-development-goals/ (accessed 17 July 2020).

30 Gordon and Hill, *Sustainable Fashion*, xv.

31 Ibid., 122.

32 Otto Scharmer, 'From Ego-System to Eco-System Economies', *Open Democracy*, 23 September 2013, https://www.opendemocracy.net/en/transformation/from-ego-system-to-eco-system-economies/ (accessed 29 June 2020).

33 With regard to the making of new clothing alone, it has been calculated that approximately 15 per cent of fabric used to make an adult-sized garment is wasted, with the scrap fabric usually going straight to landfill. See Gordon and Hill, *Sustainable Fashion*, 55.

34 de Castro, *Loved Clothes Last*, 168–9.

35 Ibid., 171.

36 Cited in Gordon and Hill, *Sustainable Fashion*, 17.

37 Sandy Black, *Eco-Chic: The Fashion Paradox* (London: Black Dog Publishing, 2008), 46.

38 de Castro, *Loved Clothes Last*, 171.

39 See Brooks, *Clothing Poverty*, 183.

40 de Castro, *Loved Clothes Last*, 9.

41 Ibid., 152.

42 Gordon and Hill, *Sustainable Fashion*, 31; 32.

43 Fiona Hackney, Clare Saunders, Joanie Willett, Katie Hill and Irene Griffin, 'Stitching a Sensibility for Sustainable Clothing: Quiet Activism, Affect and Community Agency', *Journal of Arts and Communities*, 10, no. 1–2 (2020): 35–52. https://www.ingentaconnect.com/contentone/intellect/jaac/2020/00000010/f0020001/art00004

44 Gordon and Hill, *Sustainable Fashion*, 61.

45 Thomas, *Fashionopolis*, 188.

46 Gordon and Hill, *Sustainable Fashion*, 69.

47 de Castro, *Loved Clothes Last*, 92.

48 Ibid., 93; 94.

49 Gordon and Hill, *Sustainable Fashion*, 63–4.

50 Ibid., 73.

51 Ibid., 72.

52 Ibid., 75.

53 de Castro, *Loved Clothes Last*, 100.

54 Gordon and Hill, *Sustainable Fashion*, 81.

55 https://www.greenpeace.org/international/story/6956/what-are-microfibers-and-why-are-our-clothes-polluting-the-oceans/ (accessed 18 June 2020).

56 Suna Erdem, 'Fashion's Victims: How Our Clothing Is Polluting the Arctic', *The New European*, 28 January–3 February 2021: 22.

57 https://www.thegreenhubonline.com/2019/02/27/new-research-shows-microfiber-bags-and-cora-ball-filters-are-working/ (accessed 25 May 2021).

58 Gordon and Hill, *Sustainable Fashion*, 81.

59 https://www.apparelcoalition.org (accessed 18 June 2020).

60 See https://www.ecotextile.com/2013032811968/fashion-retail-news/sustainable-textiles-coalition-launched.html (accessed 18 June 2020).

61 de Castro, *Loved Clothes Last*, 76. In a recent chemical analysis undertaken by Buzzi Lab in Prato, Italy, it was discovered that a substantial percentage of cheap clothing made in countries such as China and Bangladesh still contains contaminants that have been banned in the EU (76).

62 Thomas, *Fashionopolis*, 45.

63 The following information on country of origin designation and garment labels is from Boris Hodakel, https://www.sewport.com/learn/garment-labeling-and-requirements (accessed 6 July 2020).

64 de Castro, *Loved Clothes Last*, 211.

65 Elizabeth Ewing, *Fur in Dress* (London: Batsford, 1981), 71. This section describes mainly British and Western fur fashions and attitudes. Needless to say, there are other histories relating to other parts of the globe that lie beyond the scope of this discussion.

66 Ewing, *Fur in Dress*, 13.

67 Ibid., 15.

68 Ibid., 19.

69 Ibid., 20. Miniver refers to the white underbelly of the squirrel and was often dotted with small pieces of other black fur.

70 Ewing, *Fur in Dress*, 21.

71 Ibid., 23–4.

72 Ibid., 28–9.

73 Ibid., 26.

74 See line 30:

> 'I saw his sleeves were lined around the hand
> With fur of grey, the finest in the land.'

Geoffrey Chaucer, *General Prologue to the Canterbury Tales* (*c.* 1387–1400), https://www.owleyes.org/text/canterbury-tales/read/the-monk#root-218780-1 (accessed 25 May 2021).

75 Ewing, *Fur in Dress*, 32.

76 Ibid., 50.

77 Ibid., 35.

78 Ibid., 54.

79 Quoted in Ewing, *Fur in Dress*, 65.

80 Ewing, *Fur in Dress*, 43.

81 Ibid., 66; 67.

82 Ibid., 71.

83 Ibid., 69; 70.

84 Ibid., 88–9.

85 Ibid., 92.

86 Ibid., 102.

87 Ibid., 97.

88 Ibid., 105; 106.

89 Ibid., 112.

90 Ibid., 113.

91 Ibid., 128; 129.

92 Ibid., 126.

93 Ibid., 139.

94 Ibid., 144.

95 This section on imitation fur draws on Ewing, *Fur in Dress*, 145–6.

96 Ewing, *Fur in Dress*, 151.

97 Thomas Hardy, 'The Lady in the Furs' (1925), published in *Winter Words* (1928), lines 13–18.

98 Ewing, *Fur in Dress*, 158.

99 https://www.humanesociety.org/resources/about-canadian-seal-hunt (accessed 23 March 2021).

100 https://www.peta.org (accessed 25 May 2021).

101 Zoe Wood, 'Vegan Fashion To Get Cruelty-Free Guidelines', *The Guardian*, 1 February 2020: 42.

102 https://www.rspb.org.uk/about-the-rspb/about-us/our-history/ (accessed 30 July 2020).

Chapter 4

1 Ben Fine, *The World of Consumption: The Material and Cultural Revisited* (London: Routledge, 2002), 26.

2 Smith and Max-Neef, *Economics Unmasked*, 134.

3 Ibid., 12.

4 Ibid., 11.

5 Ibid., 28.

6 Ibid., 29.

7 Ibid., 67.

8 Sheila Backburn, *A Fair Day's Wage for a Fair Day's Work: Sweated Labour and the Origins of Minimum Wage Legislation in Britain* (Aldershot: Ashgate, 2007), 69.

9 Ibid., 2.

10 Ibid., 15.

11 Ibid., 7.

12 The 1878 Factory and Workshops Act altered the legal definition of a 'factory' from an establishment with at least fifty persons to any place with motive power, defining those without power as 'workshops'. The emphasis of this legislation was to protect women and children, who were particularly vulnerable in the workplace, the Act limiting working hours of women and children to ten, between fixed times. Meanwhile factories were to be open to inspection day or night. But by contrast women's workshops and homeworkers were exempt from legal requirements, regarding cleanliness, for example. Within factories trade unionism prospered but female outworkers had no such protection. See Backburn, *A Fair Day's Wage for a Fair Day's Work*, 63.

13 Backburn, *A Fair Day's Wage for a Fair Day's Work*, 27.

14 Charles Kingsley (Parson Lot), *Cheap Clothes and Nasty* (London: William Pickering, 1850), 21.

15 Backburn, *A Fair Day's Wage for a Fair Day's Work*, 41.

16 Ibid., 80.

17 Ibid., 91–2; 94.

18 Ibid., 77; 105.

19 Ibid., 116.

20 Ibid., 144.

21 Ibid., 160.

22 Ibid., 175. In 1918 the Trade Boards Amendment Act allowed for additional boards to be created without the controversial six months' waiting period and reduced to two months the time allowed for objections. The Act permitted the establishment of boards where pay was exceptionally low but where no adequate collective bargaining machinery existed (178).

23 Backburn, *A Fair Day's Wage for a Fair Day's Work*, 176.

24 Ibid., 182.

25 Ibid., 185.

26 16 January 1945 vol 407 cc69-116; Order for Second Reading. See https://www.api.parliament.uk/historic-hansard/commons/1945/jan/16/wages -councils-bill. Bevin later describes the 1909 Trade Boards Act as 'the first step taken to answer Thomas Hood in his "Song of the Shirt"' (accessed 3 September 2021).

27 Backburn, *A Fair Day's Wage for a Fair Day's Work*, 186; 187.

28 Ibid., 191.

29 Ibid., 202.

30 Ibid., 203.

31 Gordon and Hill, *Sustainable Fashion*, 123.

32 Thomas, *Fashionopolis*, 47.

33 Smith and Max-Neef, *Economics Unmasked*, 139.

34 Ibid., 104.

35 Ibid., 109–10.

36 Ibid., 135.

37 Ibid., 139.

38 Ibid., 99.

39 This quotation and the previous discussion references https://www.theguardian .com/global-development/2020/aug/25/the-fashion-industry-echoes-colonialism -dfid-new-scheme-will-subsidise-it (accessed 6 October 2020).

40 See https://www.theguardian.com/global-development/2020/aug/25/the-fashion -industry-echoes-colonialism-dfid-new-scheme-will-subsidise-it (accessed 6 October 2020).

41 Charles Dickens, *Hard Times* (first published in *Household Words* in serial form April–August 1854 and as a novel later that year), Book the First, Ch. 5.

42 Garfield, *Mauve*, 120.

43 Ibid., 89.

44 Ibid., 108–24.

45 Ibid., 114.

46 https://www.youtube.com/watch?v=dqNk-loy-xc (accessed 23 July 2020).

47 Garfield, *Mauve*, 170.

48 Cited in David S. Waller and Helen J. Waller, 'H&M Post-Rana Plaza: Can Fast Fashion Ever Be Truly Ethical?' Bloomsbury Fashion Business Cases, 1 November 2018: 3. The year before, in 2012, 117 people lost their lives and another 200 were injured at a fire at the Tazreen Fashion factory in Dhaka (see Hunter, *Threads of Life*, 270).

49 Waller and Waller, 'H&M Post-Rana Plaza', 3.

50 Raworth, *Doughnut Economics*, 90.

51 https://www.bbc.co.uk/news/uk-wales-politics-34721771 (accessed 17 January 2022).

52 Thomas, *Fashionopolis*, 129–30.

53 Lucy Jolin, 'Natural Capital', *Cam: Cambridge Alumni Magazine*, 93 (2021): 12–15.

54 Raworth, *Doughnut Economics*, 37 and 32, respectively.

55 Ibid., 38. The work by Lakoff and Johnson referred to is their 1980 'classic' *Metaphors We Live By*.

56 Raworth, *Doughnut Economics*, see 248, 250–1 and 268.

57 Ibid., 5.

58 Ibid., 110.

59 Smith and Max-Neef, *Economics Unmasked*, 159.

60 In the 1920s the influential Italian economist Piero Sraffa (1898–1983) argued in opposition to 'equilibrium theory', showing that as firms in many industries face falling unit costs as they expand their production, so these industries tend towards oligopoly or monopoly rather than perfect competition. Raworth offers a contemporary example of this: in 2011 just four Wall Street banks accounted for 95 per cent of the financial industry's derivatives trading in the USA, which pattern of concentration, she says, prevails in many other industries, from media and computing to telecoms and supermarkets. Raworth, *Doughnut Economics*, 148. I might add that the same could be said of the fashion industry and market dominance by a relatively small number of brands. As I write, Asos has announced that it is buying the Topshop and Miss Selfridge brands for £330m, putting 2,500 jobs at risk (https://www.theguardian.com/business/2021/feb/01/asos-buys-topshop -topman-miss-selfridge-arcadia (accessed 1 February 2021)). This will add to the already gigantic Asos online empire.

61 Raworth, *Doughnut Economics*, 151; 165.

62 Ibid., 207; 209.

63 Ibid., 245.

64 Smith and Max-Neef, *Economics Unmasked*, 155.

65 Ibid., 68.

66 Ibid., 145.

67 Ibid., 140.

68 Ibid., 145.

69 Susannah Frankel, 'Radical Traditionalists: Azzedine Alaia and Jean-Paul Gaultier', in *Radical Fashion,* edited by Claire Wilcox (London: V&A Publications, 2001), 18–27; 23.

70 Raworth, *Doughnut Economics*, 212.

71 Ibid., 245. The odds are stacked against the vision of an alternative to growth: for example, Raworth points out that one of the founding objectives of the OECD is the pursuit of economic growth and that it is very hard for the World Bank, IMF, UN, EU and almost every political party worldwide to 'even voice the idea that it might be time for some countries to start thinking about landing the economic plane' (255).

72 Jackson, *Prosperity Without Growth*, 197.

73 https://www.esrc.ukri.org/about-us/50-years-of-esrc/50-achievements/the-easterlin-paradox/ (accessed 1 July 2020).

74 Raworth, *Doughnut Economics*, 264–5.

75 Jackson, *Prosperity Without Growth*, 144; 147.

76 Ibid., 79.

77 Ibid., 51.

78 Peter Sterling, 'Why We Consume: Neural Design and Sustainability', *A Great Transition Initiative: Towards a Transformative Vision and Praxis*, 2016. https://www.greattransition.org/archive/2020/ (accessed 2 July 2020).

Chapter 5

1 See especially Rachel Worth, *Clothing and Landscape in Victorian England: Working-Class Dress and Rural Life* (London: I. B. Tauris, 2018).

2 F. R. Leavis, *D. H. Lawrence: Novelist* (Harmondsworth: Penguin, 1955), 373.

3 Hunter, *Threads of Life*, 185.

4 Jonathan Bate, *John Clare: A Biography* (London: Picador, 2004), 227.

5 Iain Sinclair, *Edge of the Orison: In the Traces of John Clare's 'Journey out of Essex'* (London: 2005; this edn London: Penguin 2006), 215.

6 Ibid., 362.

7 Bate, *John Clare*, 11.

8 Ibid., 68.

9 Cited in Bate, *John Clare*, 137.

10 Discussed in Bate, *John Clare*, 313.

11 Bate, *John Clare*, 157.

12 Ibid., 159.

13 Ibid., 160.

14 Ibid., 167.

15 Ibid., 168.

16 Ibid., 326.

17 Ibid., 328.

18 Cited in Bate, *John Clare*, 476.

19 Bate, *John Clare*, 207.

20 Ibid., 328.

21 Ibid., 211.

22 Stanza XXVII. This was Clare's longest poem to date. See John Taylor, ed., *The Village Minstrel, and Other Poems. By John Clare, the Northamptonshire Peasant; Author of 'Poems on Rural Life and Scenery'* (London: Taylor and Hessey, 1821). It consists of 119 Spencerian stanzas.

23 Cited in Bate, *John Clare*, 241.

24 Bate, *John Clare*, 265.

25 Ibid., 414.

26 Ibid., 440.

27 Ibid., 445.

28 Thomas Hardy, *The Return of the Native* (1878; this edn Harmondsworth: Penguin, 1979), Book I, ch. I.

29 See especially Worth, *Clothing and Landscape in Victorian England*.

30 W. J. Keith, *The Rural Tradition* (University of Toronto Press, 1975; published in Great Britain by The Harvester Press Ltd.), 194.

31 Thomas Hardy, *The Trumpet-Major* (1880; this edn Harmondsworth: Penguin, 1986), ch. XVI.

32 Henry David Thoreau, *Walden* (1854; this edn London: Penguin Random House 2016), ch. 1, 25.

33 Ibid., ch. 14, 244.

34 Edward Thomas, *In Pursuit of Spring* (first published in 1914 by Thomas Nelson and Sons; this edn with an Introduction by Alexandra Harris, Ford: Little Toller Books, 2016), 222.

35 Thomas Hardy, *Under the Greenwood Tree* (1872; this edn Harmondsworth: Penguin, 1872), I, ch. III.

36 Thoreau, *Walden*, Conclusion, 305.

37 Thomas Hardy, 'The Dorsetshire Labourer', *Longman's Magazine*, 2 (1883): 262–3.

38 Adam Thorpe has noted that Hudson's work has something in common with the eco-theology of Liberty Hyde Bailey (1858–1954), whose *The Holy* Earth, 1915,

https://www.gutenberg.org/files/33178/33178-h/33178-h.htm (accessed 12 January 2021) (already quoted) was a founding text for American environmentalism. See Adam Thorpe, Introduction to W. H. Hudson, *A Shepherd's Life* (1910; Wimborne: Little Toller Books, 2010), 15. For Bailey's text, see https://www.gutenberg.org/files/33178/33178-h/33178-h.htm (accessed 12 January 2021).

39 Adam Thorpe, Introduction to Hudson, *A Shepherd's Life*, 10.

40 Hudson, *A Shepherd's Life*, 124.

41 Ibid., 178.

42 Ibid., 179.

43 Ibid., 172.

44 Ibid., 38–9.

45 Ibid., 40.

46 Ibid., 54. Caleb was one of five children, with two sisters and two brothers, the boys earning their own living from an early age.

47 Hudson, *A Shepherd's Life*, 201.

48 Ibid., 59.

49 Ibid., 192.

50 Ibid., 134–5.

51 Nathalie Rothstein, *Silk Designs of the Eighteenth Century* (London: Thames and Hudson, 1999), 48. For the following section on Garthwaite, I refer principally to Rothstein's detailed research.

52 Charles O'Brien, *The British Manufacturers Companion and Calico-Printers Assistant* (1792), cited in Michael Joseph, *The Victoria and Albert Colour Books: Rococo Silks* (Exeter: Webb and Bower in association with the Victoria and Albert Museum, 1985), 9.

53 Ibid., 10.

54 John Ruskin, *Praeterita: The Autobiography of John Ruskin* (first published in 28 parts between 1885 and 1889; this edn Oxford: Oxford University Press, 1978), xi.

55 Ibid., Vol. II, ch. 1, para. 8; 226.

56 Ibid., Vol. I, ch. 1, para. 9; 10.

57 Ibid., Vol. I, ch. 1, para. 30; 21.

58 https://www.ruskinmuseum.com/who-was-john-ruskin-1819-1900/ruskin-linen-and-lace/ (accessed 12 October 2021).

59 Anna Mason, Jan Marsh, Jenny Lister, Rowan Bain and Hann Faurby, *May Morris, Arts and Crafts Designer* (New York/London: Thames & Hudson/V&A/William Morris Gallery, 2017), 176.

60 Ibid., 181.

61 Cited in Mason, Marsh, Lister, Bain and Faurby, *May Morris, Arts and Crafts Designer*, 179.

62 Mason, Marsh, Lister, Bain and Faurby, *May Morris, Arts and Crafts Designer*, 10.

63 Ibid., 11.

64 Cited in Mason, Marsh, Lister, Bain and Faurby, *May Morris, Arts and Crafts Designer*, 20.

65 Mason, Marsh, Lister, Bain and Faurby, *May Morris, Arts and Crafts Designer*, 21.

66 Cited in Mason, Marsh, Lister, Bain and Faurby, *May Morris, Arts and Crafts Designer*, 22.

67 May Morris, *Decorative Needlework* (London: Joseph Hughes & Co., 1893), Dedicatory Note.

68 Ibid.

69 Ibid., ch. 1, 1–2.

70 Ibid., ch. 1, especially 5–9.

71 Ibid., ch. 6, 73.

72 Ibid., ch. 7, 80.

73 Ibid., ch. 7, 83–4.

74 Ibid., ch. 8, 94.

75 Ibid., ch. 9, 101.

76 Ibid., ch. 10, 113.

77 Barbara Morris, *Liberty Design 1874-1914* (London: Octopus Books, 1989), 45. The journal, *Woman's World* (Vol. III (1890): 223) describes how 'when the fashionable revival of this difficult craft began . . . the artistic modistes had to send their delicate "Liberty" silks down to humble cottages in this county [Sussex] and in Dorsetshire where a few conservative rustics still adhere to the old smock-frock'.

78 Morris, *Liberty Design 1874-1914*, 48.

79 Ibid., 45.

80 Ibid., 49.

81 Ibid., 52.

82 Ibid., 54.

83 Hunter, *Threads of Life*, 251.

Chapter 6

1 Frédéric Gros, *A Philosophy of Walking* (London: Verso, 2014), 193; 201.

2 Ibid., 198.

3 Ibid., 198–9.

4 'But it is hard to make anything like a truce between these two incompatible desires, the one for going on and on over the earth, the other that would settle for ever, in one place as in a grave and have nothing to do with change.' (Edward Thomas, *The South Country* (first published 1909 by J. M. Dent & Sons; this

edn Toller Fratrum: Little Toller Books, 2009, with an introduction by Robert Macfarlane), 161.)

5 Gros, *A Philosophy of Walking*, 200.

6 Riello, *Cotton*, 52.

7 Gros, *A Philosophy of Walking*, 201.

8 *The Lady's World*, July 1887, 291–2.

9 https://www.readingdesign.org/philosophy-of-dress (accessed 26 January 2022). All references to Oscar Wilde's 'The Philosophy of Dress' are from this source.

10 Mrs Haweis, *The Art of Dress* (London: Chatto & Windus, 1879), 24.

11 Ibid., 32.

12 Ibid., 22.

13 Ibid., 10.

14 Ibid. 13.

15 Ibid. 19.

16 Ibid., 70.

17 Ibid. The whole of ch. 5 is devoted to economy in dress: see 48–59.

18 Haweis, *The Art of Dress*, 20.

19 Ibid., 35.

20 Ibid., 99.

21 Ibid., 101–2.

22 Ibid., 92.

23 Ibid., 95.

24 Ibid., 103.

25 Ibid., 46.

26 Ibid., 81.

27 Eric Gill, *Clothes* (London: Jonathan Cape, 1931), 121.

28 Ibid., 8.

29 The root of the problem – Gill sees it as emerging from his own context – is the supplanting of human labour which is the result of a combination of 'Puritanism' (a 'strong puritan government'), a 'highly developed utilitarianism' and 'a wealth of machinery and mechanical contrivances'. Gill, *Clothes*, 22.

30 Gill, *Clothes*, 33.

31 Ibid., 73.

32 Ibid., 78.

33 Ibid., 91.

34 Ibid., 111.

35 Ibid., 112.

36 Ibid., 4.

37 Ibid., 64.

38 Ibid., 62; 63.

39 Ibid., 146.

40 Ibid., 147.

41 Ibid., 16.

42 Ibid., 166.

43 Ibid., 35.

44 Ibid., 165.

45 Ibid., 167.

46 Ibid., 22; 23.

47 Ibid., 29.

48 Ibid., 34.

49 Ibid., 37.

50 Ibid., 117.

51 Ibid., 118.

52 Ibid., 89.

53 Ibid., 142.

54 Ibid., 56.

55 Ibid., 55.

56 Ibid., 47.

57 Ibid., 44–5.

58 Ibid., 38–9.

59 Ibid., 148.

60 Ibid., 40; 41. By contrast, Gill believes that to put on a dress is to 'to put on something more or less appropriate to the person wearing it' so that fit becomes less crucial (43).

61 Gill, *Clothes*, 58; 59.

62 Ibid., 68.

63 Ibid., 77.

64 Ibid., 107.

65 Ibid., 95.

66 Ibid., 96.

67 Ibid., 104.

68 Ibid., 109.

69 Ibid., 124.

70 Ibid., 176.

71 Ibid., 67.

72 Ibid., 187.

73 Ibid., 125–6.

74 Ibid., 127.

75 Ibid., 196–7.

76 Ibid., 127.

77 Ibid., 195.

78 Ibid., 155.

79 Ibid., 185.

80 Ibid., 92.

Conclusion

1 Hyde Bailey, *The Holy Earth*, 18.

2 Ibid., 75.

3 Jess Cartner-Morley, 'Fashion Must Get on the Right Side of History', *The Guardian*, 17 September 2021: 4. See also Jess Cartner-Morley, 'Crunch Time for Fashion: Does the World Still Care? The £1.1 tn Industry Is Set to Find Out', *The Guardian*, 12 September 2020: 12–13.

4 de Castro, *Loved Clothes Last*, 137. She continues: 'We now no longer bother to mess with our own jeans; we'd rather buy a pair that already has someone else's vision imprinted on them. We've run out of patience to let life happen, no longer allowing it to leave its unique fingerprint, made possible only with time' (Ibid.).

5 Cartner-Morley, 'Fashion Must Get on the Right Side of History', 4.

6 Laurie Havelock, 'Firms Seek Fast Fashion Formula That Does Not Cost the Earth', *Independent* 2 June 2022: 49.

7 Cassandra Coburn, 'Why Industry Is Going Green on the Quiet', *The Observer*, 8 September 2019: 28–9.

8 Hannah Marriott, 'London Fashion Week Gives Clothes Swaps Its Seal of Approval', *The Guardian*, 15 February 2020: 35.

9 Gordon and Hill, *Sustainable Fashion*, 97.

10 Cited in Thomas, *Fashionopolis*, 150. According to Dana Thomas, 99.9% of all the denim worn (2019) is dyed with synthetic indigo. See https://www.stonycreekcolors.com (accessed 21 November 2021).

11 See https://www.textiletoday.com.bd/air-dyeing-technology-a-review/ (accessed 21 November 2021).

12 de Castro, *Loved Clothes Last*, 143.

13 See https://www.jeanologia.com/about-us/ (accessed 23 November 2021).

14 See https://www.bluedeltajeans.com (accessed 23 November 2021).

15 Ibid.

16 See https://www.modernmeadow.com (accessed 24 November 2021).

17 Thomas, *Fashionopolis*, 189.

18 Ibid., 178.

19 Ibid., 186.

20 https://www.eu.patagonia.com/gb/en/wornwear/ (accessed 27 November 2021).

21 https://www.eu.patagonia.com/gb/en/our-footprint/fair-trade.html (accessed 27 November 2021).

22 https://www.eu.patagonia.com/gb/en/ironclad-guarantee.html (accessed 27 November 2021).

23 https://www.apparelcoalition.org/the-sac/ (accessed 29 November 2021).

24 Thomas, *Fashionopolis*, 103.

25 https://www.evrnu.com (accessed 29 November 2021).

26 https://www.wornagain.co.uk (accessed 29 November 2021).

27 https://www.econyl.com (accessed 2 December 2021).

28 de Castro, *Loved Clothes Last*, 170.

29 https://www.eileenfisher.com/circular-by-design (accessed 3 December 2021).

30 https://www.unmade.breezy.hr (accessed 2 December 2021).

31 https://www.cabbagesandroses.com/about-us (accessed 28 January 2022).

32 https://www.globalfashionagenda.com/about-us/our-mission/ (accessed 2 December 2021).

33 https://www.premierevision.com/en/magazine/smart-creation-premiere-vision -whats-that/ (accessed 2 December 2021).

34 Clio Padovani and Paul Whittaker, *Sustainability and the Social Fabric: Europe's New Textile Industries* (London: Bloomsbury, 2019).

35 Alice Payne, *Designing Fashion's Future: Present Practice and Tactics for Sustainable Change* (London: Bloomsbury, 2021).

36 Hunter, *Threads of Life*, 12.

37 Ibid., 21; 22.

38 Ibid., 33.

39 Cited in Andy Friend, *Ravilious & Co.: The Pattern of Friendship* (Thames & Hudson in association with Towner Art Gallery, 2017), 59.

40 Olivia Yallop in her study of influencers, *Break the Internet: In Pursuit of Influence* (London: Scribe, 2021), makes the point that without brands, influencers would not exist (141).

41 Yallop, *Break the Internet*, 58.

42 Ibid., 146; 147. Yallop points out that MrBeast includes his viewers in his videos and so promotes a 'philosophy of individual aspiration – the tantalising suggestion that "anyone can make it" – that fuels the Influencer industry as a whole' (148).

43 Yallop, *Break the Internet*, 149.

44 Ibid., 234. While the impact of Covid-19 is that it increased online sales, this was followed by a downturn. However, TK Maxx (in 1994 it opened in the UK and sells excess production, cancelled orders and overstocks of in-season fashion brands) is one of the sustained winners in retailing clothing in the period between 2015 and 2020. The company has been able to negotiate deals through a period of substantial discounting when so many retailers have been overstocked. See

Sarah Butler, 'The Bargain Store That Is Benefiting from Crisis', *The Guardian*, 12 September 2020: 37.

45 This figure is according to research published by business consultancy Grand View Research, cited in Yallop, *Break the Internet*, see 161–2.

46 de Castro, *Loved Clothes Last*, 185.

47 https://www.studioama.be/en/over-ama/ (accessed 31 January 2022).

48 https://www.bbc.co.uk/news/business-44885983 (accessed 30 January 2022).

49 de Castro, *Loved Clothes Last*, 155. 'Everything that you throw away carelessly without a strategy for its disposal – even if you do what is perceived to be the "good" option and take it to a charity shop – is of consequence.' Ibid., 156.

50 de Castro, *Loved Clothes Last*, 151. But de Castro also points out that the rise in rentals and teenagers trading their used clothing is due to a lack of attachment towards our possessions. Ibid., 184.

51 Sally Rooney, *Beautiful World, Where Are You* (London: Faber & Faber, 2021), ch. 4, 38.

52 Belk, 'Possessions and the Extended Self', 139–68; 144.

53 Ibid., 158.

54 Discussed in Belk, 'Possessions and the Extended Self', 139–68. For this discussion, see 145–6.

55 Eva Wiseman, 'Clothes Rental Services Won't Break Our Fashion Addiction', *Observer Magazine*, 14 October 2021: 5.

56 Belk, 'Possessions and the Extended Self', 139–68; 149.

57 Discussed in Belk, 'Possessions and the Extended Self', 139–68; 151.

58 Wiseman, 'Clothes Rental Services Won't Break Our Fashion Addiction', 5.

59 Thomas, *Fashionopolis*, 290. Orsola de Castro writes persuasively when she tells us that clothing care (how we wash, mend and look after our clothes) is not just 'a personal household duty, but a collective duty for the future health of our planet'. de Castro, *Loved Clothes Last*, 71.

60 de Castro, *Loved Clothes Last*, 179. She goes on: 'the most sustainable garment is the one you already own.' Ibid.

61 Kate Fletcher, presentation for 'Responsible Fashion Series', 'Can Fashion Save the World?', University of Antwerp, 21 October 2021.

Bibliography

Adburgham, Alison. *Shops and Shopping, 1800–1914*. London: Barrie and Jenkins, 1981.

Baclawski, Karen. *The Guide to Historic Costume*. London: Batsford, 1995.

Bailey, Liberty Hyde. *The Holy Earth*, 1915. https://www.gutenberg.org/files/33178 /33178-h/33178-h.htm (accessed 12 January 2021).

Bate, Jonathan. *John Clare: A Biography*. London: Picador, 2004.

Beazley, Alison. 'The Heavy and Light Clothing Industries 1850–1920', *Costume* 7 (1973): 55–9.

Belk, Russell. 'Possessions and the Extended Self', *Journal of Consumer Research* 15 (1988): 139–68.

Bell, Quentin. *On Human Finery*. First published in 1947, this edn London: Alison and Busby, 1992.

Black, Sandy. *Eco-Chic: The Fashion Paradox*. London: Black Dog Publishing, 2008.

Blackburn, Sheila. *A Fair Day's Wage for a Fair Day's Work: Sweated Labour and the Origins of Minimum Wage Legislation in Britain*. Aldershot: Ashgate, 2007.

Brand, Stewart. *How Buildings Learn: What Happens After They're Built*. London: Penguin, 1995.

Breward, Christopher, Edwina Ehrman and Caroline Evans. *The London Look: Fashion from Street to Catwalk*. New Haven: Yale University Press and the Museum of London, 2004.

Brooks, Andrew. *Clothing Poverty: The Hidden World of Fast Fashion and Secondhand Clothes*. London: Zed Books, 2015.

Burton-Hill, Clemency. 'The Dark Side of Nursery Rhymes', 11 June 2015. http://www .bbc.com/culture/story/20150610-the-dark-side-of-nursery-rhymes (accessed 19 April 2020).

Butler, Sarah. 'The Bargain Store That Is Benefiting From Crisis', *The Guardian*, 12 September 2020: 37.

Cartner-Morley, Jess. 'Crunch Time for Fashion: Does the World Still Care? The £1.1 tn Industry is Set to Find Out', *The Guardian*, 12 September 2020: 12–13.

Cartner-Morley, Jess. 'Fashion Must Get on the Right Side of History', *The Guardian*, 17 September 2021: 4.

Castro, Orsola de. *Loved Clothes Last: How the Joy of Rewearing and Repairing Your Clothes Can Be a Revolutionary Act*. London: Penguin Life, 2021.

Chaucer, Geoffrey. *General Prologue to the Canterbury Tales* (*c.* 1387–1400). https:// www.owleyes.org/text/canterbury-tales/read/the-monk#root-218780-1 (accessed 25 May 2021).

Chrisman-Campbell, Kimberley. 'From Baroque Elegance to the French Revolution 1700–1790'. In *The Fashion Reader*, edited by Linda Welters and Abby Lillethun, 6–19. Oxford: Berg, 2007.

Coburn, Cassandra. 'Why Industry Is Going Green on the Quiet', *The Observer*, 8 September 2019: 28–9.

Crane, Diana. *Fashion and Its Social Agendas: Class, Gender, and Identity in Clothing*. Chicago: University of Chicago Press, 2000.

Dickens, Charles. *Hard Times*. First published in *Household Words* in serial form April–August 1854 and as a novel in 1854.

Drabble, Margaret. *Arnold Bennett: A Biography*. London: Weidenfeld and Nicolson, 1974. This edition Futura Publications Ltd., 1975.

Ehrman, Edwina, ed. *Fashioned from Nature*. London: V&A Publishing, 2018.

Eliot, George. *Adam Bede*. First published in serial form in Blackwood's Magazine from February 1859. This edn Harmondsworth: Penguin Popular Classics, 1994.

Erdem, Suna. 'Fashion's Victims: How Our Clothing Is Polluting the Arctic', *The New European*, 28 January–3 February 2021: 21–3.

Ewing, Elizabeth. *Fur in Dress*. London: Batsford, 1981.

Fiennes, William. *The Snow Geese*. Basingstoke: Picador, 2010.

Fine, Ben. *The World of Consumption: The Material and Cultural Revisited*. London: Routledge, 2002.

Frankel, Susannah. 'High Hopes', *The Guardian*, 7 February 1998: 38–43.

Frankel, Susannah. 'Radical Traditionalists: Azzedine Alaia and Jean-Paul Gaultier'. In *Radical Fashion*, edited by Claire Wilcox, 18–27. London: V&A Publications, 2001.

Fraser, Hamish. *The Coming of the Mass Market 1850–1914*. London: Macmillan, 1981.

Friedman, Vanessa. 'The Biggest Fake News in Fashion', *New York Times*, 18 December 2018. https://www.nytimes.com/2018/12/18/fashion/fashion-second-biggest -polluter-fake-news.html (accessed 15 January 2020).

Friend, Andy. *Ravilious & Co.: The Pattern of Friendship*. Thames & Hudson in association with Towner Art Gallery, 2017.

Garfield, Simon. *Mauve: How One Man Invented a Colour That Changed the World*. Edinburgh: Canongate Books Ltd., 2018.

Gill, Eric. *Clothes*. London: Jonathan Cape, 1931.

Gordon, Jennifer Farley and Colleen Hill. *Sustainable Fashion: Past, Present and Future*. London: Bloomsbury, 2015.

Gros, Frédéric. *A Philosophy of Walking*. London: Verso, 2014.

Hackney, Fiona, Clare Saunders, Joanie Willett, Katie Hill and Irene Griffin. 'Stitching a Sensibility for Sustainable Clothing: Quiet Activism, Affect and Community Agency', *Journal of Arts and Communities* 10, no. 1–2 (2020): 5–52. https://www .ingentaconnect.com/contentone/intellect/jaac/2020/00000010/f0020001/art00004

Hardy, Thomas. 'The Dorsetshire Labourer', *Longman's Magazine* 2 (1883): 252–69.

Hardy, Thomas. *The Return of the Native* (1878). This edn Harmondsworth: Penguin, 1979.

Hardy, Thomas. *The Trumpet-Major* (1880). This edn Harmondsworth: Penguin, 1986.

Hardy, Thomas. *The Woodlanders* (1887). This edn Harmondsworth: Penguin, 1981.

Hardy, Thomas. *Under the Greenwood Tree* (1872). This edn Harmondsworth: Penguin, 1872.

Havelock, Laurie. 'Firms Seek Fast Fashion Formula That Does Not Cost the Earth', *Independent*, 2 June 2022: 49.

Haweis, Mary Eliza. *The Art of Dress*. London: Chatto & Windus, 1879.

Hodgson, Geoffrey M. 'After 1929 Economics Changed: Will Economists Wake Up in 2009?' In 'How Should the Collapse of the World Financial System Affect Economics?', *Real-World Economics Review* 48 (2008): 273–8.

Honeyman, Katrina. *Well-Suited: A History of the Leeds Clothing Industry, 1850–1990*. Oxford: Oxford University Press, 2000.

Hudson, W. H. *A Shepherd's Life* (1910). Wimborne: Little Toller Books, 2010.

Hunter, Claire. *Threads of Life: A History of the World Through the Eye of a Needle*. London: Hodder & Stoughton/Sceptre, 2019.

Huxley, Aldous. *Brave New World* (1932). This edn London: Flamingo, 1994.

Jack, Albert. *Pop Goes the Weasel: The Secret Meanings of Nursery Rhymes*. London: Penguin, 2010.

Jackson, Tim. *Prosperity Without Growth: Foundations for the Economy of Tomorrow*. London: Routledge, 2017.

Jeffreys, J. B. *Retail Trading in Britain, 1850-1950*. Cambridge: Cambridge University Press, 1954.

John, Angela, ed. *Unequal Opportunities: Women's Employment in England, 1800-1918*. Oxford: Basil Blackwell, 1985.

Jolin, Lucy. 'Natural Capital', *Cam: Cambridge Alumni Magazine* 93 (2021): 12–15.

Keith, W. J. *The Rural Tradition*. University of Toronto Press, 1975 and published in Great Britain by The Harvester Press Ltd.

Keynes, J. M. 'Alfred Marshall, 1842–1924', *The Economic Journal* 34, no. 135 (1924): 311–72.

Kidwell, C. and M. Christman. *Suiting Everyone: The Democratization of Clothing in America*. Washington DC: Smithsonian Institute Press, published for the National Museum of History and Technology, 1974.

Kingsley, Charles. *Cheap Clothes and Nasty*. London: William Pickering, 1850.

Knight, Lynn. *The Button Box: Lifting the Lid on Women's Lives*. London: Chatto and Windus, 2016.

Kondo, Marie. *Spark Joy: An Illustrated Guide to the Japanese Art of Tidying*. London: Vermilion, 2016.

Lakoff, George and Mark Johnson. *Metaphors We Live By*. Chicago: University of Chicago Press, 2003.

Laurence, Anne. *Women in England, 1500–1760: A Social History*. London: Orion Books, 1996.

Laver, James. *A Concise History of Costume*. London: Thames and Hudson, 1974.

Leapman, Ben. 'How an Industry in Tatters Cut Its Cloth for a Bright Future', *Evening Standard*, 21 November 1996: 36–7.

Leavis, F. R. *D. H Lawrence: Novelist*. Harmondsworth: Penguin, 1955.

Lemire, Beverly. *Fashion's Favourite: The Cotton Trade and the Consumer in Britain, 1660–1800*. Oxford: Pasold Research Fund/Oxford University Press, 1991.

Leopold, Ellen. 'The Manufacture of the Fashion System'. In *Chic Thrills: A Fashion Reader*, edited by Juliet Ash and Elizabeth Wilson, 101–17. London: Pandora, 1992.

Marriott, Hannah. 'London Fashion Week Gives Clothes Swaps Its Seal of Approval', *The Guardian*, 15 February 2020: 35.

Mason, Anna, Jan Marsh, Jenny Lister, Rowan Bain and Hann Faurby. *May Morris, Arts and Crafts Designer*. New York/London: Thames & Hudson/V&A/William Morris Gallery, 2017.

McKendrick, Neil, John Brewer and J. H. Plumb. *The Birth of a Consumer Society: The Commercialisation of Eighteenth-Century England*. London: Europa Publications, 1982.

McLaren, Malcolm. 'Hype-Allergic', *Details*, July 1992.

Morris, Barbara. *Liberty Design, 1874–1914*. London: Octopus Books, 1989.

Morris, May. *Decorative Needlework*. London: Joseph Hughes & Co., 1893.

O'Brien, Charles. *The British Manufacturers Companion and Calico-Printers Assistant* (1792). In Michael Joseph, *The Victoria and Albert Colour Books: Rococo Silks*. Exeter: Webb and Bower in association with the Victoria and Albert Museum, 1985.

Opie, Iona and Peter Opie, ed. *The Oxford Nursery Rhyme Book*. Oxford: Oxford University Press, 1955. This edn 1979.

Orwell, George. *The Road to Wigan Pier* (1937). This edn London: Penguin Group, 1989.

Padovani, Clio and Paul Whittaker. *Sustainability and the Social Fabric: Europe's New Textile Industries*. London: Bloomsbury, 2019.

Payne, Alice. *Designing Fashion's Future: Present Practice and Tactics for Sustainable Change*. London: Bloomsbury, 2021.

Pointon, Marcia. 'The Lives of Kitty Fisher', *Journal for Eighteenth Century Studies* 27, no. 1 (October 2008): 77–97.

Potter, Beatrix. *The Tale of* Peter Rabbit. First published by Frederick Warne in 1902.

Raworth, Kate. *Doughnut Economics: Seven Ways to Think Like a 21st Century Economist*. London: Penguin Random House, 2018.

Rendall, Jane. *Women in an Industrialising Society: England, 1750-1880*. Oxford: Basil Blackwell, 1990.

Ribeiro, Aileen. 'Meet the Macaronis', *History Today*, 31 July 2019. https://www.historytoday.com/miscellanies/meet-macaronis (accessed 18 January 2022).

Riello, Giorgio. *Cotton: The Fabric That Made the Modern World*. Cambridge: Cambridge University Press, 2013.

Rimbault, Edward Francis. *Nursery Rhymes, With the Tunes to Which They Are Still Sung in the Nurseries of England, Obtained Principally from Oral Tradition*. London: Cramer, Beale & Co., 1846. With lithographed plates by J. Brandard. https://www .momh.org.uk/exhibitions-detail-all.php?cat_id=2&prod_id=135&start_row=1

Rivelli, Carlo. *The Order of Time*. London: Penguin, 2019.

Roche, Daniel. *The Culture of Clothing: Dress and the Ancien Régime*. First published in 1989 and translated into English in 1994. This edn Cambridge: Cambridge University Press, 1996.

Rooney, Sally. *Beautiful World, Where Are You*. London: Faber & Faber, 2021.

Rothstein, Nathalie. *Silk Designs of the Eighteenth Century*. London: Thames and Hudson, 1999.

Ruskin, John. *Praeterita: The Autobiography of John Ruskin*. First published in 28 parts between 1885 and 1889. This edn Oxford: Oxford University Press, 1978.

Scharmer, Otto. 'From Ego-System to Eco-System Economies', *Open Democracy*, 23 September 2013. https://www.opendemocracy.net/en/transformation/from-ego -system-to-eco-system-economies/ (accessed 29 June 2020).

Sharpe, Pamela. '"Cheapness and Economy": Manufacturing and Retailing Ready-Made Clothing in London and Essex, 1830-50', *Textile History* 26, no. 2 (1995): 203–13.

Sigsworth, Eric. *Montague Burton: The Tailor of Taste*. Manchester: Manchester University Press, 1990.

Simmel, Georg. 'Fashion', *International Quarterly* 10, no. 1 (October 1904): 138–9.

Sinclair, Iain. *Edge of the Orison: In the Traces of John Clare's 'Journey Out of Essex'*. London, 2005; This edn London: Penguin, 2006.

Smith, Adam. *An Inquiry into the Nature and Causes of the Wealth of Nations*. First published in 1776. This edn New York: Modern Library, 1937.

Smith, Philip B. and Manfred Max-Neef. *Economics Unmasked: From Power and Greed to Compassion and the Common Good*. Cambridge: Green Books, 2013.

St Clair, Kassia. *The Golden Thread: How Fabric Changed History*. London: John Murray, 2019.

Sterling, Peter. 'Why We Consume: Neural Design and Sustainability', *A Great Transition Initiative: Towards a Transformative Vision and Praxis*, 2016. https:// greattransition.org/publication/why-we-consume (accessed 2 July 2020).

Sutton, George Barry. *C. and J. Clark, 1833–1903: A History of Shoemaking in Street, Somerset*. York: William Sessions Ltd., 1979.

Taylor, John, ed. *The Village Minstrel, and other Poems. By John Clare, the Northamptonshire Peasant; Author of 'Poems on Rural Life and Scenery'*. London: Taylor and Hessey, 1821.

Taylor, Lou. *Mourning Dress: A Costume and Social History*. London: George Allen and Unwin, 1983.

Tebbutt, Melanie. *Making Ends Meet: Pawnbroking and Working-Class Credit*. London: Methuen, 1984.

Thomas, Dana. *Fashionopolis: The Price of Fast Fashion and the Future of Clothes*. London: Head of Zeus, 2019.

Thomas, Edward. *In Pursuit of Spring*. First published in 1914 by Thomas Nelson and Sons. This edn with an Introduction by Alexandra Harris. Ford: Little Toller Books, 2016.

Thomas, Edward. *The South Country*. First published in 1909 by J. M. Dent & Sons. This edn with an introduction by Robert Macfarlane. Toller Fratrum: Little Toller Books, 2009.

Thomas, R. S. *Pietà*. London: Rupert Hart Davis, 1966.

Thoreau, Henry David. *Walden*. First published in 1854. This edn London: Penguin Random House 2016.

Veblen, Theodore. *The Theory of the Leisure Class: An Economic Study of Institutions*. New York: The Macmillan Company, 1899.

Waller, David S. and Helen J. Waller. 'H&M Post-Rana Plaza: Can Fast Fashion Ever Be Truly Ethical?', Bloomsbury Fashion Business Cases, 1 November 2018.

Wilde, Oscar. 'The Philosophy of Dress', *New York Tribune*, 19 April 1885. https://www.readingdesign.org/philosophy-of-dress (accessed 26 January 2022).

Wilson, Elizabeth and Lou Taylor. *Through the Looking Glass: A History of Dress from 1860 to the Present Day*. London: BBC Books, 1989.

Wiseman, Eva. 'Clothes Rental Services Won't Break Our Fashion Addiction', *Observer Magazine*, 14 October 2021: 5.

Wood, Zoe. 'Vegan Fashion to Get Cruelty-Free Guidelines', *Guardian*, 1 February 2020: 42.

Woolf, Virginia. *A Room of One's Own*. First published in 1929. This edn London: Penguin, 2004.

Worth, Rachel. *Clothing and Landscape in Victorian England: Working-Class Dress and Rural Life*. London: I. B. Tauris, 2018.

Worth, Rachel. *Fashion for the People: A History of Clothing at Marks & Spencer*. Oxford: Berg, 2007.

Yallop, Olivia. *Break the Internet: In Pursuit of Influence*. London: Scribe, 2021.

Websites (information with no specific author)

https://www.api.parliament.uk/historic-hansard/commons/1945/jan/16/wages-councils-bill (accessed 2 December 2021).

https://www.apparelcoalition.org (accessed 18 June 2020).

https://www.apparelcoalition.org/the-sac/ (accessed 29 November 2021).

https://www.aspiga.com (accessed 18 May 2021).

https://www.bbc.co.uk/news/business-44885983 (accessed 30 January 2022).

https://www.bbc.co.uk/news/uk-wales-politics-34721771 (accessed 17 January 2022).

https://www.bluedeltajeans.com (accessed 23 November 2021).

https://www.cabbagesandroses.com/about-us (accessed 28 January 2022).

https://www.collections.vam.ac.uk/item/O11107/pin-unknown/ (accessed February 2022).

https://www.econyl.com (accessed 2 December 2021).

https://www.ecotextile.com/2013032811968/fashion-retail-news/sustainable-textiles -coalition-launched.html (accessed 18 June 2020).

https://www.eileenfisher.com/circular-by-design (accessed 3 December 2021).

https://www.esrc.ukri.org/about-us/50-years-of-esrc/50-achievements/the-easterlin -paradox/ (accessed 1 July 2020).

https://www.eu.patagonia.com/gb/en/ironclad-guarantee.html (accessed 27 November 2021).

https://www.eu.patagonia.com/gb/en/our-footprint/fair-trade.html (accessed 27 November 2021).

https://www.eu.patagonia.com/gb/en/wornwear/ (accessed 27 November 2021).

https://www.evrnu.com (accessed 29 November 2021).

https://www.globalfashionagenda.com/about-us/our-mission/ (accessed 2 December 2021).

https://www.greenpeace.org/international/story/6956/what-are-microfibers-and-why -are-our-clothes-polluting-the-oceans/ (accessed 18 June 2020).

https://www.historic-uk.com/CultureUK/More-Nursery-Rhymes/ (accessed 20 April 2020).

https://www.humanesociety.org/resources/about-canadian-seal-hunt (accessed 23 March 2021).

https://www.jeanologia.com/about-us/ (accessed 23 November 2021).

https://www.modernmeadow.com (accessed 24 November 2021).

https://www.peta.org (accessed 25 May 2021).

https://www.premierevision.com/en/magazine/smart-creation-premiere-vision-whats -that/ (accessed 3 February 2022).

https://www.referenceforbusiness.com/history2/3/Littlewoods-plc.html#ixzz6IXlsBIQD (accessed 3 April 2020).

https://www.rspb.org.uk/about-the-rspb/about-us/our-history/ (accessed 30 July 2020).

https://www.ruskinmuseum.com/who-was-john-ruskin-1819-1900/ruskin-linen-and -lace/ (accessed 12 October 2021).

https://www.sewport.com/learn/garment-labeling-and-requirements (accessed 6 July 2020).

https://www.stonycreekcolors.com (accessed 21 November 2021).

https://www.studioama.be/en/over-ama/ (accessed 31 January 2022).

https://www.textiletoday.com.bd/air-dyeing-technology-a-review/ (accessed 21 November 2021).

https://www.theguardian.com/business/2021/feb/01/asos-buys-topshop-topman-miss
-selfridge-arcadia (accessed 1 February 2021).

https://www.theguardian.com/global-development/2020/aug/25/the-fashion-industry
-echoes-colonialism-dfid-new-scheme-will-subsidise-it (accessed 6 October 2020).

https://www.thegreenhubonline.com/2019/02/27/new-research-shows-microfiber-bags
-and-cora-ball-filters-are-working/ (accessed 25 May 2021).

https://www.tonyseymour.com/people/elias-moses/ (accessed 19 May 2021).

https://www.un.org/development/desa/en/news/population/world-population
-prospects-2017.html (accessed 9 June 2020).

https://www.un.org/sustainabledevelopment/sustainable-development-goals/ (accessed
17 July 2020).

https://www.unmade.breezy.hr (accessed 2 December 2021).

https://www.vvrouleaux.com (accessed 27 March 2020).

https://www.walkerandling.co.uk (accessed 3 April 2020).

https:// www.wornagain.co.uk (accessed 29 November 2021).

Index